MIGRANTS FROM THE PROMISED LAND

NEW OBSERVATIONS

Howard S. Becker, series editor

The close and detailed observation of social life provides a kind of knowledge that is indispensable to our understanding of society. In the spirit of Robert E. Park, the books in this series draw on an intimate acquaintance with their subjects to make important contributions to the development of sociological theory. They dig beneath the surface of conventional pieties to get at the real story, and thus produce ideas that take account of the realities of social life.

MIGRANTS FROM THE PROMISED LAND

ZVI SOBEL

Transaction Books
New Brunswick (U.S.A.) and Oxford (U.K.)

Library of Congress Catalog Number: 85-8440
ISBN: 0-88738-046-8 (cloth)
Printed in the United States of America

Library of Congress Cataloging in Publication Data

Sobel, Zvi
  Migrants from the Promised Land.

  (New observations)
  Bibliography: p.
  Includes index.
  1. Israel—Emigration and immigration. 2. Israel—Social conditions.
  3. United States—Emigration and immigration. 4. Israelis—United
States. I. Title. II. Series: New observations (New Brunswick, N.J.)
JV8749.I8S63   1986   325.5694   85-8440
ISBN 0-88738-046-8

Contents

Acknowledgments

It is often only toward the completion of the task that an author realizes to what extent a presumably individual effort was actually a joint undertaking. I would like to acknowledge my indebtedness to Eve Kadar, Genoveba Breitstein, Tami Kreindler, and Mike Doran, whose contributions made this book possible. Eve Kadar transcribed and translated the bulk of the taped interviews upon which the book is largely based. Every tape required dozens of decisions with respect to nuance, translation of slang, and often problems with slurred syntax on the part of both interviewee and interviewer. Genoveba Breitstein demonstrated not only superb skill but saintly patience in deciphering my crabbed hand and quickly, accurately, and almost magically producing a coherent type text from the handwritten material. Tami Kreindler took on a heavy load of responsibility in checking bibliography and references and managed to not only save me from some rather embarrassing errors but also to suggest, in not a few instances, background material about which I was unaware. Mike Doran helped in innumerable ways, ranging from the preparation of the index to gently pointing out to me that I harbored a most unhealthy relationship to the comma.

I would also like to express my thanks to James Hughes, the council-general of the United States in Tel Aviv, and to his staff for their patience, openness, and interest in the research.

Finally, for Mechal, my wife—not only appreciation but deepest assurance that "Portugal has not and will never lose interest."

Glossary

Agudat Yisrael: Ultra-orthodox political party begun as an anti-Zionist religious grouping at the turn of the century and while remaining staunchly anti-Zionist it has assumed an active role in Israeli political life.

Agunot (pl.): Women deserted by their husbands without Rabbinic divorce and/or those who cannot prove death of spouse and are thereby forbidden to remarry.

Ain brerah: There is no alternative.

Al t'nai: On condition, conditionally.

Aliyah (literally "ascent"): Migration to Israel.

Ashkenazim (pl.): Jews of Central and Eastern European descent.

Bagrut: Matriculation examination.

Bituach L'eumi: National insurance, somewhat akin in services rendered to the American social security system.

Chalutziut: Pioneering.

Chutz la'aretz (literally "outside the land"): Anywhere but Israel.

Dayenu: Enough, sufficient, as in "it would have sufficed."

Edot hamizrach: Israeli Jewish citizens of Afro-Asian origin.

Eretz Yisrael: The Land of Israel.

Gadna: Paramilitary youth organization operative in most Israeli high schools.

Galut: See *Golah*.

Geulah: Redemption.

Golah (var. *galut*): Exile.

Gush Emunim (literally "bloc of the faithful"): A religiously orthodox group advocating Jewish settlement of the West Bank and Gaza Strip and their incorporation into Israel.

ix

Haganah: The underground forces founded in 1921 within the Histadrut. The prestate foundation of the present Israeli Army.

Halachah (adj. *halachic*, literally "the way"): Jewish law.

Havlagah: Self-restraint; a guideline with respect to retaliatory acts in the prestate underground organization Haganah.

Histadrut: General Confederation of Labor which is both employer and representative of labor in Israel. A central and still powerful economic and political force in Israel.

Kashrut: Jewish dietary laws.

Katyusha: A Soviet manufactured rocket used extensively by terrorists against Israeli border communities.

Kibbutz: Israeli agricultural collective expanded in recent years to include nonagricultural undertakings.

Kibbutznik: Kibbutz member.

Knesset: Israel's parliament.

Lachatz: Stress.

L'chayim (literally "to life"): Traditional Jewish drinking toast.

Lirot (pl.): The Israeli currency unit (sg. *lira*) replaced in 1980 by the *shekel*.

Ma'abarot: Transitional camps, begun in 1951, housing the mass immigration of the poststate period.

Mamlechet Yisrael (literally "kingdom of Israel"): Presently used in religious nationalist circles to suggest Jewish sovereignty.

Mamzer: The offspring of an *halachically* illicit union between a married woman and a man not her legal husband.

Matzpen: A far left political grouping of essentially young people that enjoyed a brief growth following the 1967 Six-Day War, although begun prior to the war.

Mechdal: Malfeasance; referring to *hamechdal*, or the multiple failures surrounding Israel's performance in the 1973 Yom Kippur War.

Mechina: A yearlong preparatory course for entrance to institutes of higher education for candidates lacking certain prerequisites.

Mellah (Arabic): North African ghetto.

Metach: Pressure.

Miluim: Reserve military duty that most Israeli men fulfill until age 55.

Mitzvot (pl.): Commandment and/or good deeds based on biblical and rabbinic tradition.

Moshav: A small-holders cooperative settlement almost exclusively agricultural.

Moshavnik: Moshav member.

M'sudar (literally "ordered" or "in order"): To be "set up" or "established."

Oleh (pl. *olim*): An immigrant to Israel.

Palmach: The elite striking arm of the prestate underground army, *Haganah*, begun in 1941.

Protektzia: Unofficial influence or "clout" whether of a personal, political, economic, or purely social character.

Rakah: The Moscow-oriented Israeli Communist party.

Sabra: A native-born Jewish Israeli.

Sephardim (pl): Jews of Iberian, Balkan, and North African descent.

Shekel: Present Israeli basic unit of currency.

Shulchan Aruch (literally "prepared table"): Compendium of rabbinic and biblical regulations.

Tachles (Yiddish): Pragmatic, practical.

Tzahal: Israel Defense Forces (IDF)—the Israeli Army.

Yerida (literally "descent"): Emigration from Israel.

Yeshiva bucher (Yiddish): A student in a rabbinic academy devoted to higher Talmudic studies.

Yishuv (literally "settlement"): The Jewish community of Palestine prior to the creation of the State of Israel. The Old Yishuv was the Jewish community of Palestine in the period before the rise of Zionism.

Yored (pl. *yordim*, literally "descender"): One who emigrates from Israel.

Introduction

This is home. This is my country.
These are my people. My own family.
I know them by heart. I am at home.
Home. Home. Let me out. Let
me out of here.

—J. Lind, *The Trip to Jerusalem*

In December of 1983, Israel Radio and Television blitzed the nation with a near orgy of programming on the subject of *yerida*[1] or emigration from Israel. On five consecutive nights programs were broadcast from 6:00 P.M. to 7:00 P.M. and again between 11:00 P.M. and 1:00 A.M., bracketed by a TV presentation on the same subject on the nation's only channel in midweek. In addition to the local Israeli audience, the programs were beamed to Europe and North America and listeners abroad were invited to call in questions and observations—an opportunity of which many availed themselves. Together with the TV broadcast, approximately sixteen hours of air time was devoted to the problem of *yerida*, which might suggest to the casual observer that *the* central threat to or concern of Israeli society was the phenomenon of emigration. Based on this information, one might have formed the wrong notion that Israelis were deserting in tens of hundreds of thousands and that a veritable depopulation of the country was in process.

While the number of Israelis who have emigrated is much in dispute, almost no enlightened observer has or would suggest that matters have reached the red line of a demographic crisis.[2] It is significant to note that in a country facing a plethora of near mind-boggling problems and challenges ranging from war to a fragile economy, no other problem has been the subject of such concentrated media attention. Recognizing the agenda-setting function of the mass media, one might assume (correctly) a hand from above, but this would only obscure what must be seen as a deep-seated and rather pervasive fear among many "ordinary" Israelis concerning the viability of the collective national enterprise and, more specifically, the willingness of large numbers of people to remain a part of it.

The present volume attempts to shed some light on the *why* of these concerns and to explain some of the key factors underlying the emigration phenomenon.

1

Conventional wisdom and establishment explanations in Israel tend to attribute the existence of what is viewed as a rather large Israeli Diaspora to greed and selfishness on the part of those who choose the fleshpots over Zion. Our findings indicate that while the economic motive is strong, a no less significant stimulus to emigration is the widespread dissatisfaction with a host of factors associated with Israeli society. Some of these are—or should have been—obvious, such as the threat and reality of constant war, a high level of associated tension, natural limitations on opportunities resulting from the small size of the country, an absurdly high level of taxation, a byzantine bureaucracy and generally unresponsive political structure, the relative absence of civility in everyday life, and more.

Less obvious, but no less significant, are factors such as a desire to reassume a deeply embedded and culturally sanctioned stance of marginality in preference to the unfamiliar dimension of sovereignty, an increasing inability to evolve new societal challenges and allegiances following the completion of the pioneer phase and the beginnings of routinization, a not-so-eccentric response to the overwhelming Americanization of Israeli society, and an almost inchoate and inexpressible fear with respect to the long-range future of the country. In addition, we must be cognizant of the importance of having reached a critical mass of former Israelis established abroad who then draw others after them, and the not-to-be-entirely-ignored factor of fad often associated with emigration.

Thus reasons for emigrating abound and are explored in the following pages. Also discussed are factors easing the process such as the critical mass of previous emigrants and the element of mobility generally associated with groups or individuals who have already moved or have the idea or possibility of mobility etched into their consciousness through historical and personal memory. Few social groups can equal the Jews in this dimension, which perhaps more than any other factor plays a significant role in the evolvement of such deep concern of so many Israelis with the problem of *yerida*. As Lee has observed, "The factors that hold and attract or repel people are precisely understood neither by the social scientist nor the persons directly affected," but the plain and well-known fact that the overwhelming burden of Jewish history was played out in the Diaspora rather than in Zion is an unescapable datum with which Israelis and Jews in general must contend. Thus the present work does not deal only with emigrants but, and if only indirectly, also with those who stay; not only with the nuts and bolts of high taxes and a devilish bureaucracy, but also with the overarching Zionist vision and the very fabric of a Jewish epistemology that serves as the state's backdrop.

For the present, *yerida* cannot be conceived of as an objective threat to the survival or viability of the Jewish state, but its assumption of such a central concern does suggest an almost subliminal awareness of danger having more to do with the consciousness of history and the quasi-articulated matrix of cultural preference than with people already left or preparing to do so. *Yerida* has assumed a place as one of the, if not *the*, major and weighty problems confronting the third Jewish commonwealth along with the peace-war, East-West, Arab-Jew, and religious-secular conflicts. How Israel meets and deals with these challenges in the coming decades will determine its outline and substance if not its very survival as a state, and yet none of these dichotomously paired categories have received the type of concentrated media treatment enjoyed by *yerida*.

Israeli society faces two categories of problems that might be termed *general* and *specific*. Under the heading of *general* one is confronted by a whole bevy of disturbances such as an inordinate level of inflation, a low economic growth rate, a rising crime rate, rapid rates of urbanization, ecological problems, and so on, namely, the same type of problems faced by many or most Western societies. However, Israel is also faced by the aforementioned dichotomous categories of problems whose equivalents may or may not exist in other societies but which assume a peculiar valence in Israel in that each discreet grouping or any combination of groupings if not resolved or left unattended as it were, could bring about the collapse of the society or its reconstitution along lines not presently entirely clear.

Thus, for example, if the cycle of constant war leading to a still further growth and deepening influence of an already gargantuan military structure should continue unabated, we can only assume that "something will give." The "something" that springs to mind is the essentially civilian nature of Israeli governance and the desirable (and desired) inclination to view the military as responsible and subordinate to the civilian political structure. How long can a society place an army and all that derives from it at the very core and center of its existence and still hope to escape unscathed in terms of civilian-controlled democratic institutions?

The situation is similar with the problem of East-West or the relationship between Jews of Sephardic and Ashkenazic origin. The gulf of bitterness on the part of one and indifference on the part of the other threaten to explode with catastrophic force when and if the various constellations holding the matter in check such as an external unifying threat or lack of organization and focused power among the Sephardim, or different objective needs and positioning among the *edot hamizrach*[3] themselves, should undergo change.

The problem of how the society will resolve the issue of a growing Arab minority *within* its borders and assume a role as a tiny Jewish majority in a regional sea of non-Jews has been skirted and avoided during the past thirty-seven years. But the desire to establish a Jewish state, which would at the same time respect and enhance full civic freedom for its non-Jewish citizens, has proven more than a little problematic. This is so especially in view of the ongoing conflict for dominance and ownership of the land between Jews and Arabs, but it is sensed by many that even with the resolution of this question the position of the "stranger" in a religio-ethnic political configuration such as Israel's would remain clouded. It is recognized, if not talked about, that Moslem Arab citizens of Israel must confront unmitigated dilemmas in saluting a national flag whose central motif is the Star of David, singing a national anthem that speaks of the Jews' return to Zion, observing the Jewish Sabbath, participating willy-nilly in a state-sanctioned and defined religious calendar, and more. That after three decades of independence no clear structure of citizenship, symbolic or practical, has emerged which could prove democratically inclusive for Jews and Arabs is of the highest and perhaps most fateful significance, and has established the outline of a future agenda with respect to the possible form Israeli society can assume.

Very much tied to the foregoing question is the role of Jewish religion in the State of Israel, not only with respect to apparent implications for non-Jews but also for Jews who define themselves as secular, nonobservant, or irreligious. Israel is referred to as the Jewish state, but substantive content for the term *Jewish* has been left largely void and rather deliberately vague. In a situation of social stasis this vagueness would prove functional, but where dynamic realignments and upheavals are occurring on this front, the lack of definition can be and is troubling. Orthodox minorities are successfully claiming both political power and an inordinate share of public treasure with which to sustain and enlarge their institutions and role. As a direct outgrowth of the inherently unstable Israeli political system encroachments on what had been undefined or even secular preserves—institutional, political, educational, and geographical-physical—on the part of Orthodox religious groups has led to bitter encounters between the two camps which in a significant number of instances have involved actual violence. The level of verbal violence characterizing the growing conflict with hurled epithets like "Nazi," "Hitler," and "*Zhid*" provides sufficient attestation to the depth of emotions involved.

An additional complicating impediment is found in the emergence between Orthodoxy and religious indifference or secularity of a religious-nationalist camp bearing a messianic tone against a matrix of, at times, right-wing and unashamedly antidemocratic and racist stances. The Jewish nature of the state occupies a key corner on an already crowded platter of conflicts and dilemmas confronting the third Jewish commonwealth.

Nothwithstanding the demonstrable seriousness and centrality for Israeli society, none of the foregoing questions has received anything like the concentrated media attention or hand-wringing cries of threat that have been elicited by the emigration problem. Admitting that the depth and complexity of these dilemmas do not readily make for Madison Avenue treatment in a light-hearted format, the question still arises why they are largely, and almost exclusively, left to academic analysis rather than public exposure and discussion. One obvious answer is the perceived lack of consensus with respect to even the definitions, to say nothing about the solutions, to at least some of the above-noted conflicts. This in turn raises fears about the effects of a probable conflict that can derive from focusing on these issues and a resultant silent agreement to defer discussion until a more propitious time.

Not dealing with an issue of weight and importance does not lead to its going away, just as approaching it head on does not assure resolution. The dilemmas and problematics of Israeli society sketched above tend, at the very least, to contribute to an atmosphere of tension and pervasive feelings of gnawing dissatisfaction afflicting so many in Zion. This, together with an undiminished consciousness of the Jewish historical preference for marginality over rootedness, time over space, has led to a realistic rather than "baseless" fear and dread of what growing *yerida* could mean for the collective enterprise. *Yerida* can be addressed in a way that the religious-secular conflict or the social and political gap between Jews from East and West cannot. In some fashion it can serve as a telegraphic umbrella category, suggesting the inclusivity of these problems, sans blatant definition and exposure, which might prove too disruptive and threatening. For there is in addition the subversive fear that the choice of emigration is not entirely unrelated to the festering irresolution of these very dilemmas.

The present volume is based on intensive interviews carried out with 117 people preparing to leave the country, almost all for the United States. I was fortunate in securing the cooperation of the U.S. embassy in Tel Aviv which permitted me to work within the consular division for a period extending over one and a half years and thus to interview dozens of visa recipients as they received their documents. I was also permitted to review and organize basic data on additional hundreds of emigrants whom I did not interview. I was thus given systematic access to a fairly large number of emigrants which, when given the reluctance of so many "leavers" to define themselves as emigrants when confronted, "at large," proved an important research boon for which I am thankful.

Interviews were generally quite lengthy, most lasting between two and three hours. An open-ended interview guide was utilized, though an attempt was made in almost all cases to conduct a sort of free-wheeling conversation with those involved. Most interviews were taped, although a

TABLE 1

Occupation	15 June 1981–8 July 1982
Unskilled	18
Manual	36
Artisan, mechanic, farmer	186
Professional	249
Housewife	129
Business person	69
Clerk; sales person	139
Student	77
Artist (inc. performing arts)	14
Para-professional*	41
Retired*	9
Total	962

*Data available only for 2 December 1981–8 July 1982.

fair number declined to be recorded, while others asked that the machine be shut at particular times which they viewed as sensitive or otherwise threatening.

Without being in real control of the sample—I took all who were willing to be interviewed—later checks suggest that a pretty fair cross-section of the *yored* population was in fact reached.[4] Reviewing data for the period from 15 June 1981 through 8 July 1982 for departees who were not interviewed, reveals the distribution of their occupation as presented in Table 1.

This breakdown reflects most closely the distribution found among those interviewed in depth with the interesting and unexplained exception of retired persons who almost uniformly refused to be formally interviewed, although three consented to talk with me in a less-structured context.

With respect to birth place, again the interview sample jibed well with other visa recipients, although here we were confronted by a serious problem which has not been resolved. In the interview setting I was of course able to ask those born in Israel where their parents came from and to which ethnic group they belonged, an exercise I was unable to perform in reviewing the cold data of the consular day book. Thus I was unable to determine what proportion of those born in Israel were from Eastern or Western background, or whether they were second generation or of longer provenance. Table 2 presents the distribution of country of origin for 571 visa recipients who were documented between 2 December 1981 and 8 July 1982.

In terms of age both the interview sample and the additional data suggest a classic migration pattern, with a tremendous bunching up in the age group 20-39. Of 907 cases for the time period from 15 June 1981 through 8 July 1982, 621 fall into this group, as shown in Table 3.

TABLE 2

Origin	2 December 1981–8 July 1982
Africa; Asia*	136
West Europe	24
Anglo-Saxon	12
East Europe	107
Israel	292
Total	571

*Including one case from Japan and one from Thailand.

Once again, the fit between the interview sample and those not talked with in terms of age, occupation, and I suspect origin, is high, suggesting that the relatively small group of 117 interviewees should nonetheless provide a more than adequate picture of green card recipients.

But here we are confronted by a serious difficulty: A large proportion of Israelis who emigrate to America do not do so as bona fide immigrants but rather enter the United States as tourists or even illegally and then adjust their status while already in the country. Is there any evidence to suggest that they too reflect the same profiles as those recorded above? I believe that there are in fact differences between the two groups—the legals and the illegals—with the latter on the whole being younger, less skilled, poorer, more Eastern and probably less educated. There may be other important differences between the two categories, but for very obvious reasons it would be most difficult to properly research the matter. While differences no doubt exist, there are some data, mostly based on newspaper stories and interviews, pointing to a large area of shared attitudes.[5] In addition, in my own sample there were a number of instances of people who had initially gone to the United States as illegals and then returned to Israel in order to regularize their status. These tended on the whole to reflect few if any differences in attitudes, beliefs, or background from others who chose the long, legal approach from the outset. While I am convinced that some possibly important differences exist between the two groups, I am equally convinced that the differences do not make for a significant qualitative gulf.

TABLE 3

Age Distribution	15 June 1981–8 July 1982
Under 20	32
20-29	351
30-39	270
40-49	107
50-59	77
60 and over	70
Total	907

Jansen (1969:65) has observed that "perhaps the question most asked and least understood about migration is 'why do people move?' The reason for this is that in a majority of cases the actual migrants themselves do not know the answer to the question." In reviewing the literature of migration studies one is repeatedly struck by the frequency with which both theorists and empiricists return to a variation of this observation. Why one and not another? Why now and not at another time? Why move rather than stay? Why a foreign move rather than an internal move or vice versa?

While answers will of necessity be inexact, the significance of migration to the destinies of nations, societies, and individuals is such that however halting and tentative our attempts at making sense of the matter, the effort must nonetheless be pursued. The only place where one can begin such an effort is with the migrant himself. Then begins the difficult process of weighing, sifting, balancing, weaving, and ultimately constructing a system of meaning and understanding which goes beyond Yi-Fu Tuan's (1974:3) flip assertion about the social sciences merely being an exercise "where common sense is repeatedly confirmed with a great show of professional solemnity." As Taylor (1969:100) notes, there is the problem of sifting between "real" and "stated" notions when dealing with the migrants' own account of motives, but this is a problem not limited to the study of migration or to the social science task itself but is rather metaphysical in nature. Ultimately one is thrown back—after making sure that the technical tools are as sharp as they can be, and are fitted to the task at hand—on something a bit beyond common sense. I remain persuaded by the wise observation of Louis Wirth (1936:xx), that

> insight may be regarded as the core of social knowledge. It is arrived at by being on the inside of the phenomenon to be observed . . . by sympathetic introspection. It is the participation in an activity that generates interest, purpose, point of view, value, meaning and intelligibility, as well as bias.

But "sympathetic introspection" is often clouded by unavoidable bias or even too much distancing from the people or subject being observed. An important datum of the present research is the author's personal commitment to the continued growth and health of Israeli society, and his recognition of the threat—personal and communal—suggested by large scale "desertion" on the part of thousands of his countrymen. Feelings of regret and in some instances of hostility and even bewilderment had to be confronted in numerous cases. Distaste was another feeling to overcome, as when one was privy to acts of near desperation in order to leave the dust of Israel behind, such as the appearance of a tired-looking woman in her sixties who had American citizenship and was attempting to get a visa for a

40-year-old Russian immigrant whom she was about to marry. She was both widowed and divorced; he was a divorcée, and it was fairly clear that at least this prospective marriage was not contracted in heaven. Neither was this the case with a 23-year-old mechanic who appeared with his youthful and quite beautiful mother in order to arrange "papers" for his marriage to a 45-year-old American.

Sad were the many attempts to defraud the visa authorities such as the couple who tried to lie about their army-age son's birth date even though the objective evidence was unassailable, or the man who claimed he had "forgotten" his original family name "because we Hebraized it so long ago." Similarly striking was the combination of sheepishness and aggression, as when people apologized for emigrating by assuring me that "it's only temporary," or "admitting" to unfathomable depths of weakness. Many applicants mistook me (until corrected) for an embassy employee and would often ask for my professional attention. In many instances questioners would not believe that I did not work for the embassy and would assume that I was either an American diplomat who knew Hebrew or an Israeli representing the Americans, and in either case I was rewarded with some choice demonstrations of hostility. When I did in some instances ask questions like, "What sort of visa are you here for, immigrant or tourist?" the fact that I asked in Hebrew caused pause, and no little consternation. In one case the questioner merely said "I work there," meaning the United States; in other cases I was treated to explanations on the spot such as "I have a family over there," "I'm out of work here," or the above noted "It's only temporary."

At times this ready sense of guilt was poignant as when one applicant asked, "How do we look from back there on the other side of the window— like animals, eh?" A typewriter serviceman coming in to service the embassy machines asked "And if I want to go to America you can help me?" When I asked, "Do you want to emigrate?" he said, "No—do I lack for anything here? I just want to see."

Reflective pause is an immediate and automatic reaction to what seems to be shocking instances of departure on the part of elites: the full colonel (retired) who has come back to bring his mother out to Texas, where he successfully sells insurance; the native-born judge married to a leading surgeon who are both going to seek what could only be a replication of what was already achieved in Israel. The professor who wants to preserve her Israeli ties just in case "her son starts going with *shiksas*." The rich and successful businessman whose "horizons" are too crabbed in Israel. The successful artist who needs "oxygen" in the form of a wider audience and more stimulating ambience. The politician who will view Israel's continuing decline from New York—on an Israeli government pension.

Similarly poignant were the numerous instances of parents being "brought over" by children who had preceded them and made it in America. In almost all instances the departees were apologetic, somewhat ashamed of their emigration, and reluctant to admit its finality. "We'll be back and we'll bring the kids with us" was asserted as a reason for going by more than a few in this category. In a curious way, the fact of having made *aliyah*, of having immigrated, which was the case for most of these parents, tended to legitimize *yerida*, or emigration: if one can move and make it a virtue—why not an additional move bearing its own virtue or justification?

Evoking less sympathy were the aggressive ones who pugnaciously (and unasked) announced that they "owe Israel nothing," and "where I choose to live is my own business." Among these were emigrants who resented Israeli society and denied its rights to make demands on the individual, whether it be credentialization or standards of performance, while openly extending these rights to foreign societies. "Here I need *bagrut* [matriculation exam]—What for?" "Here they have taxes on everything." "And if it doesn't work out there—I can always come back, no?"

Not a few lectured me for shirking my duty in merely interviewing rather than presenting myself as an example of successful *aliyah*. Why did I not "try to talk people out of *yerida* instead of just asking why, why?" I was often privy to an almost childlike desire on the part of emigrants to be punished for leaving, perhaps to be stopped from doing something shameful and unacceptable. Many departees demonstrated this desire to be treated as infants with the implied sanction of punishment and/or help for their weakness. In some cases it put me in mind of potential suicides who announce in a variety of ways, "I'm going to kill myself: stop me!" Indeed, in many cases I was asked: "Why has no one tried to stop me?" or "Why has nobody tried to ask me *why* I'm leaving?"

Almost all interviewees as well as those who declined to be interviewed assured me of two things: (1) "I'm not really an emigrant"; and (2) "my reasons for going are special." Each emigrant had his or her story: medical care, business, education, family or legal complications, need for "clearing the head" or a change, seeing the world, etc. These assertions were essentially "true" in the sense that very few could assume the full burden of guilt still attaching to *yerida* (emigration) from Israel by admitting to the finality of the act, and indeed there were about as many reasons for departures as there were emigrants. While immigration to Israel was for many a collective act, departure is by its very nature individual and thus many faceted, elusive, and somewhat chimerical. The phenomenon of *yerida* is a societal and historical datum and its implications are clearly beyond individual vicissitudes reaching to the very core of the collective enterprise—in Israel and the Diaspora.

Notes

1. *Yerida*, literally "going down," refers to emigration from Israel. One who emigrates is a *yored* (*yordim*, pl.). *Aliyah* is "going up" and refers to immigration to Israel. An *oleh* is one who immigrates (*olim*, pl.). While the appellation *yored* is no longer a pejorative, it is far from carrying a positive connotation. The Hebrew word for migrant—*m'hager*—is almost never used when referring to movements to or from Israel on the part of Jews. In these cases *aliyah* and *yerida* are used almost exclusively.

2. What has come to be called the "numbers game" will be returned to at various junctures in the present work, but as will become amply clear, the "real" numbers of departees from Israel are, for the purposes of this work, not of central concern. Estimates run from the recent low suggested by Pini Herman and David La Fontaine in an M.A. essay, *In Our footsteps: Israeli Immigration to the U.S. and Los Angeles*, wherein they assert a mere 100,000-130,000 *yordim* in America, to the high of Shmuel Lahis, former director general of the Jewish Agency who speaks of at least half a million.

3. Definitions here are very hazy and in some cases misleading. All *edot hamizrach* are Sephardic, but not all Sephardim (pl.) are *edot hamizrach*. *Edot hamizrach*, or Eastern communities, generally refers to Jews deriving from either African or Afro-Asian backgrounds, and it is here rather than among Sephardim at large that the "problems" within Israeli society lies.

4. There exists, however, one "geographical" problem which could conceivably have skewed matters with respect to the religious-secular composition of the sample. My interviewees came from all parts of the country *except* the Jerusalem area with its heavy concentration of observant Jews.

5. See Gidon Alon, "Yordim B'tel Hashomer," *Ha'aretz*, 4 July 1983 (Hebrew); Gidon Alon, "10-15 Achuz Min Hayordim—Yordim Shuv," *Ha'aretz*, 18 November 1983 (Hebrew); Amos Elon, "Tashtit Klita," *Ha'aretz*, 20 May 1981 (Hebrew); Gidon Alon, "Hegiau Mayim Ad Nafesh," *Ha'aretz*, 26 February 1982 (Hebrew); "The Exodus from Israel," *Newsweek*, 12 January 1981; Amos Elon, "Yoram B'Eretz Haplaot," *Ha'aretz*, 21 May 1981 (Hebrew).

1

The Jewish People and the Land of Israel

The Current Concern with Emigration

In the summer of 1982, the Falk Institute for Economic Research published a study by R. Lamdany in which the following points were made: approximately 340,000 people have emigrated from Israel from 1948 through 1979, the average number of emigrants was 4.6 per 1,000 inhabitants per annum or, looked at differently, 225 emigrants for every 1,000 immigrants. It was further noted that when compared to other countries of immigration, such as Canada or Australia, the Israeli rate of emigration is, objectively speaking, not high. One might argue with the accuracy of the statistics involved—no one really knows just how many Israelis have permanently left if for no other reason than we have no agreed upon conception of either *permanent* or *left*. In some accounts each person who leaves the country for a month is counted together with those who leave for longer periods or for good. In the case of some countries—notably the United States—most Israelis who will ultimately stay do not arrive as immigrants but as tourists and in the course of time (sometimes ten years and longer) "adjust" their status in that country. One might take further exception with Lamdany's findings after a casual stroll in certain neighborhoods of New York, Montreal, Los Angeles, Johannesburg, Amsterdam, Frankfurt, and numerous other cities in the world, where one can only assume that his estimate falls to the modest side of the ledger.

Additionally, these figures do not tell us how many have emigrated if by emigration we mean *permanent* residence in a country other than Israel. For Israelis are among the most peripatetic of peoples and seemingly are willing to travel at the merest hint of opportunity to do so. In a country sheltering only 4 million people (3.5 million Jews), it was estimated that had the Lebanon crisis not descended in the summer of 1982 some 500,000 to 700,000 Israelis would have availed themselves of the opportunity to travel abroad—a truly astounding proportion. Working, studying, or traveling abroad for a certain period of time has become a *sine qua non* for, if not acceptance, then at least minimal social honor in any number of social circles, not least among young kibbutzniks (kibbutz members) and other similarly "motivated" segments of the Israeli social rainbow. For thousands of youngsters being released after years of onerous army service, a trip abroad rather than "settling down" and becoming *m'sudar* is the first order of business. Thousands will stay abroad for short periods only, either because of financial considerations, plans back home, homesickness, or just because the itch was satisfied and the muse answered. For others the time abroad might stretch from months to years, but ultimately they return.

Many hundreds of Israelis live abroad in service to government and quasigovernmental agencies and organs like the Jewish Agency, the World Zionist Organization, the national airline and shipping company, as well as private and semiprivate business concerns including Histadrut enterprises. For still others, the "trip of a lifetime" will have turned into a complete change of direction and venue and these will stay abroad indefinitely, swelling the ranks of what have come to be known as the *yordim.* Thus, quantifying the number of real (i.e., permanent) emigrants from Israel remains an inexact exercise at best, and while Israelis do travel at an inordinate level of frequency (and distance as well), Lamdany may or may not be correct in asserting that emigration rates as such are not inordinate.

For what is inordinate in one national or social context might be easily assimilable in another. The departure of more than one-quarter of a million Israelis over the years and the continuing departure of tens of thousands presently is viewed somewhat differently in a beleaguered, self-conscious society such as Israel than it would be were similar or comparable numbers to leave Canada or Australia. While a demographic emergency in a purely objective sense might not exist, it is clear that a psychological emergency does.

Whatever the "facts" of the matter, large numbers of Israelis—the man in the street as well as establishment figures—*perceive* emigration as a problem and one of serious dimensions. Emigration has in some respects come to be treated as a national emergency. Government figures, academic authorities, and media gurus have all commented. Symposia have been organized on the subject. A director-general of the Jewish Agency resigned in protest over the asserted lack of serious attention being paid to the problem by official bodies, and the same official has since established a public committee to combat emigration. An assistant minister without portfolio has been given responsibility for dealing with the issue on a governmental level. Dozens of articles have been published in the past few years in all the country's newspapers and in most of the quality journals, albeit relatively little of a scholarly or research-based nature has emerged.

A ministorm was created a few years ago when former prime minister, Yitzhak Rabin defined *yordim* as *nefolet shel nemushot* (dregs of the earth), initiating something of a public debate on the nature of the problem, and what could be done to stem or reverse the tide. Programs have emerged to win back at least the children of *yordim* by organizing summer programs for them along the lines of and within the framework of *Gadna,* and a suggestion has been muted to organize an Israeli scout movement among the children of *yordim* in the major North American centers. The pros and cons of supporting TV shows in Hebrew geared to *yored* communities are discussed from the perspective of whether their very existence will legitimate emigration and perhaps aid in the process of acculturation and acclimatization of *yordim* in their new homes, or maintain the needed contact with home and hearth that might eventually result in or at least aid in their return. Arguments for and against special tax benefits or mortgage aid for potential returnees are posited on two levels, the practical: will it help to tip the scales in favor of return; and the quasi-theological: can sin be rewarded? Tax benefits and mortgage rights are fairly straightforward affairs; their efficacy or lack of same (i.e., the return of *yordim*) can probably be demonstrated with relatively little effort.

But this pragmatic approach is generally eschewed in favor of what I have referred to above as the quasi-theological dimension, wherein *yordim* at best are viewed as fallen angels and at worst as the handmaidens of Satan. Thus the question persists: What can be done? Can returning *yordim* be employed, for example, in government ministries? If so, should they be allowed access to the highest positions or should they be relegated to lower-level functions only, so as not to penalize the "sons" who stayed at home and not to reward those who opted for and indeed achieved rewards of a kind not available at home?

Whatever the actual dimension of emigration, Israelis and Israeli society view the phenomenon as problematic and threatening. Questions about reward and punishment, sin and the cleansing of sin, characterological failings, salvaging of the young, legitimation or condemnation are indications of a deep substratum of unease concerning the phenomenon of *yerida.* No matter how many articles or research reports are published attempting to demonstrate that in statistical and comparative terms there is no problem,[1] or a limited problem, it would appear that something of a consensus has emerged to the effect that a serious problem does exist.

The reaction to the phenomenon of emigration in Israel parallels to a marked extent that noted by Kai Erikson (1966:69) in his remarkable book dealing with deviance in the Puritan colonies in America:

> The severity of a "crime wave" cannot always be measured by the number of deviant offenders involved or the volume of deviance in fact committed. In the sense that the term is being used here "crime wave" refers to a rash of

publicity, a moment of excitement and alarm, a feeling that something needs to be done. It may or may not mean an actual increase in the volume of deviation.

But this is to some degree begging the question. One might ask why the perception of growing deviance emerged at that particular historical juncture rather than at another point in time. Why is Israeli society suddenly bombarded with a seemingly perverse and almost compulsive concern with emigration now, if in fact it can be demonstrated that the phenomenon has ever been present albeit showing some periodic fluctuation in the numbers involved?

The evidence does seem to suggest a spurt in emigration in 1974 following the Yom Kippur War and a renewed surge in the 1980s, but a perusal of the available data from 1954 to 1979 would not give sufficient objective cause for the type of societal response alluded to above. It does not explain discussions of a hand-wringing nature in the Knesset plenum, resolutions at the World Zionist Congress, or many of the other responses previously noted.

The Factor of Insecurity

In a certain sense one cannot be shocked by an overall concern with problems of this nature on the part of Israelis. Israel is, after all, a society and a country that can be said to be obsessed with the very idea of migration. Aliyah—coming up to the land, immigration—is and has been a central concern and has received formidable emphasis since the beginning of the modern Zionist dream of return in the twilight years of the nineteenth century.

Indeed the history of the *Yishuv*, or the Jewish community in Palestine since 1882, is marked by *aliyot* (immigration waves) rather than other factors, and is generally recorded as follows: first *aliyah*—1882-1903; second *aliyah*—1904-1914; third *aliyah*—1919-1923; fourth *aliyah*—1924-31; fifth *aliyah*—1932 and onwards. (Eisenstadt 1954:42).

The first and most basic challenge of the emerging Zionist epiphany was the Jewish repopulation of Palestine, which could not be accomplished other than by immigration. For demographic as well as sociological reasons, the small, indigenous Jewish population of the country could not under any circumstances peform this role, and if in fact the third Jewish commonwealth was to emerge, it could only be as a result of significant numbers of Jews leaving their various places of abode and "going up" to the Land of Israel.

Tens of thousands did so. Approximately 450,000 immigrants arrived between 1882 and 1944 (Eisenstadt 1954) and well over 600,000 in the immediate post-World War II years.

Given the rather harsh facts on the ground—that the indigenous Arab population of Palestine (1) outnumbered the Jewish settlers to begin with; (2) had a higher birth rate and a fast declining death rate, the latter as a by-product, to some extent, of Jewish settlement; and (3) experienced a burgeoning and expanding national consciousness that could only conflict with the growing consensus that a Jewish state rather than a simple concentration or refuge was the desirable outcome of the Zionist dream—a preoccupation with *aliyah* rates was a foregone conclusion.

If the foregoing pragmatic considerations were not sufficient, there was, in addition, the ideological parousia to the effect that the Diaspora was doomed and if the Jewish people did not in considerable numbers reform themselves in the ancient homeland, the romance of a dispersed religio-national entity that had survived unparalleled adversity for 3,600 years would draw to a close under the battering effects of persecution, assimilation, and the sheer decline of will to exist. The Holocaust and various postwar upheavals in Eastern Europe and in the Moslem lands clearly enhanced this vision so that the central importance of *aliyah,* of bringing as many Jews as was possible to Israel, became paramount, and foremost, as was the need to strengthen in a very physical (i.e., numerical) manner the existing community in its struggle with the Arab world.

Thus it is for Israel and Israelis anything but a marginal subject of concern. Immigration and emigration in the Israeli context—past, present, and probably future—assume an importance that would be difficult to exaggerate, again, both on pragmatic and ideological grounds. Each immigrant is considered a victory of sorts, a kind of bodily enhancement of the vision, while each emigrant is conversely seen as a defeat for the common enterprise and not unimportantly a challenge to the inner viability or worth of the psychosocial premises of those staying. This is not a unique response given the context. The unsettling effect brought about by a sense of desertion from what must still be viewed as an essentially shaky enterprise finds its parallel in other venues and other times. John Winthrop (1971:298-300), for example, writing in the seventeenth century about *"yerida"* from the Plymouth colony sounds curiously (if exotically) *au courant* when he bewails the departure of settlers to greener pastures:

[September 22, 1642] The sudden fall of land and cattle, and the scarcity of foreign commodities, and money, etc., with the thin access of people from England, put many into an unsettled frame of spirit, so as they concluded there would be not subsisting here, and accordingly they began to hasten

away, some to the West Indies, others to the Dutch, at Long Island, etc. (for
the governor there invited them by fair offers), and others back for England.

They fled for fear of want, and many of them fell into it, even to extremity, as
if they had hastened into the misery which they feared and fled from, besides
the depriving themselves of the ordinances and church fellowship, and those
civil liberties which they enjoyed here; whereas, such as staid in their places,
kept their peace and ease, and enjoyed still the blessings of the ordinances,
and never tasted of those troubles and miseries, which they heard to have
befallen those who departed. Much disputation there was about liberty of
removing for outward advantages, and all ways were sought for an open door
to get out at; but it is to be feared many crept out at a broken wall. For such as
come together into a wilderness, where are nothing but wild beasts and
beastlike men, and there confederate together in civil and church estate,
whereby they do, implicitly at least, bind themselves to support each other,
and all of them that society, whether civil or sacred, whereof they are members, how they can break from this without free consent, is hard to find, so as
may satisfy a tender or good conscience in time of trial. Ask they conscience,
if thou wouldst have plucked up they stakes, and brought thy family 3,000
miles, if thou hadst expected that all, or most, would have forsaken thee
there. Ask again, what liberty thou hast towards others, which thou likest not
to allow others towards thyself; for if one may go, another may, and so the
greater part, and so church and commonwealth may be left destitute in a
wilderness, exposed to misery and reproach, and all for thy ease and pleasure,
whereas these all, being now thy brethren, as near to thee as the Israelites were
to Moses, it were much safer for thee, after his example, to choose rather to
suffer afflication with thy brethren than to enlarge thy ease and pleasure by
furthering the occasion of their ruin.

The essential insecurity of the enterprise, whether in the Plymouth
colony or contemporary Israel, is a veritable "given" of settler societies
where constant reinforcement of the initial decision to migrate is sought
and a defensive stand assured against any and all forms of desertion. Even
more is this the case when the very physical survival of the structure remains at question, and not only the viability or efficacy of the personal
decision. That the long-term survival of Israel remains in doubt cannot be
denied. Its present and future security is not in any way vouchsafed notwithstanding its substantial military strength and the remarkable victories
in war it has thus far enjoyed. Thus, questions of immigration and emigration are not academic and are in fact existential in their very nature, and go
to the core of the society's collective being.

The question of a basic sense of insecurity is not however exhausted in
taking note of the physical or survival notion alone. There is, in addition,
the insecurity of a psychosocial nature that no less than the physical dimension fulfills an important function in the society's concern with questions of immigration/emigration.

For tens of thousands of Israeli citizens, coming to this land was not so much a matter of choice as of no alternative—or as Israelis phrase it: *ain brerah.* They were either the displaced survivors of the horrors of 1933-45 who had no place else to go, victims of renewed anti-Semitic terror in their former homelands, or people who had had enough, as it were, of the world of the hostile and dangerous gentiles. In some cases they viewed Israel as a temporary "resting" place before moving on to more desired and desirable locations. Other postwar immigrants were moved by semiarticulated notions of a return to Zion whose temporal dimension remained sketchy at best and at worst phantasmagoric. Many of these came from the Moslem lands of North Africa, the Middle East, and from societies being buffeted by the winds of change and upheaval from which they naturally enough did not emerge unscathed. Still others, a minority both then and now, came out of idealistic or ideological concerns and commitments. Thus, in some cases refuge was sought and found; in others a sort of religious even quasimessianic fulfillment was hoped for, while in still other cases a canvas for social and national experimentation was pursued.

What was not sought and hardly expected was that Palestine and later Israel would provide a context for any kind of economic or material success, a solid base for an energetic and talented people whose traditional response to the trials and challenges of physical survival was to overcome—and then some. What I am suggesting is that with the possible exception of serving as a refuge of last resort, reasons for coming to Israel (not *being* there) were essentially arational, thereby constantly posing the question, why Israel and not somewhere else? Am I a fool for plighting my troth with an endangered enterprise at the western tip of "far off Asia"? Are there not more promising lands beckoning? Cannot my talents be more readily realized in a larger country having a more highly developed economy and more sophisticated structure, and greater outreach? Such a context veritably cries out for patterns of constant reinforcement and reassurance about the essential correctness of the decision to be in Israel rather than elsewhere. When immigration is high or on the rise this constitutes a prominent and visible form of reassurance: others are choosing the path I chose. There is, after all, something of positive value to be found in Israel if other people choose to immigrate, especially if the decision is volitional and other choices were not considered superior. Conversely, when emigration is or seems to be in the ascendency, the reverse mechanisms are operative and questions as to the valildity of "my" selection come to the fore. These doubts assume prominence when alternatives seem to be in the offing, and readily, if not easily, achievable. News reports to the effect that in 1980 and 1981 emigrants outnumbered immigrants to Israel have a predictable effect on large numbers in a population still unsure of itself and manifesting a self-consciousness of almost paranoic proportions. Visitors to the country are often taken aback by the almost hectoring insistence of their Israeli hosts to get "positive feedback" on themselves and on the country. When Israelis are assured that their country is indeed beautiful, their men courageous, their women attractive, and their achievements unparalleled, it tends to be received much like the children of Israel in another time responded to mana from the heavens—not only nice but essential! Leaving the country is viewed not as the choice of an alternative option, but as the rejection of the ordained pattern of things. The appearance of long lists of ads in the press advertising apartments, household furnishings, automobiles with the "come on" phrase of "leaving the country" evokes a sense of pain, loss, and anger among most Israelis.

Not only pain, loss, and anger, but fear as well. Because if emigration can be attributed to x, y, and z causes, those very same factors likely as not are at work among those who remain as well. The primary reason, in the last analysis, for *yerida* being so high on the national agenda of concern is because all Israelis face the same stimuli and issues that result in some of them leaving. In some very real sense, all Israelis are candidates for *yerida,* and this rather than x number of thousands of emigrants per year is what lies at the root of concern.

There exists widespread fear that ties and attachment to the country are ephemeral, that roots are shallow, that, in short, Israelis lack an identity.

The Factor of Identity

Erik Erikson (1974:124) in a somewhat jocular but nonetheless serious observation has remarked: "Identity, you may be glad to hear, is not everything, either for a person or a nation—once you have it of course." Erikson might have added: "And it does not come easily!" Three and a half decades of renewed national existence are, it would appear, not sufficient for the development of a deep sense of place or a feeling of comfort in the collective skin.

It would appear that a certain litmus test of national identity exists wherein it can be said to be present when the various problems and frustrations that invariably beset the individual in the course of daily existence are viewed situationally rather than against the matrix of presumed collective bankruptcy. Thus, when the plumbing does not work, or the schools do not teach "Avi" to read, or when neighbors are unkind, these situations will be viewed in perspective as failures of this or that mechanism or individual rather than be attributed (and usually given equal weight in importance) to the collectivity as a whole. I do not suggest or assert that such a tendency is not present in all national groupings. How often will one hear an Englishman attribute certain behavior to an innate phlegmatism inherent in his "race," or Germans explain their political history *and* their love life in terms of certain set-in-concrete characterological inclinations peculiar to their "race," or similar statements for Frenchmen, Italians, and other groupings. What would not occur with any frequency, however, is a certain ferment or doubt as to whether or not the individual can continue to stay a part of such an enterprise, continue to identify himself with the nation, or perhaps leave and strike roots elsewhere.

There exists a certain conditionality with respect to the ties that bind so many Israelis to their land and society. Many identify with their society *al t'nai* (on condition): "I will stay if it is 'good' for me, I will leave when and if it isn't." Numbers of Israelis (and not only those born or raised elsewhere) suffer from periodic "*yerida* flashes" or feelings of wanting to chuck it all, which can be stimulated by even the most prosaic of events. A veteran settler of American background put it thus:

> When I get stopped by a cop in Israel and am given a ticket, I tend to get mad as hell about it and blame the government, its stupid and inefficient organs and all its flunkies who manage to get *me* while all the real criminals wander around freely. In the States I would write the same event off to bad luck or at worst, stupid cops. Here, I actually get a momentary bug up———where I'm prepared to say "the Hell with *them,* they don't deserve me and I deserve better."

The foregoing was not volunteered by an emigrant, but by a "committed" and rather solidly "rooted" Israeli. Indeed, I would venture that few Israelis reading these words would find them far from the mark or distant from similar sentiments they have heard voiced on numerous occasions by fellow countrymen. How many have not heard on varied occasions and in diverse ways questions raised about "whether or not Jews were made to live together in a 'normal' framework." "Are we not too much for each other?" "Is it not better, or more 'normal' for us to live among the goyim?" One emigrating interviewee put it in a most succinct, pithy if utterly gross fashion when he suggested that "the Jews are like manure. When you put them on [or together with] goyim, both flourish. Here, where we are all Jews and you put Jews on [or together with] Jews—you only get manure."

Israel must be among the rarest of nation-states where the threat of emigrating can be and is actually used to achieve results of one kind or another with government ministries and officials, health authorities, educators, and religious leaders. Threats to return to (or leave for) Morocco, France, the USSR, or the United States can and have resulted in the desired action or results being forthcoming. Can one easily conjure up a parallel recourse in any other country? The very fact that citizens will contemplate emigration as a potential solution to a wide range of frustrations or problems is not in itself surprising. What is, however, is the recourse to this device not as an ultimate step in response to despair but as one among many potential weapons that can legitimately be utilized for diverse ends and will *mirabile dictu* stand a good chance of success. And while resentment will be elicited among fellow citizens, a sense of surprise will not.

Israelis are prepared to hear of doubts concerning the viability or even the desirability of the national enterprise expressed by others simply because the very same doubts are widely shared in the society at large.

It is not, it should be noted, a sense of Jewish identity that is lacking or problematic, but rather a developed and tuned sense of national identity that has proven a snare and a stumbling block. There has been a certain smugness abroad among Israelis who were positive that practically alone among the emerging nation-states following the great war *they* would have no problems with a national identity. Were they not after all an ancient people merely throwing off an imposed foreign overlay and reasserting a previously established place on the stage of history? Alas, this judgment might have been somewhat hasty and Israelis, I would assert, are in fact in search—with much company—of an illusive and chimerical national identity. Notwithstanding the historical and sociological "advantage" with which Israelis reconstituted a national existence, certain key and basic elements were and are missing that would inevitably prove troublesome. But the least of these is, simply put, time—the sheer passage of years, the rising up and going down of generations. In speaking of community identity or what he defines as "a belief that one shares a place with like-minded others who are psychologically embraced as 'we,'" Robert E. Lane (1962:305) notes of his sample: "The conditions are not present for such a feeling. It is the product of generations of common living; it is hard to create in one or two disoriented generations."

He concludes on a note of particular relevance for our concerns in noting that "community identity is a product of an immobile society, a static society," and however else Israel may be described, it cannot be in these terms. For however many thousands of years of longevity may be ascribed to the Jewish people, modern Israel is a mere 37 years old. Despite a remarkably high sense of "we" that can be called upon in view of a perception of a shared past, one cannot avoid the fact that Israel's is a polyglot population with at least as much diversity as similarity marking it and defining its essence. In the light of these facts it is, I think, rather impressive to note what *has* been achieved rather than what has not (i.e., a national sense of identity), but still it cannot be forgotten that we are dealing with a somewhat frail rather than a particularly robust entity.

The Factor of Declining Commitment and Alienation

Clearly, factors such as the absence or relative weakness of a sense of national identity and certain elements of basic insecurity play a role in the subjective positioning of emigration as a perceived central core problem of Israeli society. It is difficult to overemphasize the fact, however, that these factors are not unique to Israeli society, but their relative weight and importance are of a particular valence in view of certain historical and sociological factors such as the time frame in which the state was created and the natural life span of collective enthusiasm.

There exists decided sociological limits to the length of time wherein collective enthusiasm or ideal visions can be maintained in a central societal position. While the simple dream of national revival and the excitement of creating a state and a society can sustain for perhaps one generation—if that long—this will not suffice much beyond. Deep rootedness and binding ties to place are not, in contrast to our naive expectations, created overnight. When a collective ideal is buffeted by a sense of smashed dreams, broken promises, failure of leadership, and the growth of something of a moral vacuum, the tensions and fragile ties that bind begin to unravel. In this respect it would appear that 37 years of statehood are both too much and not enough: too long for the dream to remain untainted and too little for expanding and deepening roots.

A complicating overlay to the above is to be seen in the fact, as noted previously, that so many of the immigrants who flocked to Israel before, during, and immediately after the World War did not share in the "dream" to begin with. Both the personal and collective identities for this significant segment of the Israeli populace were in flux. This operated against the fulfillment of Erikson's dictum to the effect that:

> A sense of identity means a sense of being at one with oneself as one grows and develops; and it means, at the same time, a sense of affinity with a community's sense of being at one with its future as well as its history or mythology (Erikson 1974: 27-28).

But even for that large segment of the population that did share a common dream and a collective vision, an erosion of sorts has taken place resulting in a growing sense of alienation not unlike that which can be found in other contemporary societies. As Keniston (1965: 325) has noted: "The frontiers of certainty have vastly shrunk in the last four centuries, leaving few if any modern equivalents of the Cartesian axioms of 'self-evident' reason." In the context of Israeli society those same "frontiers" have taken only one generation to decline, and rather precipitously at that.

The struggles between hawks and doves, maximalists and minimalists, religious and secular, East and West tend to take on a tone wherin they can only be understood as a struggle for certainty against its unplumbed slippage. Where certainty is absent or in doubt, tenacity and fanaticism will tend to be substituted and a progressive sense of alienation results on all sides. The growth and development of polarization is both cause and effect. The more tenacious the attempt to latch on to certainty, whatever its nature, the greater the developing gulf between people of differing persuasion and opposing ideas. Thus, one finds in Israeli usage a proliferation of denunciatory appellations such as "traitor," "fifth columnist," "Nazi," "fascist," "anti-Semite," or "saboteur" being substituted for reflection, thought, and the more pacific forms of intercourse that characterize an integrated society or collectivity. Increasingly, the holder of contrary opinion is cast into the void and out of the camp, with the result that congeries or opinion folds demand ultimate loyalties in place of the larger social order.

A sort of paradigm of this emerging constellation can, I believe, be seen to have arisen in Israeli society between the Six-Day War of June 1967 and the outbreak of the Yom Kippur War in October 1973. In searching for trends and guidelines to the status of societal commitment or growing signs of alienation, no better focal point can be provided than the factors following upon the events of June 1967.

June 1967–October 1973: The Decline of Sustaining Myths

Although numerous books, articles, songs, poems, and varied analyses have been published in the years since the Six-Day War, few if any of these even begin to touch upon the long-range influences this conflict has had on manifold aspects of the Israeli reality. The present work is decidedly not the place to undertake this mammoth task. However, insofar as that conflict represents a sort of watershed in Israeli history, having what I believe to be wide-ranging implications for the understanding and analysis of contemporary Israel, a somewhat lengthy treatment seems not only excusable but will perhaps prove profitable as well. What is intended here is not a history of the period but rather an essay on its ramifications for understanding our central concern, which is the matter of *yerida*.

The war first and foremost brought about a situation wherby for the first time since the birth of the State in 1948, Israelis and indeed world Jewry could begin to believe in the possibility of Israel's ultimate security and physical survival. Notwithstanding the victories of the War of Independence and the Sinai campaign, there existed the feeling that Israeli military prowess in these conflicts was still less than totally convincing. These feelings appeared to be shared by outsiders (witness the worldwide concern in the weeks leading up to the war) and by the Arab enemy. The latter made convincing arguments to the effect that the defeat of 1948 was attributable to corruption in their ranks and that of 1956 to collusion between Israel and two ranking powers—France and Britain. There was, however, little basis for doubt regarding the outcome of the 1967 conflict.

Thus, both for Israelis and for world Jewry at large, 1967 represented a watershed experience characterized by a feeling that at long last "we are home safe." Israel became intoxicated not only with the idea of safety, but with the idea of its power and military prowess. "One hundred and seventy minutes" to eliminate the Egyptian air force screamed one headline (*Jerusalem Post* 2 July 1967: 2), when clearly putting it in minutes rather than hours enhanced the idea of unstoppable power. The new "empire" was toasted and celebrated in Lucullan terms, such as is indicated by the menu of a Knesset victory luncheon for high army officers:

> The food and wines which were of an excellent standard were not given on the menu in French as is customary on such occasions. Instead the menu read: Sharm-e-Sheikh fish, Golan Heights duck, Emek Hayalon (Latrun) salad, Jerusalem fruit and Six-Day ice cream (Parve) (*Jerusalem Post* 2 August 1967: 6).

Disdain for the Arab enemy and an elevated sense of Israeli power became manifest not only with the "average" man in the street, but was widely shared by almost all strata of leadership. Ezer Weizman observed that "no Arab army in any sort of combination even with the backing of 'volunteers,' can get the better of us" (*Jerusalem Post* 27 July 1967: 4), while his overall commander in the war, Yitzhak Rabin added that he did not believe "the Arabs were capable of waging war against Israel again" (*Jerusalem Post* 6 August 1967: 2)—not in ten years or twenty years, but simply "again," which is to say "never." In the general euphoria following the war even a balanced and rather sober diplomat like Abba Eban could unblinkingly suggest that "we can maintain our present situation indefinitely" (*Jerusalem Post* 4 August 1967: 4, Weekend Magazine), while Moshe Dayan went a bit further yet in suggesting or hinting that Israel could handle not only the Arabs but perhaps the Russians as well. He is on record as having said it was possible that Soviet troops "might fight with the Arabs in a future war because the recent crisis had shown them Arab soldiers were of little use against Israelis" (*Jerusalem Post* 9 July 1967: 2). The interviewer quotes Dayan as having said that he would not hesitate to advise his government to fight against Russia if Soviet troops were ever used against Israel, noting that the Viet Cong have shown "how a world power could be kept in check" (*Jerusalem Post* 9 July 1967: 2).

The triumphant phrase "things will never be the same again" assumed some of the trappings of a national mantra, repeated over and over again with respect to a set of highly diverse phenomena. Superlatives became the order of the day, whether in noting that 18,000 Jews in Switzerland raised 10 million dollars for Israel, or that 100,000 persons in Britain gave to the Joint Appeal for Israel, which would mean virtually every Jewish family in the country (if the donors could be shown to be all Jews); the possibilities seemed unlimited (*Jerusalem Post* 2 July 1967).

Signs existed showing an emerging faith that a new era in Jewish and Israeli history had been embarked upon. Even the Communists split, with part "coming home" bearing aloft the banner of the secular counterpart to the emerging religious messianism of the day. The old Communist warhorse Shmuel Mikunis sanctified the occasion with the observation that "Israel's war was waged to preserve the physical existence of the nation against Arab threats" (*Jerusalem Post* 5 July 1967: 6), adding commentary to text in noting that Leninist theory supported a war of this kind and it is not important who fired the first shot. Expectations with respect to a meaningful rise in *aliyah* emerged. The hope was expressed that, in view of the fact that Israel was now finally secure physically, Jews from the Diaspora would flock to Israel. Indeed *aliyah* figures did rise in the years immediately following the war, and the suspicion that push factors might have been about as strong as pull factors (at least concerning the U.S. immigrants) failed to dampen enthusiasm.[2] Jewish youth from the United States—the largest Diaspora community by far—began to appear in highly increased numbers as students in Israeli universities and institutes of Jewish learning such as yeshivot.[3] Volunteers from the Diaspora became a force to reckon with and grandiose schemes full of ambition and hope made their appearance, to wit: "Volunteers will join forces with Israelis in creating sixteen new settlement points—near Manara, at Mukebia facing Jenin, at Danjur facing the Gaza Strip, in the Korazim area, in the Gilboa hills." (*Jerusalem Post*, 2 July 1967: 3). Continuing in the same enthralled vein the item goes on to report that forests will be planted by volunteers, and some of the volunteers can be expected to fill over 300 vacancies that exist for men with specialist qualifications, such as in electronics. Thousands, according to a leading Jewish agency executive, were prepared to join from the Western countries—if only conditions were right (*Jerusalem Post*, 1 October 1967: 6).

An International Economic Advisory Conference was held in Jerusalem in August 1967 to lay the groundwork for a full-fledged coming together of Jewish economic power from around the world to be held on the eve of Independence Day, 1968. This, too, was thought to herald a new relationship between Israel and the Diaspora notwithstanding the voicing of harsh criticism of the Israeli economic reality on the part of participants from abroad who noted *inter alia* that Israel is beset by high taxes, excessive bureaucracy, government competition with private enterprise, low labor morale and discipline, and high production costs (*Jerusalem Post*, 9 August 1967: 6). Though its promise was never fulfilled, this conference did result in a marked increase of investment from abroad.

Overlaying all was a sense that nothing was beyond the country's ability to achieve or realize. A strange aura of unreality, of being unconnected, affected almost all phases of national existence whether in politics, religion, economics, the military, or how Israel's positioning on the world stage was to be understood. Transport Minister Moshe Carmel could suggest at the end of July 1967 that "if Israel governs the occupied areas *wisely* [emphasis added], world opinion will get used to the idea that the State of Israel controls the whole of Palestine" (*Jerusalem Post*, 30 July 1967: 2). This suggests a naivete of significant dimensions.

Not only regarding the "world" do we see this myopia, but more pointedly even with the respect to analysis of the internal situation of the country with respect to its Arab population. A public figure like Shimon Peres, known for his political acumen and analytical skills and certainly not untutored with respect to the minority situation in Israel up to 1967, felt no constraints suggesting that talks should be begun with the Palestinians on the basis of the good relationships built up with Israel's own Arabs over the years prior to 1967. "The sound relationships Israel had built up over twenty years with her 300,000 Arabs could be maintained just as well with one million" (*Jerusalem Post* 31 October 1967: 1). That there were few among the Arab minority who would agree with this assessment and no evidence to suggest that a minority of 300,000 and one of 1,300,000 would result in the same type of social configuration was not apparently worthy of consideration.

Again, it must be emphasized that these do not represent the views of marginal or indeed unintelligent or unthoughtful men. The fact that quite the opposite is the case should suggest something of the valence involved in the euphoric cloud that covered Israel—in all its dimensions—following the events of June 1967.

This euphoric atmosphere provided a backdrop against which two related but contrary developments occurred. The first is to be seen in the eclipse of certain core myths long current in the Israeli gestalt, and the second in the expansion of the political and social polarization of the society.

No doubt many of the underpinnings of various societal myths had begun to slip prior to the Six-Day War and were already doomed by the beginnings of mass, undifferentiated immigration attendant upon and pursuant to the creation of the State in 1948. Though periodization is a tricky business, it is rare to come upon such clear historical turning points as are afforded in this conflict, where the contradictions and tensions between myth and reality, values and behavior became palpable.

Generations of Israelis, since the second *aliyah* (1904) were in effect nurtured on images such as the soldier-farmer ideal, equalitarianism, redemption through work, simplicity, cultural innovation, and voluntarism—all against a backdrop of being both a light unto the nations and achieving for the Jewish people what they had never before coveted—normalcy. One must ask what is the status of these key societal myths in the aftermath of the war?

Following close upon the conclusion of the Six-Day War, and once it had become clear that peace was not to be Israel's immediate destiny, changes in the army's configuration emerged. While the citizen army concept, based on near universal conscription remained and indeed still forms the basis of the army's character, an elite officer corps and the core of a highly professional army also arose. The professional kernel existed at least since 1948, but following the Six-Day War subtle changes occurred lessening the aura of uniqueness that had heretofore characterized this force. The Cincinnatus model had receded (as was no doubt inevitable given the increasing complexity of modern warfare) and had been replaced by a force bearing much more similarity to other armies in our time. Fewer were the generals who served table in their kibbutzim on weekend leaves, or who returned to the plow following military actions and wars. A more likely path of what might be considered horizontal mobility if not interlocking interests tended to be a movement into high political positions or into the business elite. When returning to the farm it was more likely to be the large ranch owned by General Sharon, or to the prosperous holdings of Dayan in Nahalal, though in an attempt to feed the myth former Foreign Minister Yigal Allon never failed to take visiting dignitaries to his home kibbutz on the shores of Lake Kinneret.

Generations of young Israelis have been raised hearing the story of an early secretary of the vast general confederation of labor, or Histadrut—a central if not *the* central economic force in the country during its early formative years—who earned less than the gateman at Histadrut headquarters. The reason, proudly advanced, was that the gateman had a much larger family than the director had and thus was compensated accordingly and in line with the current and accepted standard. From each according to his ability, to each according to his need, was not thought of as idle sloganeering or empty jargon but rather as a firm basis of social and economic organization.

Large income differentials were minimal and the general trend of the *yishuv* and during the early years of statehood was to maintain this. Here again the changes did not start precipitously with the Six-Day War, but could already be observed with events such as the signing of the Reparations agreement with West Germany in 1954, which served to inject large sums not only into the economy at large but to funnel it to individuals (and a significant number of them) as well. But if the trend can be seen to have begun in 1954 the events of June 1967 and the years that followed ended the vaunted income equalitarianism of Israel in its early years. Millionaires began to emerge whose fortunes were made in housing, defense, manufacturing, tourism, and trade—all of which enjoyed immense growth spurts in the years between 1967-73. A labor shortage developed that automatically introduced the element of competition into salaries, and differentials grew apace.

The foregoing inevitably led to the appearance of all manner and form of conspicuous consumption and the previous societal myth of simplicity in living style crumbled before the juggernaut of mind-boggling sums of cash, the likes of which had not previously been experienced in the Jewish State. Where prior to this even Israelis who had substantial resources would assiduously avoid flaunting them, the new and emerging framework put premiums on square footage of apartments, imported furniture and appliances, automobiles, and trips aborad. Where in the early years of the State the principle of simplicity reigned, the post-1967 years saw the reverse achieve prominence and salience.

The pursuance of more and more had many effects, not least being the latent but highly important one of spotlighting the existence of failure in the society, where previously this was cushioned by the general similarity in goods and living standards. Where earlier few put into evidence the signs and symbols of the social or economic distance that separated them from their fellow citizens, the postwar phenomenon of grandiosity and highly conspicuous consumption quickly served to separate those who had the "right stuff" from those who clearly did not. The element of pressure—psychological and social—which this led to or allowed to surface cannot be underestimated in importance.

It soon became not only a matter of how much one made, and how much one had, but also how one made one's living. From the days of the second *aliyah*, and the philosophy of A.D. Gordon that emphasized personal and national redemption through labor, preferably hard physical labor on the farms, roads, and docks of the holy land, one was able to witness a growing reluctance to do not only the dirty jobs but to engage in physical work as such. This had corollary effects in the lowering of work morals among those who did engage in physical tasks and the growth of the phenomenon whereby Jews increasingly withdrew from these jobs with their places being taken by tens of thousands of Arabs from the territories who were only too willing to fill the void. Inevitable though this trend might be, the universities could be filled with thousands of Jews seeking "the degree," and the office and service industries with still additional thousands only because a ready pool of non-Jewish labor was present to fill the less desirable, less sought-after posts. Not only were these jobs less sought-after but were to be avoided even when economic rewards were made more attractive than what was available in the service sector. For example, skilled building workers in the Israeli economy can make highly attractive salaries, but this industry is marked as almost *judenrein* (Jewish) at this juncture, with a very high proportion of Israeli Arabs as well as those from the territories occupying these slots.

It must be recognized that the trends outlined above were due in no small measure to predictable patterns of growth and development shared by other societies and are not specific to the Israeli situation. But the Six-Day War and its aftermath accelerated and radicalized the process leaving little time for the emergence of replacement myths of comparable social impact. The society was overpowered by a spirit of collective intoxication for which there was no recallable parallel. As noted previously, all things became possible and limits to both societal and personal ambitions receded into the background. Israel catapulted from an endangered, beleaguered, essentially weak nation-state at the eastern end of the Mediterranean into the category of superstar among nations. Thus the State was shuttled from subnormalcy (unaccepted, threatened, on guard) to supernormalcy (pugnacious, powerful, highly capable) without ever achieving status as "just another country" or plain normalcy. Before Israel could really begin to develop a healthy sense of itself as a nation among nations it had thrust on it a series of burdens not easily sustained, even under more favorable circumstances and in a more objectively powerful container not the least of which was the gladly assumed mantle of the center and leader of world jewry.

One of the unarguable outcomes of the June conflict was the remarkable growth of identity of the Diaspora with the fate of Israel and the comparable growth of a sense of Jewish connectedness among Israelis. While this development may have desirable effects in certain directions, when viewed against the backdrop of Jewish history it does not aid in the development of a specifically *national* enthusiasm or add to its vitality. It does not and did not add anything to the process of developing an indigenous culture whose parameters would be Israel and the Israelis. Partly as a result of the introduction of television during this period, with its attendant Americanization of almost all aspects of the culture, and partly because of the deepening contacts with world Jewry in America, Europe, South Africa, etc., Israeli culture in the period following the Six-Day War became highly derivative, immitative, and lacking in originality. Popular music became essentially American music, magazines were copies (in Hebrew) of Western types, clothes, food, furnishings, films, and even plays tended to be largely adaptations of what was "in" abroad rather than reflective of an indigenous muse.

The Americanization of culture went hand in hand with another characteristic generally associated with the American pattern—a rise of individualism and a decline of interest in group-oriented, collective, or even volunteer activity. Israelis in the post-1967 period were on the make with a vengeance that can only be associated with a tendency that must have existed over a long period of time but was bottled up and frustrated. When the dam burst, when the constraints were lowered, the waters of desire nearly engulfed the society in a paroxysm of self-seeking and sheer grasping. Getting volunteers to pick oranges or for the Civil Guard or for charitable agencies proved to be more and more difficult. So much so that Prime Minister Golda Meir, otherwise not known for having a particularly sensitive finger on the social pulse of the country, saw fit to appoint Knesset member Esther Herlitz to set up a special government-appointed organization to encourage volunteerism in various spheres. This, in a society that had taken justifiable pride in the fact that it had voluntarily done everything from tax itself to protect itself during the pre-State, halcyon days of the British Mandate, where in effect an almost complete analogue of government was successfully undertaken by the *yishuv*. True, war and the threat of war, or most things connected with defense, could and did still elicit the "volunteer spirit," but with the increasing sense of receding threat there ensued a commensurate adumbration of privatism and a retreat from collective demands.

This affected not only collective demands, but a collective vision as well wherein the concept of a "light unto the nations," while admittedly always somewhat of an exercise in puffery, still nonetheless held a certain content in terms of a set of self-imposed standards of a rather high-minded character. Israel and Zionism itself in most of its classical formulations have from early on been beset by the conflict between normalcy—becoming like all the nations—and the bearing of a prophetic burden, a nation of priests and a holy people. How does one fight war after war and continue to maintain a concept of *havlagah*, or self-restraint? Does not an idea such as "the purity of arms" undergo too much buffeting in the heat of battle to be able to sustain much beyond the mere rhetoric? How does one act the conqueror and wield control over hundreds of thousands of subject people while convincing oneself of one's credentials as a pacific defender of the peace and the lofty sentiments emblazoned in the prophetic texts?

The answer of course is that this is difficult if not impossible and in any event leads to a kind of inner tension and conflict with predictable results for the body politic and social. Israel since 1967 has demonstrated more and more of a kind of pugnacious defensiveness about its moral credentials than either specific acts would warrant or even the often unfair, biased accusations of its "comforters" can justify. A subtle shift has occurred away from assertion of moral superiority (or self demands toward that goal) in the direction of a reluctant embrace of the notion of "a nation like all other nations": "We are, after all, no worse than the United States in Viet Nam, the British in the Falkland Islands, or certainly the Soviet Union in Afghanistan."

This move away from the notion of the collective and toward individualism as well as that from uniqueness to normalcy must be viewed again, as inevitable consequences of the effect of time and events on ideology as well as reflecting unresolved and always present inner tensions and conflicts within the ideology itself. Thus the events that followed the Six-Day War must be viewed as a trigger rather than a cause, an element rather than a complete etiology.

Keniston (1965: 355) is doubtless correct in noting that "the dominant demands of every society are closely related to the special human qualities it considers most virtuous. Men usually define as their highest virtues the human qualities their society most needs of them." Could it not be that with the Israeli emphasis on "winning," "personal courage," and "improvising and taking charge" we witnessed an inevitable and progressive decline of emphasis on cooperation thus encouraging the rise of individualism and ultimately disconnectedness from goals of the collectivity? The idea does not seem to be utterly without foundation or particularly farfetched. An underlying commonality of goal is essential for calling forth even normal levels of group commitment, not to speak of the loftier qualities heretofore demanded by the Israeli myth, for

> men are unique among all creatures in that their visions of the ideal, their myths of the good and bad life, their conscious and unconscious expectations about their just desserts and their merited sufferings—all profoundly affect not only their interpretation of their experience, but the subjective "feel" of experience itself. Thus, among the central factors underlying contemporary alienation is the absence of any shared conscious myth, vision, or conception of the good life that would make the demands of our society worth accepting (Keniston 1965: 313).

This very decline of a "shared myth or vision" was the basis on which the growing polarization of Israeli society could proceed.

The post-1967 period witnessed the development of various left-oriented phenomena such as Matzpen and the growth of Rakah as a voice if not *the* voice of Israel's Arabs. No less important was the rise (and rather precipitous decline) of the Black Panther movement which set out to articulate the sense of disinheritedness of Israel's Oriental community, or more correctly of the Jews stemming from Moslem societies, who though close to being a majority in the population suffered from a sense of second-class citizen status, poverty, lack of educational achievement, and in general—powerlessness!

Here too we can trace a certain connectedness to the events of June 1967. The Jews of this community shared in the general sense of uplift and euphoria and after having performed no less well in the war than their Ashkenazic brethren there was a sense that the time was right to take their rightful place in society now that earlier fears of levantinization had proven groundless and could be laid to rest. Were they not as courageous and resourceful as their brothers of European origin?

Courageous and resourceful though they might have been, systems of stratification to say nothing of hoary prejudices are not easily shaken. The slums did not disappear and the doors of the executive suites did not open any wider than previously for the children of the east. Indeed, very little change was experienced by this segment of the population once the general overall euphoria began to dampen. They were still the hewers of wood and drawers of water, who could be expected to fill the less desirable tasks and occupy the bottom rungs of the societal ladder.

In 1971 Israelis were shocked and shaken at the appearance of a group calling themselves the Black Panthers who emerged from the slums of Jerusalem to demonstrate rather forcefully in the streets of the capital. "Black"? "Panthers"? Was this not the name of a group of young negroes who had recently achieved some notoriety in the United States for, among other things, their rather rabid anti-Semitic rhetoric? How could the Jewish Sephardim identify with such a group? What basis, in fact, existed for such expresssion of alienation and frustration? Did not all Israelis share the same *ma'abarot*, the same poor conditions until they worked themselves out and up? Would not the same opportunities be available to *edot hamizrach* if the necessary will and energy were to be demonstrated?

Initially, the stark effect of the movement's appearance led to some soul searching, some questioning among various segments of the Israeli establishment. Some meliorative programs were launched: poverty was recognized, a dialogue of sorts was begun. But a basic understanding of what the problem might have been seemed to escape most Israelis from the prime minister down. In a notorious meeting between Golda Meir and some leaders of the Black Panthers she was quoted as having summed up the affair with the observation that "they were not nice boys."

Some of the leadership was quickly coopted either to the establishment parties or to other political forces who could advance them while making capital with their cause, and within a few short years the Panthers ceased to be a threat, let alone a force. The small voice they provided to existent frustrations did, however, leave a residue and given the continuance if not deepening of a social and economic gulf separating the two halves of the house of Israel, future upheavals of a much greater magnitude and a tonal level considerably more "shocking" than was apparent with the Panthers are predictable.[4]

While the "ethnic gulf" will probably prove to be the most persistent internal challenge to the successful realization of the Zionist dream, the most startling, if perhaps ephemeral development growing out of the Six-Day War was to be found in the rise of a coalition between an almost idolatrous, land-based nationalism and the forces of religious orthodoxy.

Prior to the June War, a curious but eminently workable symbiosis existed between the religious parties on the one hand, and the dominant labor coalition on the other. The non-Zionist Agudat Yisrael party was interested in what could be discerned as purely religious issues only, such as abortion, autopsy, Sabbath observance, army service, and financial support for its institutions. As long as their minimal needs could be fulfilled in these areas they were content to support the government (or at least to leave it alone) in all other matters. The National Religious Party (NRP), a Zionist grouping, had somewhat wider concerns, but here too they were essentially satisfied with a trade-off wherein the status quo in religious affairs would be preserved in return for support on foreign policy and broader social and economic issues. There existed no discernible or significant policy differences between the Labor Party and the NRP on matters such as borders, security, the internal Arab population, relationships with outside powers, the economy, or much else for that matter.

Following the Six-Day War, the Agudat Yisrael expressed a continuing fidelity to the old patterns—although by the late seventies these patterns had changed from Labor to the Likud Party of Menachem Begin. They were still essentially committed to the same issues and they merely transferred their electoral dowry to the opposition, who in turn rewarded them beyond their wildest fantasies for so doing. They continued, by and large, to evince no particular interest in matters such as borders, territories, security, or foreign policy affairs. If consistency is a virtue, this group demonstrated such to the highest degree!

The NRP on the other hand underwent a series of upheavals and changes that left them with part of the party adhering to the old concerns and hoping to maintain their prior status, while new voices were being heard advocating very definite viewpoints with respect to issues heretofore ignored. Most of these views had to do with what was fast becoming the burning issue of the day in the postwar years—what to do about the territories, or *Eretz Yisrael*? Can places like Hebron, Nablus, the hills of Judah and Samaria, the philistine coast, or Gaza be returned to foreign rule? While this question occupied a central place among other groups in the country—right, left, and center—with some very peculiar new political constellations emerging from the boiling cauldron, it assumed an immeasurably heightened virulence when combined with a deep religious view of the Zionist enterprise. In this view a Jewish anthropology was being advanced, based on fulfillment and proto-messianic elements. Seemingly political steps were quickly perceived in terms of religious desiderata, and steps going counter to a reading of the Jewish ethos in terms of people, book, and land were seen as being in violation of divinely provided opportunity.

Strangely, this dynamic was operative beyond the camp of the religiously committed and observant, with echoes of it being heard in the words of rather avowed secularists. Biblical rhythms transformed the political rhetoric of the time with statements like:

> The Golan is no less part of ancient Israel than Hebron and Nablus, for did not Jephta judge there? (*Jerusalem Post*, 16 August 1967: 6).

or

> If you have the Book of the Bible, and the People of the Book, then you also have the Land of the Bible—of the Judges and of the Patriarchs in Jerusalem, Hebron, Jericho (*Jerusalem Post*, 16 August 1967: 1).

The first statement comes not from a savant. or a Talmudist, but from Yigal Allon of the Palmach and Kibbutz Ginnosar; the second is from General Moshe Dayan.

By September 1967, a movement was formed to prevent the return of *Eretz Yisrael* to its Arab "usurpers" and among the signers of the manifesto were leading secular figures like Dan Tolkowsky, Moshe Shamir, Haim Hazan, Avraham Yoffe, Dov Sadan, Natan Alterman and others (*Jerusalem Post*, 24 September 1967: 6).

But the real enthusiasm—the bone, muscle, and sinew of the movement toward a Zionism of land before other values, of the integrity of all of *Eretz Yisrael*, of seeing in the Six-Day War an entryway or corridor to the coming days of messianic return and fulfillment—was to be found not among the secularists quoted above, but in the religious camp and in variegated hues. The chief rabbi of the Sephardic community citing Maimonades as his authority declared:

> The Land of Israel is the heritage of every Jew and no religious or secular authority including the government of Israel has the power to yield a single inch of it (*Jerusalem Post*, 29 October 1967: 8).

The broad and far-reaching implications of this need no further explication. All the key words and terms are present: "a single inch," "no . . . power to yield," "religious or secular," "the heritage of every Jew," and of course "the Land of Israel." In one way or another each of these words had assumed a heavy emotional valence that in the years following the Six-Day War were to assume centrality in the belief and political systems of a potent energetic minority of religiously observant Israelis who came to be known as Gush Emunim, or the bloc of the faithful.

Here was a movement in opposition to current conventional wisdom. Was pioneering dead? No, the Gush answered with hundreds of young people willing to settle the barren hillsides of Samaria and Judah. Can a minority prevail? Certainly. Did not the precursors come to a land populated by a vast majority of "strangers" and yet prevail? Did not the scriptures and the tradition promise a return to *Eretz Yisrael* and was this not (the war and the conquest) a God-provided opportunity to aid in God's plan for His people?

The Gush represented a delayed entry of the Orthodox into the ideological context that underlay earlier pioneering Zionist ventures in the Holy Land, with two significant differences. First, the movement appeared not at the height but rather at the nadir of these events and its legitimation system was not socialism or secular nationalsim of a nineteenth-century variety, but a messianic almost mystical nationalism more reminiscent of Bar-Kochba than Theodore Herzl. It represented a rejection of negative myths and a ringing affirmation of what the rest of the world seemed to think was either impossible, undesirable, or both. In a world where "symbols of analysis replace those of synthesis; fission, fusion; assymmetry, symmetry; regression, growth" (Keniston 1965: 320), the Gush saw its mission as being the standard-bearers of the old, tested and true way—a voice of hope, of affirmation in a society of nay-sayers and the faithless.

The Gush, rather than remain a fringe or marginal grouping within the NRP, soon demonstrated that if that were the case it was clearly a matter of the tail wagging the dog. The NRP was to all intents and purposes captured (and indeed captivated) by the Gush with the result that the political map of the country, which had assumed the aura of semipermanence, underwent radical and far-reaching changes that reached a logical summation in a new coalition being formed with Menachem Begin's right-wing grouping in 1977.

But if the NRP was captivated so were large numbers of nonparty members and secular Israelis who saw in the Gush a sort of last hurrah of commitment in a country gone the way of all flesh. Statements to the effect that "I don't agree with them but I respect their idealism," "they are the only real pioneers left," "they really believe," or "you must admit that if we have a right to Tel Aviv we have a right to Hebron" made the rounds with increasing frequency in the years following the war.

These are telling sentiments indeed. They reflect the thrust of the main point being made in this essay to the effect that the Six-Day War has proved to be a turning point in the history of the third Jewish commonwealth. The Six-Day War ushered in a period of unbounded hope, expansiveness, and radical internal change. Sustaining myths, which had begun to recede earlier, fell from view entirely. Polarization in a variety of dimensions emerged to the fore together with the growth of a gnawing sense that along the way more than illusions were lost: also gone was a sense of purpose, commitment, justification.

The capstone to these developments was to come with the *mechdal*, the great failure of the Yom Kippur War of 1973, where the factors alluded to above reached peak expression and where it was clearly demonstrated that while the old myths were crumbling replacement myths were not readily at hand. In the interwar period it was possible to witness the growth of a kind of false consciousness in Israeli society that won expression in a sort of boundless enthusiasm, a sense of finally achieved national identity that was to prove somehow less than fully viable.

This was the period where a call went out to return to the old ways, truths, and values. This was the time when the Gush became the unlikely vessel for the preservation of collective enthusiasm and societal values that were already long eclipsed.

In the year following the Yom Kippur War Israel experienced its highest rate of emigration to date. Though intellectuals like E. Schweid could demand an antidote in a return to Zionist values such as Jewish labor, a return to the land, the denial of the *galut* as a desirable or acceptable alternative, settlement and reclamation, the revival of Jewish national culture, etc., it remained unclear to whom he was addressing his remarks (*Maariv*, 7 June 1981: 35 [Hebrew]). For in the three decades following the creation of the State not only had circumstances radically altered, but so had the population and inevitably its consciousness of role and place.

Where the Six-Day War clouded perspectives in a miasma of euphoria and unrealistic perception with regard to Israel's capabilities and objective positioning in the world, the Yom Kippur War brought in its wake clouds of collective despair and fear. The delicately wrought structure of faith in the country's central institutions was shaken and badly so. The army's leadership, which had come to be thought of as sacrosanct and above criticism, saw its reputation, at the highest levels, sink to unheard of depths. The political system was considered to have failed badly in allowing rot and deterioration to set in and afflict the military, and also fell guilty in not reading the purely political signs of impending disaster correctly.

The vaunted intelligence arm of both the military and the civilian systems suffered unprecedented scrutiny and criticism. Settlements on the Golan, which were supposed to serve as a buffer against attack, were in fact found to be a military liability and were evacuated calling into question a key building stone of past Israeli policy and a prime legitimating base for the settlement of the territories.

The Six-Day War had triggered a process that was to be capped in the Yom Kippur War of October 1973, but which had its roots in broad sociological processes and in the peculiar and particularistic history and psychology of the Jewish people and the *yishuv*.

Commitment and Completion: Mystery to Mastery

The notion set forth earlier that whatever the objective facts with respect to emigration—that is to say whether or not a dangerously large and growing number of Israelis are leaving the country or not—the society does perceive the phenomenon as a serious problem. It has further been asserted that the definition of the problem's existence in and of itself stamps the matter with a cover of reality and importance and is suggestive of any number of social phenomena that bear examination within the society. For example, it has been posited that the matter of a sense of collective and deep-ranging insecurity with respect to the nation's future survival is an element to be reckoned with. Another is to be seen in the matter of the solidity and viability of a collective identity, which while largely and extensively ignored as a factor by most observers in the mistaken confusion of Jewish identity with Israeli identity, is not as clear-cut as was assumed. The events emerging out of the Six-Day War and the near tragedy of the Yom Kippur War highlighted these factors in a particularly obtrusive fashion.

But one cannot assume that Israeli society is subject only to the law of cataclysmic upheavels such as wars and the threat of ultimate destruction. More prosaic sociological processes play a role in the unfolding of the Israeli drama as well and these no less than the more dramatic dimensions must be examined.

Earlier, note was taken of the fact that collective enthusiasms or ideal visions have a limited life span and cannot be long maintained as a central strut of communal existence. This is a general proposition and in no way specific to the Israeli reality. Whether it be revolutionary fervor, or Utopian ecstasy—these phenomena tend not to live much beyond the generation of initiators and their charismatic leaders. If the phenomenon persists and does not fade out completely with this founding generation, the age of the institutionalizers follows with all that this implies by way of routinization and a decline in initial fervor, to say nothing of purity of vision.

If anything, Israel and the Zionist enterprise have maintained a sort of "founding fervor" beyond what is normally to be expected in historical terms, and this is even more true of specific aspects of the enterprise, such as the kibbutz movement.

But dreams end, soaring visions descend, ecstatic hopes are dashed. Perhaps even more shocking and more devastating, however, from the point of view of the efficacy of the social propellant supplied by these is that some dreams are realized, some visions are sustained, and some hopes come to fruition. Ennui can be no less formidable an enemy to a societal vision than outright defeat! A measure of success can undermine a social experiment no less surely than failure for there exists no threat greater than ordinariness to an enterprise predicated on exalting the extraordinary.

What Kai Erikson says about the decline of the Puritan enterprise at the end of the seventeenth century has, I think, unique applicability to an understanding of Israel at this stage of its existence.

> The Puritan experiment ended in 1692, rather because the sense of mission which had sustained it from the beginning no longer existed in any recognizable form, and thus the people of the Bay were left with few stable points of reference to help them remember who they were. When they looked back on their own history, the settlers had to conclude that the trajectory of the past pointed in quite a different direction than the one they now found themselves taking: They were no longer participants in a great adventure, no longer residents of a "city upon a hill," no longer members of that special revolutionary elite who were destined to bend the course of history according to God's own word. They were only themselves, living alone in a remote corner of the world, and this seemed a modest end for a crusade which had begun with such high expectations (K. Erikson 1966: 155-56).

Once again, the comparisons with Israel circa 1985 are impressive. Drawing too strict a parallel between events representing different historical periods and a totally different anthropology can be misleading, but one cannot fail to be impressed with the seeming fit between the later developments within the Puritan experiment in America and the present Israeli reality.

In both cases we see societies that flourished on the basis of a perceived mission that had either succeeded or not but had in any event certainly passed. In both we can sense a certain fatigue having replaced prior enthusiasm. In both we see a falling back inwards, a decline in the feeling of representing a spearhead of either history or God. In both, one senses the often devastating effects of routinization on what had previously been fueled by enthusiasm, resulting in a feeling of not only no longer representing the wave of the future, but of perhaps being irrelevant.

In some ways—ironic though predictable—both the Puritans and the Israelis might indeed be considered to be suffering from the effects of success more than from the opposite. As put so forcefully by Kai Erikson (1966: 156-57) in the matter of the Puritans:

> By the end of the century, the Puritan planters could look around them and count an impressive number of accomplishments. Here was no record of erratic providence; here was a record of solid human enterprise, and with this realization, as Daniel Boorstein suggests, the settlers moved from a "sense of mystery" to a "consciousness of mastery," from a helpless reliance on fate to a firm confidence in their own abilities. This . . . left the third generation of settlers with no clear definition of the status they held as the chosen children of God.

From a sense of mystery to a consciousness of mastery! From a sense of mission with all of the excitement attendant upon such a burden to a type of steady, if not plodding, conquest of the commonplace.

One sees in Israel a growing sense of completion or closure in terms of the creative, unique aspects of state building or Zionism. A corollary is the breaking down of a feeling that people "owe" the enterprise to remain when in fact the State is built, Zionism is realized, and the country is more or less secure.

The time seems propitious to tend one's own garden, to pursue individual paths to fulfillment, and this, it would appear, for at least tens of thousands of Israelis is best achievable in the world rather than in Zion.

Land, Sovereignty, and History in Terms of Exile,
Marginality, Time and Space

Why the concern, why the nearly hysterical worry over some tens of thousands—even half a million or so—Israelis who have chosen over the past 35 years to live their lives elsewhere? If 15 percent or so of the Jewish population has left over the years, 85 percent has stayed, and this does not constitute a particularly dreadful record for a land of immigration. Furthermore, for those who take the long view of things or react against the backdrop of past experience, comfort can be drawn from two factors: (1) a shared dynamic with all lands of immigration—past and present, and (2) the cyclic nature of the phenomenon in Israel wherein periods of strong *aliyah* are generally followed by periods of emigration (Eisenstadt 1954: 42).

It seems clear that the concern is predicated on two specters, one which might be termed pragmatic and the other historical-psychological.

The first need not detain us unduly. In a country where the factor of a real physical threat to its continuance is present, every loss through emigration and every decline through lack of immigration or lowered birth rate is rightly conceived of as threatening. Israel is certainly not suffering from an overly large population, even when Jews and minorities are viewed as a single whole. There is, for example, no problem of unemployment, little overcrowding, more than enough food to go around, and adequate shelter. If anything, there is a problem in reverse: sufficient manpower for the army and any number of other central institutions.

Thus emigration, in a very real numerical, bread-and-butter sense weakens the society, even if one takes into consideration a possible function of emigration as a sort of social strainer, filtering out malcontents and perhaps deviants as well. This weakening might be said to be the case in view of the known penchant of Jews other than the poorest and most orthodox to be among the world's most successful practitioners of family planning. In this sense Israelis, though lagging, are moving in the direction of their brethren in the Diaspora. Thus, concern on a practical level with emigration rates cannot be said to be misplaced or without foundation.

The key element of disquiet is to be found in what may be termed the historio-psychological vein or dimension, wherein emigration seems uncomfortably and worrisomely consonant with some rather consistent trends in the Jewish past, both recently as well as in antiquity.

There is no lack of awareness among Israelis that although almost any Jew living almost any place in the world can, if he or she wishes, come to join his brethren in the Jewish State, relatively few have chosen to do so. The fact is that 37 years after the creation of modern Israel approximately 75-80 percent of the world's Jews still choose, for one reason or another, the Diaspora over Zion. Furthermore, at least a proportion of the small number of Jews who have returned to Zion can be said to have done so with less than a full measure of enthusiasm, and simply because of the absence of viable alternative places of settlement. Thus thousands arrived in the early years of the State more as a result of lack of opportunity to go elsewhere than out of any presumed passion for the cessation of exile. One might therefore see in the new departures a move to complete an essentially interrupted process, rather than an out-of-the-blue response to suddenly changed objective or ideational circumstances.

What raises anxiety among so many is the fear that Jews remain what they have always been—rootless wanderers who have in fact chosen this course and this identity as much if not more than having it forced upon them. A.B. Yehoshua (1981: 24), in a biting but brilliant analysis of what he conceives of as a centuries-long Jewish love affair with the *golah*, suggests that this reflects something in the nature of a collective neurosis. In speaking of the *golah* he asserts that rather than viewing it in terms of lachrymose falsity, Jews should recognize that "we foisted it upon ourselves," which in turn means that "it should be regarded not as an accident or misfortune but as a deep-reaching national perversion."

Indeed, even a surface perusal of the Jewish historical drama reveals more than a small measure of truth, or at the very least basis for Yehoshua's assertion. As he (and other observers) have pointed out, the recorded history of this people begins with an act of *aliyah*—Abraham leaving his father's house in Ur of the Chaldees and going up to the Land of Canaan, only to be followed rather quickly by this same central characters' *yerida* or departure from the land in the face of famine. In the case of Abraham we see a return to the Land, but his grandson Jacob—who also left for "economic" reasons (again, a famine)—actually dies in exile and is only brought home for burial.

From the very beginning the twin polarities of exile and redemption have been tied in and irrevocably bound up with the reality of *Eretz Yisrael*, the land of Israel, the land of the Jews. When the Jews (as their basic text the Bible records) sinned or departed from the ways set forth by their God, the punishment, more often than not, was separation from the land. When forgiveness was posited and promised, the center piece of redemption always suggested a temporal, spatial dimension implying a return to the land.

Notwithstanding this absolute centrality of the land in the Jewish epiphany, we cannot escape the implications of the fact, as Yehoshua (1981: 28) notes, that this people was not born, not created in the land. "The elementary primal tie between a people and its homeland is for us not natural." The *golah* is thus deeply ensconced in the Jews' very being, and this depth of enrapturement is symbolized in searing fashion by the fact that the Torah, the formative and formed instrumentality of Jewish existence, was given not in the homeland but in the desert between Golah and Geulah. And this desert did not cease to play a part in the dynamic unfolding of the historical drama following its nation-creating role, but in fact continued to assert preeminence in religio-symbolic terms.

Thus, built into the core of the Jewish praxis we find a central tension between being in the land and without, with reward for virtue always being a physical return and punishment for sin being physical expulsion.

But what kind of reward? The creative impulse found sublime expression in the desert, which might be considered the ultimate symbol of exile—empty, bereft, alone, unforgiving of error, unfruitful—but which in the hands of the Jewish people gave forth with unparalleled richness and of the profoundest variety. Israel was formed in the crucible of Sinai, not on the temple mount. One might extend the metaphor even further by observing that not only in spiritual-creative terms did this first paradigm of exile serve the Jewish people well, but even in material terms. The fleshpots of Egypt were the height, but the mana of Sinai was not to be scorned. It demonstrated a rather benign regularity and a certain leisurely, indeed minimum, outlay of energy was required for its gathering—which cannot be said of what awaited the people after their final ascendency to Canaan. There it was a matter of constant struggle, of a calculus more akin to the expected rhythms of mankind at large where harvest bore some relationship to sowing, where results were in direct if not always dependable relationship to efforts expended.

I am here suggesting in agreement with Yehoshua that from the very earliest there has existed a deep ambivalence about the land among this people, but going one step beyond, I would aver that the ambivalence was long resolved in a preference for exile over life in the land in very pragmatic fashion. The land assumed symbolic centrality reflecting an inner yearning for wholeness, for union, but not more than symbolic centrality; the dispersal among the nations became the true expression of the Jewish sociology in here and now everyday meanings. Exile might very well have been "foisted" upon the Jewish people—but the Jewish people embraced it. Marginality might very well have been a natural outcome of an unnatural existence, but the Jewish people endowed it with a certain aura of positive immutability. Yehoshua suggests that Zionism began with a fear of the *golah*; I would suggest that such a fear has never been manifest and, in fact, Jewish history seems to suggest greater fear of *geulah* [redemption] than of *golah*.

How can this be? Simply because the Jewish drama is acted out within history rather than being some kind of suprahistorical excrescence. Being part of history means that specific events bearing certain unavoidable implications have shaped and formed the Jews no less than other peoples. Straightforwardly put, exile and marginality have been the hallmark of Jewish existence and it is these elements—albeit in tension with their opposites—that have left an indelible mark upon the psyche of this nation. Most of Jewish existence, by far, has been lived in exile rather than in the Land of Israel. The most distinctive sociological classicism that sums up the *modus vivendi* as well as the condition of this people is marginality, not indigenousness. The basic framework or canvas against which the dynamic is spun out is that of time rather than space.

Peoples, like individuals, if they are to survive learn what must be learned in order to do so. Jews over a 3,600-year history have learned how to handle adversity: they do less well with acceptance and affection. They have learned how to deal with dispersal and exile; they remain untutored in the finer points of rooted, collective existence.

From the first Babylonian exile forward the Jews have demonstrated a certain genius for exile. As Paul Tabori (1972: 54) pointed out in talking of this first dispersal:

> Only half a century—yet because it was the exile of a whole nation rather than of individuals . . . it left a traumatic imprint upon the Jewish soul from which only the establishment of the modern State of Israel has released them; and even this release isn't a complete one.

So "traumatic" that when the time of return presented itself only a fraction chose this path; so complete that even until this day and the creation of the modern State the vast majority choose to stay away.

The pattern and habit of exile was early embedded into the heart of Jewish culture and became the foundation stone upon which it was developed. Rather than crush the Jewish spirit, exile enhanced and embellished it, and it became the anvil upon which an almost cosmic toughness was hammered into this people. It became a tool in the age-old battle of the Jews with their God. As Peter Halasz has noted: "For the exile by the mere fact of leaving his country has accepted full and total responsibility for the shaping of his fate. Whoever emigrates, plays God" (Tabori 1972: 167).

The exile must try to master what the stay-at-home (the rooted) can leave to time. The exile must constantly create and recreate the container of his existence leaving little to chance, to habit, to comfortable repetition of what went before. This process elicits a constant price, but the prize in a certain freedom from constraint, from culture, is substantial.

Sociological marginality has always been conceived of as something to be avoided or escaped from rather than embraced. This is a narrow conception of the matter, taking little note of the fact that marginality in itself can be an adjustive pattern, a cultural framework and one bearing with it considerable rewards as well as obvious disabilities.

Stonequist and Park, the classic formulators of the concept, saw it in essentially dysfunctional terms, but there exist positive functions as well. True, the definition of the concept as set forth by Stonequist leaves little room for this type of dual weighting in that the key phrase emphasizes the absence of a "satisfactory adjustment." Stonequist (1961: 2-3) defines marginality as follows:

> The individual who through migration, education, marriage, or some other influence leaves one social group or culture without making a satisfactory

adjustment to another, finds himself on the margin of each but a member of neither. He is a "marginal man."

The bias here is obvious. The classic theorists felt strongly about being either fish or fowl, here or there, white or black. Little room was left for sociological ambiguity, which was not necessarily dysfunctional in adjustive terms. The view, which saw in the Jew the epitome of marginality, assumed in its classic formulation far too much and far too little. It was (and is), in short, somewhat simplistic:

> The Jew has a peculiarly complex problem of adjustment. Centuries of experience with this problem have left their imprint upon his character. His group life is organized upon a marginal basis, characteristically expressed in his proclivity for living in the cosmopolitan city by means of trade and banking—"business." The flexible and restless nature of his mind enables him swiftly to seize an advantage and to discount the future (Stonequist 1961: 81).

The above suggests more caricature than is warranted, with more than a little hint in the direction of a "thief in the night," "here today—gone tomorrow" perception of the Jews than a realistic dealing with their peculiar positioning.

Without denigrating the factor of personality instability, or the existence of discomforting conflict that often afflicts people who live on the margins of two cultures (an inner and an outer as it were), one must also be cognizant of marginality as a chosen cultural vehicle with decided social and personal benefits accruing to the participant.[5] Thus Simmel's concept of the stranger might add to our understanding in this regard in that the element of volition plays a role other than sheer determinism alone. In speaking of the "objectivity" of the stranger, Simmel (1950: 404) notes:

> But objectivity does not simply involve passivity and detachment; it is a particular structure composed of distance and nearness, indifference and involvement.

Simmel (1950: 405) goes on to suggest that objectivity might also be defined as freedom, for "the objective individual is bound by no commitments which could prejudice his perception, understanding and evaluation of the given. . . . He is freer, practically and theoretically; he surveys conditions with less prejudice; his criteria for them are more general and more objective ideals; he is not tied down in his action by habit, piety, and precedent."

Simmel, too, would aver that the status of stranger is ascribed via a given route of societal dynamics, rather than sought as a personal identity. Few indeed would be the individuals who consciously choose either a marginal existence within a given society or status as a stranger. But would it be absurd or without foundation to suggest that both conditions can be turned to benefit? Do not, in fact, the attributes Simmel suggests as being those of the stranger, or Stonequist those of the marginal man, in a certain sense provide a high degree of freedom from social constraint and stultifying standards of full commitment? Cannot these be ensconced and embraced as a cultural value or desiderata on the part of a group that has learned over a period of centuries how to utilize them in a positive fashion?

I would assert that this is the case with the Jews and serves to explain much with regard to the placement of the concept of exile in their cultural firmament and their continuing reluctance, in the main, to assume the burden and pain of freedom and responsibility subsumed and suggested in national autonomy, and a return to Zion.

This is clearly not a cut-and-dried matter. I am not maintaining the existence of a vast historical fraud perpetrated by the Jews upon themselves wherein on the one hand the idea of exile is posited as a negative value, while on the other they gleefully undermine every act, step, or possibility that would abrogate this "unnatural" condition. The lusting after Zion is real enough, but I would assert more in its symbolic, relatively abstracted guise than as a temporal goal. One might almost see the centrality of Zion in Jewish praxis as a metaphor for what lies behind and beyond, which is an eschatology defined very naturally in time and which has very little to do with space. In this regard I find Yi-Fu Tuan's (1978: 10) contrasting of the Hebrew and Greek conceptions of time and space apt:

> Western conceptions of space, time and place have roots in Greek and Hebrew thought (Russell, 1968). To the Greeks the world was essentially spatial. Places also had deep significance. As Pericles's oration indicated, the Greeks valued autochthony, the fact of being native to a place. Time was either cyclical or it was negated in the image of timeless ideas, the eternity that Plato liked to contemplate. To the Hebrews the world was essentially time, sequential or directional time. The Hebrew God was the God of History, and history began with the Creation and reached towards the Consummation. The Hebrews were nomads; their chronicles were packed with events, including mass movements of people. Migration provided a linear structure of time: as a journey had a starting point and was consummated at the goal, so time was sequential with a beginning and an end.
>
> Hebrew prophets denigrated place—the tie to the soil of sedentary peoples. They associated attachment to place with the worship of Baalim, that is, the worship of "place" gods. For the Hebrews, according to Robert Aron, there was "something scandalous about building in space. The Jews' vocation is to build in time; their true temples are in the human heart and consubstantial with history, never finished and indeed owing their endurance to this very

incompletedness. . . . The very fact of construction, of an attempt to isolate a unit of the immense space created by God and thus to check the flow of time, was . . . shocking and almost idolatrous." After heaven and earth have been created the mythical mind would expect God to create a holy place—a holy mountain or spring—on which a sanctuary is to be established. Yet in the Bible it is holiness in time, the Sabbath, that comes first: "And God blessed the seventh day and made it holy." In the New Testament Jesus consistently opposed the idea of sacred places. He rejected the promptings of Zealots to save the homeland from the pagan Romans; he rejected his disciples' suggestion that a monument be raised on the Mount of Transfiguration in his honour; "he repeatedly promised to destroy the Temple of Jerusalem, the existence of which was always on the verge of respatializing God" (Cox 1966: 57).

Jews have repeatedly demonstrated this inclination to express their people's genius in a time- rather than a space-oriented framework. Zion in its temporal manifestation has ever served as a symbolic anchorage for a culture utterly devoted to a sort of existential dispersion which has, it would appear, expressed its truer nature. Commitment to the temporal Zion, the land of Israel has more often than not been proven to be a sort of collective talisman rather than profoundly real in any identifiable historical or sociological sense.

This tendency I would submit is not a recent development, or tied to the European dispersion or to biblical mythology, but can rather be shown to have manifested itself in every historical period through which the Jewish drama has unfolded, suggesting deep roots rather than ephemeral responses to persecution or expulsions.

Not only in the biblical rendition, or the meager results of the call to return after the first exile, but also after the second penultimate dispersal following upon the defeat of the revolt against Rome we are able to see the problematic nature of the attachment to the here and now Zion. Even in the period when one might have thought the habits of "landedness" so to speak were still deeply embedded and relatively undisturbed (notwithstanding the long-term parallel existence of a Diaspora), we are able to trace examples of the leadership of the time inveighing against a strong drift outwards.

Avi-Yonah (1976: 25), for example, notes that in the period following the Bar Kokhba War "the first danger which threatened Jewry was emigration." This lead to a series of measures among those leaders who stayed behind to stem the tide. A perusal of some of these evokes a decided feeling of deja vu—a sense that indeed the more things change, the more they stay the same.

Avi-Yonah records two parallel courses of action: one legal, the other religious or moral. The legal measures adopted aimed at encouraging *al-*

iyah and included economic benefits with respect to currency, land and property sales, etc., while trying to curb any economic gain to be derived from emigrating. The latter included a ban on the purchase of property in Syria (probably the Golan). This apparently was a popular device to avoid the laws of tithing and sabbatical year which apply only in Palestine. The rabbis decreed that, for a Jew who buys a field in Syria, "it is as if he bought it in the suburbs of Jerusalem" (Avi-Yonah 1976: 26). Measures were also taken to discourage the emigration of students and priests whose departure was viewed as particularly unacceptable. One action in this regard was that formal ordination (of rabbis) could take place only in the Holy Land.

Numerous aphorisms emerged from the mouths and pens of learned rabbis suggesting the moral and spiritual uplift to be gained from residence in Palestine, and the loss to be sustained from either leaving it or not returning.

> Whoever lives in the Land of Israel is free of sin.

> The Holy One measured all the Lands but found none worthy of Israel but the Land of Israel.

> Whoever walks four cubits in the Land of Israel gains Paradise.

> A man should always live in the Land of Israel . . . for whoever lives in the land of Israel is like one who worships the true God . . . and whoever lives abroad is like one who worships false gods (Avi-Yonah 1976: 27).

Most interesting of all was perhaps the following:

> A man should live in the Land of Israel, even in a city with a Gentile majority; and he should not live abroad even in a place inhabited by Jews only (Avi-Yonah 1976: 27).

This is a recognition of the portability of Zion and of the fact that from an early period in their history Jews recognized the centrality in their lives of the confraternity of believers rather than landed rootedness. There was a struggle to embrace the space dimension by a leadership sensing its importance (and its shallowness) and a seeming rejection on the part of the masses of the people in favor of a pattern of dispersal that has become synonymous with Jewish existence.

Thus the modern Zionist movement as it emerged at the end of the nineteenth century in Europe, and as it developed over the next half century or so, should not be viewed as in any way a secular recapitulation of a formerly religious based passion for physical return and normal national existence. It represented something utterly new and, I believe, basically flawed in its understanding of the role of a temporal, here and now, Zion in Jewish experience. Not only is its basic interpretation in error, but its emergence at this juncture of Jewish history and in the West might be considered to have constituted a fatal error of timing as well, this time in purely sociological terms.[6]

With respect to the dominant and pervasive Jewish *Weltanschauung*, it would appear that Herman Cohen rather than his confounders had the right approach. It is reported that the famous German Jewish philosopher, who was notorious for his anti-Zionist attitudes, was once reproved and asked why he was so rejective of what seemed to many to be not only the wave of the future but perhaps the only salvation of the Jews as well. He is reputed to have answered with great passion, saying "the fools, the fools, they actually want to be happy." Alas, perhaps not!

Over the course of field research for this volume, and in the face of the evidence provided by the demography of the Jewish world at this point, one would have to posit that the ideology of political Zionism was at all points in deep conflict with a pervasive understanding that went counter to any reputed desire for normalcy.

The classical Zionist theorists (again, the political rather than cultural Zionists, such as represented by Ahad Haam)—Herzl, Pinske, Borochov, Nordau—left no doubt that they were envisaging a real flesh-and-blood country for the Jews, with all that this implies and implied by way of the entire range of problems and satisfactions bound up in the notion of statehood. So passionate was the desire (it was thought) for normalcy that the relative absence of social deviates from the *yishuv* was a cause for at least feigned concern on the part of no less a personage than Bialik, the poet laureate of the early community. In the history of the *yishuv* and during the early years of statehood every development—the great and the modest— that seemingly rejoined the Jewish people to the wheel of history was celebrated often in the most touching if intemperate tones: "the first Jewish Army in 2,000 years," "the first Jewish coinage," "the first Jewish ship," "the first Jewish steel plant," etc.

But no sooner did it become evident that a Jewish ship is run very much like a gentile ship, or that Jewish tax people can be as nasty as others of that breed, or that armies were hierarchical, nondemocratic machines of destruction, that it became equally evident that something more (or less) was, in fact, hoped for. In talking with Israelis—young and old, those staying as well as those leaving—or in reading the press and the literature it becomes clear that the level of "disappointment" with Israel seems so total as to raise serious doubt with respect to whether any apparently "normal" society would suffice, or is indeed desired. It is the "City of God" that has been sought and found absent rather than any recognizable temporal entity.

The Zionist movement thought that it was opting for a physical solution, while the masses of Jews—those in Israel as well as in the Diaspora—

proved to be quite content with a more ethereal device. For many the state was, seemingly, a misunderstanding! How does one understand the numerous departees who told me in one way or another, "Yes, I am leaving but I am an Israeli. I will remain an Israeli, and this is my country," other than seeing in this a strong skein of continuity with the Jewish role in history and a radical misreading of the modern Zionist presentation. What is really being said is, "I am a *Jew* and will *remain* a Jew no matter where I live." Israel for this group is as it has always been for the masses of Jews— an idea, or a metaphor, rather than dirt, boarders, and policemen. It became clear during the course of interviewing dozens of departing Israelis that there existed a certain confusion with regard to distinctions between Jewishness and Israeliness. It was thought that just as Jewishness was portable and transferable from place to place, that one could be a good Jew and a good American or Frenchman or Italian, so one could do the same with a purely national identity like Israeliness. There existed honest confusion when confronted with the possible paradox of fulfilling one's destiny as an Israeli, while driving a cab or running a computer in New York. An Italian or Greek immigrant in New York fulfilling the same role might very well continue to identify hinself personally as an Italian or Greek, but I venture to say he would not think of the fact that he was in New York rather than in Rome or Athens as of no consequence regarding his national credentials. He would at the very least see it as a bifurcated national identity, whereas there exists a tendency for Israelis to identify themselves as Israeli-Americans meaning as it were Jewish-Americans. In other words, when the Italian or Greek immigrant lives in America he at least recognizes that his national input in Italian or Greek terms has drawn to a close either temporarily or permanently. The Israeli immigrant, on the other hand, sees a high degree of continuity that suggests a confusion or slurring of distinction between the religio-ethnic and purely national aspects of his identity. And this, I would assert, is not without significance suggesting *inter alia* a sort of collapsing of Israeli into American ideals that is reflective of a strong skein of continuity with past patterns among Jews.

I have been attempting to establish the point that Zionism in its classic formulation has tended to misread Jewish history with regard to the nature and role of a temporal Zion. In addition, however, I noted earlier that there exist some sociological difficulties as well, and primary among these is the fact that the creation of a here-and-now, flesh-and-blood state called into question not only the long established and assiduously defended love affair with marginality but also the traditional class structure of postemancipation Jewry as well.

While strata of the very rich and very poor exist among Jews as they do among the peoples and societies wherein Jews live, there is little doubt that the Jews in the majority of instances and places are heavily concentrated in the middle classes. This is especially the case in the post-World War II era, where in addition to a heavy middle-class concentration two other factors have become even more preeminent than previously: a very high degree of urbanization and a significant weighting in the direction of business and the professions such as law, medicine and, lately, engineering.

One of the central and most important thrusts of the Zionist movement—even its nonsocialist, nonpioneering configurations—was on the creation of a "normal" social framework in *Eretz Yisrael* that would, in the nature of things, presage a bottom, a middle, and a top. Indeed, at least for an important group among the early Zionists, the creation of a Jewish proletariat and a Jewish pseudo-peasantry was elevated to an ideological value. Not only was the first Jewish thief or first Jewish deviate to be celebrated, but more importantly (and understandably) the first Jewish farmers, guards, street cleaners, and factory workers were eulogized and raised up to Homeric heights. But it dare not be forgotten that the vast majority of the Jewish people, while cheering and indeed cheered by this development, never shared in the vision on the personal level. Jewish "normalcy" like Jewish sovereignty was always desirable more in the abstract, or symbolically, or for others more than for themselves. But a state or society cannot function with only doctors, lawyers, businessmen, and Ph.Ds. Someone has to deal with the garbage, people have to man an assembly line, and not everyone can go to the university. Who will fulfill the less desirable, the less sought-after tasks in the society? Indeed, who will occupy the bottom rungs of the social ladder?

One can respond to this dilemma in a number of ways, and according to some fairly obvious, existing models.

- The Jews of Israel could opt for a supervisory role while Arabs from within the green line (or since 1967 from the territories) did the physical labor.
- One could attempt a revamping of the reward structure wherein both in financial and status terms the undesirable and unwanted could be transformed into the desirable and sought after.
- One could seek something on the order of the South African apartheid model with the Arabs fulfilling the role of the blacks.
- One could think in terms of imported contract labor from more distant parts such as Southeast Asia.
- One could allow a gulf of distinction to grow between immigration waves or ethnic groups within the Jewish group so that, for example, Jews of European background could function in various elites while those of eastern backgrounds assumed low-status roles.

It has in fact been suggested that the first and the last models alluded to reflect the direction in which Israeli society has gone and is continuing to move.

I would nonetheless suggest that all of the above models are either unworkable or undesirable in view of the financial, political, moral, or even ideological premises of Israeli society—currently or in the foreseeable future. Notwithstanding cries and warnings to the effect that Israel was on the way or has already become a Rhodesia or South Africa because of its class or ethnic structure, these judgments must be seen as still somewhat premature when not entirely mischievous or ingenuous.

Israel does have a class structure that approximates those in Western countries at a comparable stage of economic development. And Jews, albeit not equally distributed in terms of countries of origin, do occupy all slots and levels within this structure. Thus, one of the most obvious "benefits" of marginality—the ability to enjoy a skewed class structure because of the availability of outgroup members to fill unsought and negatively valued roles—can be said to have been upset by the creation of the State of Israel. Not only does this mean that in Israel Jews will be truck drivers as well as executives, farmers as well as doctors, but also, and more importantly, competition for high status roles will be tougher. Given the relative eclipse of the societal myth that elevated previously low-status tasks to ideologically positively sanctioned ones and the comparative smallness of the enterprise, this competition must be seen to be growing apace bringing in its wake tension and displacement. Recognizing this factor, the authors of a report on the implication of peace for world Jewry suggest it as a key factor in the relative unattractiveness of Israel as an alternative for large numbers of Jews. The authors address themselves to the reasons, as they see it, for the many who have come and those who have not:

> The large majority of these, however, were refugees who had nowhere else to go. Of those who had a choice, the majority chose the Western democracies. This is most clearly demonstrated by the current destinations of the emigrants from the USSR, as it was earlier by that of the emigrants from Algeria. Similar patterns have been also exhibited by recent Jewish emigrants from South Africa, Iran and Latin America. When Jewish emigrants have the choice, they recoil from the high taxes, the long army service, the threat of wars, the relatively low standard of living and of public services *and the much greater competition for jobs in the traditional Jewish occupational structure* [emphasis added]. The attractions of life under Jewish sovereignty have not been sufficiently strong to outweigh those offered by the more secure and prosperous Western democracies (Walinsky & Hirsh 1981: 45).

The more ideological press for structural normalcy declines, and the more Israel assumes the dimensions of "another country," failing to provide the canvas for the more traditional and deeply rooted Jewish social pattern, the more the ties that bind will begin to unravel. In effect we might be seeing the unfolding of a near perfect example of Romer's Rule, which posits that every innovation is, in the last analysis, conservative (Thompson 1976: 9).

The innovation in Israel was, of course, statehood and all that it brought in its wake, while providing perhaps only a springboard for a more legitimate, more established, more unshakable value that is no less surely dispersed.

Notes

1. See Eitan Sabatello, "The Emigration from Israel and Its Characteristics," *Bitfutzot Hagola* 19, no. 85-86 (Summer 1978) (Hebrew); and Zion Rabi, "Emigration from Israel 1948-77," *Rivon L'Qualkala* 25, no. 99 (December 1978) (Hebrew).
2. Just as the Six-Day War ended in complete victory and hope and euphoria, America was being racked by race riots. In July both Newark and Detroit erupted and the combination of the Six-Day War victory and American troubles and fears resulted in a new surge of American Jewish interest in *aliyah*. But then *aliyah* had to maintain too high a mix of "push" over "pull," with a resulting erosion and *yerida* in the six-year period following the war. All in all, 12 cities had riots that summer, among them Flint, Grand Rapids, Toledo, Lima (Ohio), Englewood, Pontiac, New York, Cambridge (Md.), Tucson, and Houston.
3. It would appear that as late as August 1967 the overseas student program at the Hebrew University was still a modest affair. An item in the *Jerusalem Post* stated that 180 students were due to arrive from the United States and Canada and that this number represented a 36 percent increase over the past year. This was the beginning of the student "avalanche" that began after the 1967 war.
4. For a good discussion of the growth and development of the Black Panther movement see Peres (1976).
5. Subsequent theorists who have dealt with the concept of marginality—and one must take note of the fact that the entire concept seems to have lost standing in the sociological firmament—have in fact taken up this very point. Antonovsky (1956: 62) notes that "membership in a marginal group is not necessarily a position in limbo" and that "individuals . . . seem to develop definitions of the situation which are relatively smooth, satisfying and livable." David Golovensky (1952: 333-39) posits that "the greater number [of marginals] want—not are condemned—to live simultaneously in two civilizations." See also Goldberg (1941: 52-58) and Green (1947).
6. See S. Avineri (1981) for a superb analysis of the meaning of Zionism against the backdrop of Jewish history. Avineri observes *inter alia* that "Zionism is, after all, also a revolution against Jewish history, not only against the gentile world" (p. 226).

2

The View from Israel

The scene has by now become commonplace: Long lines of people wait at the United States Embassy at Tel Aviv vying for both the hard-to-get immigrant visas or the easier (but still difficult to obtain) tourist visas, which can—as often as not—be finagled into a "green card" and, ultimately, permanent residence in America. An ad in the Israeli press placed by a South African firm asking for 50 technicians is answered by some 1,500 job seekers. News reports about Israeli "wet-backs" wading the Rio Grande from Mexico into the United States or sneaking across the Canadian border into Alaska and then flying to Los Angeles on a domestic flight are not uncommon. Much less common, but certainly shocking, are the occasional tales of Israeli "boat people"—young Israelis who jet to the Bahamas and then rent fishing boats for the trip to Miami, stepping ashore at the first convenient marina. Israeli neighborhoods spring up in the world's major cities like Amsterdam, London, Munich, Frankfurt, Johannesburg, and, of course, New York, Los Angeles, and Montreal. Fictitious marriages are arranged with citizens of various countries in order to get permanent residence or citizen status. Israeli doctors staff, at times, full departments in foreign cities; Israeli engineers are prominent in various industries; Israelis drive cabs, wait tables, bake bread, and, in some cases, engage in considerably less savory occupations. Israeli artists and musicians, *kibbutznikim* and *moshavnikim* from east and west, native and immigrant, religious or secular, educated and uneducated, army veterans and shirkers, rabid nationalists and peaceniks, academics and carpenters—all are represented in the movement outwards.

A mere three and one-half decades after the establishment of the State of Israel following the greatest tragedy to befall the Jewish people in its history, the third Jewish commonwealth feels itself to be challenged by the most prosaic and ironic of threats to its continued viability—a perceived growing lack of will on the part of tens of thousands of its citizens to stay within it. Furthermore, at a time when almost any Jew in almost any land can come home and plight his troth with the Jewish people in its land, a mere 20 to 25 percent have so opted. Not only has Israel so far failed to

55

spark any significant voluntary movement of Jews to its shores, but something of the reverse seems to be gaining ground with thousands of Israelis opting for a new exile and an almost innocent—sometimes it appears triumphant—return to the *galut*.

A recent news item quotes an Israeli government statistician to the effect that for the past two years emigrants have outnumbered immigrants. Immigration figures are (with the possible exception of 1953) the lowest in the country's history: about 11,000 were expected in 1982, while emigration that year was around the 20,000 mark. Somber as these figures might be, they can be viewed as even more so when one realizes that while the figures for immigration are more or less correct, those reflecting emigration are certainly underreported. While accurate figures are difficult if not impossible to attain with respect to emigration, most sources agree that a minimum of 300,000 Israelis have left since 1948. This figure is government supplied; independent estimates range from a low 130,000 to the frightening and seemingly absurd figure of 700,000. Whatever the true numerical dimensions of the phenomenon, widespread agreement exists among observers that, while cyclic, the trend is upwards and is likely to increase rather than decrease.

One is constrained to ask very simply at this point—why? What has happened that can explain not only the reluctance of Jews in the *galut* to come, but also the apparent wish of so many already in Israel to leave? A.B. Yehoshua (1981: 24) may have struck a chord of historical and sociological truth when he asserts of the *golah* that "we foisted it upon ourselves. It should be regarded not as an accident or misfortune, but as a deep-reaching national perversion." Is the phenomenon to be explained perhaps along less existential, less cosmic lines bearing less relatedness to "national perversion" than to here-and-now pragmatic, measurable, easily definable, and totally understandable factors such as the constant physical threat to their existence under which Israelis live, an unpromising economic situation, an absence of career possibilities, reserve duty, high taxation, an inflexible and capricious bureaucracy, and so on?

Even if the thrust of evidence suggests the centrality of all or some of these "pragmatic" variables, the serious question posed by Yehoshua retains its efficacy. If perhaps not "perversion," then at the very least a deep-seated peculiarity or idiosyncrasy that determines collective roots and national existence conditionally is deserving of exploration, and Yehoshua's phrasing becomes both felicitous and pointed. If thousands of Israelis are leaving because of this or that lack or failure of the national enterprise; if thousands weigh their commitments on a scale of measurable devices moving themselves to the left or the right, to stay or leave based on ephemeral variables, does this not suggest a most peculiar relatedness to "normal" national existence?

One must keep in mind that the thousands who are leaving Israel now are not penniless emigrants, "displaced rural peasantry," an exploited proletariat, or a frightened oppressed minority seeking freedom to live its own life and culture according to its own mandates. The overwhelming proportion of Israelis leaving the country are at the very least literate, in a significant proportion of cases professionals of one kind or another, and, if not wealthy, certainly far from the penniless prototype Jewish immigrant of the somewhat lachrymose and romantic image of the nineteenth century. I would, with respect to this latter point, venture a guess and suggest that at least in the case of the United States the Israelis presently arriving represent the most gilded of immigrant groups to reach American shores in this century. Unlike the Greeks or Italians, the Israelis arrive not from the depressed Peloponnese or the grinding poverty of southern Italy but from all parts of the country, all walks of life, all economic strata, and with a nest egg resulting from the sale of an apartment and/or an automobile in Israel's overcharged and inflationary economy. Not only are the majority of Israelis leaving for foreign parts not escaping personal economic distress of any objectively serious dimensions, but they are in addition leaving a flourishing country with a high Western standard of living; a place where at least on the material plane, a certain ease in Zion has been achieved. Visitors to the country are constantly amazed at the number of autos clogging Israeli roads, the stylish dress of the women, the plethora of banks in every nook and cranny, the stereo shops, the color TVs, the phenomenon of a half million Israelis going abroad for summer vacations, and the "villa" sections growing even in development towns like Ma'alot and Carmiel. One notes, either with dismay or satisfaction, depending on one's view of the enterprise, the vigor demonstrated by the Israeli Stock Exchange, the existence of diversified and sophisticated portfolios, the high level of personal saving, and the instant millionaires whose wealth springs from everything from admitted commercial and technical wizardry to land speculation.

Opportunity exists, clearly. The goods of this life can be attained in Zion! No Sicily, no Peloponnesus this.

Thus we are faced by something of a dilemma, a conundrum. Why is Israel—a land of milk and honey, a country with a constantly growing and expanding economy, a fine climate, a free political atmosphere; a country still enjoying the patina of romance engendered by its remarkable rebirth, astounding growth, breathtaking victories in war; the only country which both in actuality and potential can provide the sustaining valence for the development of rooted Jewish culture—witnessing instead of an inflow of tens of thousands of Jews from the four corners of the earth, an outflux of tens of thousands to the four corners of the earth?

It seems evident that four key areas, some of which have already been touched upon, must be explored in any attempt at reaching an understanding of what is currently taking place with respect to the immigration-emigration phenomenon in the State of Israel. In interrogative fashion I would formulate them as follows:

1. While the material dimension in Israel is comparatively satisfactory, does it answer the expectations of many thousands of its citizens who aspire to more? Is the prime factor underlying emigration economic in nature?
2. Is the quality of life in Israel (and by this I refer to everything from the threat of war to an instrusive bureaucracy) so lacking when compared to other Western lands as to readily loosen ties to the mother country, giving rise to emigration? Or, is the quality of life in other lands perceived as so far and away superior to what is presently available in Israel as to exercise an unparalleled attractiveness?
3. Are there some deep-rooted, seemingly intractable elements in Jewish history and culture that persistently work to undermine developments leading to autonomy and an independent national life?
4. Are the perceived sense of socioeconomic deprivation suffered by segments of the population (Jews of Oriental origin) and the existence of an "ethnically" influenced class structure factors in fomenting emigration both among those who experience this personally and others fearful of the long-range societal implications?

The Economic Factor

There can be little doubt that the economic element—the desire to earn more, buy more, have more—runs like a red thread through the current and past emigration waves. Jews historically and contemporaneously have not been marked by undue abstemiousness in the material vein (perhaps no people are so noted) and Israel has, since the early 1960s, followed an upwardly curving line of expectations fueled by a high level of intense economic development and achievement. From a point a scant 20 years ago where a two and one-half room apartment, a week a year at the seashore, and sufficient food on the table (with some luxuries like a radio and a refrigerator) represented the norm of expectation and hopes, Israelis have entered the promised land of luxury flats, trips abroad, stock options, fine automobiles, and the like. Needless to say, most Israelis are not rich, as most Americans are not rich, but the revolution in expectations is relatively fresh in Israel and the resulting growth in appetite and panic at "missing out" or being left behind is palpable. Observers, friendly and otherwise, have taken note of the high level of materialism seemingly rampant in Israel, contrasting this development with the very recent and recallable past where Israel was (rightly or wrongly) held up as an example of puritan, indeed spartan, equalitarianism.

"Making it," however, in terms of goods and wealth is still not easy in contemporary Israel. The possibilities, realistically as well as mythically, are more evident and indeed more probable in foreign parts—especially places like the United States, Canada, and South Africa.

But how is one to explain the thousands of Israelis who leave with tens of thousands of dollars resulting from the sale of their apartments and cars only to start up again in a new and, for most, strange environment abroad? A goodly proportion of those leaving have "made it"—at least in Israeli terms. Are large numbers of Israelis more committed to money and goods than to Zion? Does there exist a far-ranging willingness to trade roots for cash?

I don't think the evidence available supports the supposition. In 94 interviews (117 people) with departing emigrants carried out during the latter part of 1981 and the early months of 1982, I was repeatedly struck by the following:

1. Most emigrants would leave *even if by so doing they do not significantly improve their economic situation.* Most, however, said they would not if it meant lowering it.
2. Most (who emigrated formally and officially as opposed to those who used circuitous routes) own apartments, appliances, autos, and have well-paying jobs. My estimate is that disposable property ranges between $40,000-$70,000 for a significant proportion of emigrants, and higher for a minority.
3. Failure to put aside enough cash for an apartment or for "luxuries" motivates only a small minority to emigrate and is not even extensively resorted to as a legitimatizing device.
4. Joblessness is not a significant factor, although lack of job satisfaction might be.
5. Emigrants are willing, at least temporarily, to fill almost any job abroad though not in Israel.

Again, while the interviews suggested an economic element as most evidently present among most departees, very few were willing to state simply that they wanted money and goods alone and were therefore leaving for greener pastures.

For Israelis, materialism still carries with it the hint of a negative value. But while diffident about or even somewhat disapproving of what is considered to be crass materialism, there is nonetheless widespread recognition of its not insubstantial pull upon considerable numbers of Israelis, albeit with a dollop of sheepishness:

> I'll tell you, from the economic point of view you can get a lot of things there [U.S.] but from the spiritual dimension life there is completely empty. I decided that if at some point I decide to remain in America, it will be only because of money. Only because I want to get ahead materialistically and that's all. I don't have anything pulling me there except that. There isn't anything else.

Materialism tends to be viewed as necessary, perhaps ordained, but not really all that palatable. There exists a barely disguised notion that Israelis more than others will tend to lose their sense of proportion, becoming obsessed with the matter at hand:

> One of the things that I noticed about the Israelis in America is that they become so materialistic, that sometimes you can throw up from it. . . . Today in Israel, much to my regret, it's become very materialistic, but there they get stuck on things which are easier to get than here. You can put down a 20 percent down payment and you have a house, two cars, and all the accessories for the kitchen, plus all sorts of things, like pools, and jacuzzies, and stuff like that. If it is electric—an Israeli must have it. We have surpassed the Americans! The average American can't live at the standard of living that the Israelis do. We Israelis want to buy and run, and get, and get more; don't misunderstand me, I also went and bought things, and I also like to have a nice apartment, and nice accessories and dishes and the space and a car and everything else, but to get stuck on it?

There is a strong and often expressed feeling that the system in Israel goes counter to nature in making it inordinately difficult to fulfill materialistic "needs" without beggering the citizen:

> There is no reason that I should pay a million and a half for a car when it's only worth 750,000 or 600,000. There is no reason. Why should I pay double the norm? Or for a TV why should I pay so much, when outside Israel, in another place, it's half the price? Or a stereo, or simpler things, like the mixer, or a refrigerator that I have to pay thousands for when it's worth, without taxes, a fraction. Let's say we have to pay taxes because of the needs of the State, but why should I pay three times what it's worth? So they say, outside of Israel it's not like this, I give a lira, I get for the lira, and I don't get something for the value of 20 agorot.

There is also the matter of time, of how long one must wait for various things in Israel as opposed to the almost instant gratification that can presumably be had in America.

The reason [for going to the U.S.] is to *get* more; the idea that it's easier to make money outside; the fact that others have succeeded, and they've heard only about those that have succeeded; the amount of time it takes you to, say, buy a mixer here as opposed to there where you can get it immediately. Here it's not so easy! Here to get the smallest thing it takes a long time; there, it's there, it's in your hands right away.

Interestingly, two relatively new factors seem to be complicating widely held views in the matter of materialism: a lessening sense that the deprivation or abstinence that was characteristic of Israeli society in the early years of statehood is still justified by the objective condition of the society, and a growing, almost pervasive feeling that Israel has become the 51st state of the United States in just about everything including attitudes to "things" and "standards of living." When large numbers of Israelis were convinced that sacrifice was necessary and that the burden of these sacrifices was more or less evenly shared by all, the fact that Israelis paid outrageous sums for cars, mixers, apartments, and what have you, went down with relative ease. When the "need" for sacrifice seemed to diminish with a growing sense of security and growing affluence (and differentials) there arose a corresponding reluctance to suffer these deprivations. When it became legitimate to "crave" material things, to expand horizons, so to speak, it became equally legitimate to want the most, and the best, and it was not unclear to Israelis that a more natural arena for the satisfaction of material wants lay elsewhere than in Israel—more specifically, in America.

There is a Hebrew phrase much in use which goes *im kvar, az kvar,* which freely translates to "as long as you're going—go all the way." As one young departing woman put it:

The way people live and work, I'll tell you the truth, it's an imitation of America today: clothes, things you can buy, needs—it's like the 51st state in a lot of things. Here it's a race for those things; why should I miss out? It's terrible, it's blinding. It's the education.

Thus, the growing materialism of the society and the visible cornucopia that is America are present as factors in the decision to emigrate. But for the majority of respondents a more important irritant (or stimulus) is to be found in things like taxes, the need for financial brinkmanship, and a sense that life—more specifically life in Israel—has been unfair to them at least insofar as the distribution of economic rewards are concerned.

Most respondents were reluctant to place the matters of debt, financial fluidity, or taxes too high on the scale of reasons behind their departure, but it is nonetheless clear that these factors constitute a rather pervasive irritant. A real estate agency owner said plainly what others hinted at or skirted about when he said, "The way things are set up here with taxes you must steal to make a living! The government insists that I become a thief and I don't want to." His wife added: "After 20 years of working hard and making some success, don't I deserve to be able to afford a daily maid to clean a bit while I work, or to prepare a meal? Here, it is impossible because of unbelievable taxes."

Leaving aside the perhaps exaggerated sense of what one "deserves" after 20 years of effort, what is being asserted here is that effort does not bring with it what is at least *thought* to be commensurate gain. And the primary reason for this situation is to be found in a burdensome and excessive system of taxation. Even among interview respondees with less grandiose demands than those quoted above, one senses the importance of this element: effort is not properly or fairly rewarded in Israel, while it is in various countries of the West. Among many respondees I sensed greater resentment with regard to the "unfairness" of the system, rather than to personal financial or economic loss thay may have suffered as a result of it.

This sense of "unfairness" will be seen to be a theme that runs through other dimensions of our concern and not just with respect to economic issues. But the economic context does provide a useful vessel for its initial expression, which often then spills over into other areas. For example, one of the few recent Russian arrivals whom I was able to interview in answer to my question as to whether his apartment was bigger in Russia or here answered, "In Russia I had what I should have." The system, as he viewed it, was above all fair though in this or that detail it might have fallen below what he has achieved in Israel, whereas in Israel everything was fraught with qualifications and complications giving him a sense that all was not right with the world. In place of a safely ascribed status based on clearly defined and delimited options and rewards, Israel represents the uncertainty of the scramble, where the throw of the dice might very well favor the undeserving over the deserving. As he put it:

> In Russia I had enough to eat. I had a car. I could afford to go to restaurants. Once a year we went to the sea and the price wasn't the determinant. I would go on a ship [a river boat] with American millioniares and I didn't feel less than them. I felt free among them. Here, I can't even go to Elath. They would take my pants! It's all a matter of money here.

The same informant told me in great anguish how a fellow he knew from Russia—a butcher—had become wealthy in Israel, indicating that in a fairer, more stable, more predictable system this same person would have (deservedly) been much lower than him on the economic ladder. When asked whether he thought a "fairer" pattern awaited him in America he indicated that he expected nothing from America except a greater chance to succeed *himself,* whereas he did have expectations of Israel on a societal plain as well, which were, he said, dashed.

In certain ways the response of the Russian emigrant must be seen as relatively unrepresentative of the broader pool of emigrants in that he more than anything is reflecting a very specific socialization and cultural pattern not prevalent among most Israelis. While among them the "unfair" theme is also prevalent, it is not seen as the failure of one system as against another, but merely as a malfunction that could be corrected if the will existed to do so. In most cases there is the feeling that the system is out of control or has lost proper proportions, leading to unnecessary suffering. One respondee in the development town of Kiryat Shmona suggested that the State could, if it chose, live without taxing every so-called luxury like TV sets:

> I don't say that we don't need to pay taxes at all because then we can't exist. But in my opinion it's too much. There's a limit to how much you can squeeze out of a person.

A shopowner in Tel Aviv in response to my blatant question, "Why are you leaving the country?" answered in no less direct fashion:

> I can tell you why I and at least fifty others that I know personally are leaving the country, and the answer is one word: *TAXES.* Another word is *Income Tax Department.* They fall upon people and devour them like wolves—justly or unjustly—it doesn't make any difference.

Again we see repeated the theme of "unfairness," lack of concern for the individual, capriciousness, and unpredictability. Here, as well as in other interviews, raising the specter of taxes was to be seen as a metaphor for a sense of being ill-treated by the mechanism of government and even society that found expression in a sense of being financially trapped or at a dead end. Being trapped or feeling choked, as in the case of unfairness, is a theme that goes far beyond the economic realm, and will be discussed with respect to a number of different factors at other points. Suffice it to note at this juncture that most respondees had a very decided sense about the limitations seemingly built into the economic structure in Israel, and the expected fluidity and expansiveness to be found in places like America and South Africa. It is widely felt that the limits of economic advancement or even security were exceedingly finite in Israel while being boundless or at least very open abroad. Thus, whereas most people in most places who feel the effect of economic or financial constraints might consider changing jobs or cities, waiting a situation out, or striving still harder, there is a sense in Israel of terribly circumscribed possibilities that only departure from the country, temporary or permanent, will alleviate. A 35-year-old technician, married and father of two youngsters, stated that he is leaving only temporarily in order to "get refreshed and also to make a few lirot, so that when I come back I can add another room to the apartment, or get out of the debt we have been rolling around in all the time." When asked whether he could not do this by changing jobs or moving to another city, he replied:

> But if I'll go . . . with the wage I presently make which is pretty good for Israel—if I go someplace else in Israel I won't make what I make now . . . probably less . . . less for sure . . . and my wife might not be able to get as good a job as she has.

This same individual expressed over and over again a sense of living on the brink, of being about to fall into the precipice.

> Look, I'm not hungry for bread; I have everything, thank God. I have a good income, but it's simply not enough. So I say that if I want to get refreshed and to try a new country, to get out a little, to experience some change,then why not? Why not make it possible to earn a bit so that when I come back I will have a little saved for the kids' future, or to add a room, or have a few lirot in the bank? Why should we be living on the edge all the time?

He was, as he expressed it, looking for the possibility of buying something he wanted without "having to make payments and go into debt." A dream of his was simply to go into a bank, withdraw money, pay for the object of his desire, "without payments and without interest."

Not unremarkably many respondees expressed the feeling that they were being "choked" by an unmoving and immovable system,which they defined in economic terms but which clearly goes much beyond.

One young man, aged 23, a Yemenite who grew up from the age of 13 in a kibbutz where his older brother was a member said, "120% inflation and the need to run like a madman to 'make it' drive people from the country." This young man had never really confronted the purely economic implications of inflation and had not even begun to "run like a madman" in order to make it, but was leaving for the United States, thinking that a prime stimulus to the move was an unfavorable economic situation.

I do not suggest that he and others are not affected or influenced by the economic facts on the ground in Israel. Quite the contrary. I would aver that while the Israeli system has managed to camouflage the true dimensions of economic malaise that characterizes the country with various systems of indexing, subsidies, and social services, a brooding sense of threat and lack of promise in the economic realm do in fact affect more Israelis than are consciously willing or able to give vent to their feelings.

It is not so much wealth or still less a "killing" that is being sought by so many who leave as it is rather peace of mind in this dimension as in others.

> I don't want to make the apartment the focus of my life for the next 20 years—the problem involved with paying it off. I want to be able to provide my children with a home, with a mom and a dad, who will have time—even five minutes during the day—will have time for them rather than being worried about paying off an apartment for the next 20 years. I'll finish when I'm 70. That's not for me.

The above is taken from an interview with a kibbutz woman who, having decided to leave the kibbutz, felt that the move had to continue beyond in order to maintain certain values heretofore central to her life that could not be sustained in the face of the system as it is. Rather than devote what she thought would be most of her time to fencing with the system, she was opting out all together.

Another interviewee, a computer programmer, was leaving the country without selling his apartment in hopes that "it will work for me together with inflation, so that if I come back I will be able to buy 'upwards' with the 'profits.'" This same person expressed the view that as things are he is trapped, whereas only if he leaves will the pressure be alleviated and a dimension of hope (movement) open up.

Of the 117 people interviewed for this study, a mere four individuals expressed a desire for riches, for wealth, as being the primary reason for their decision to emigrate. Indeed, my findings seem to bear out the assertion of Lamdany (1982:43) who noted that while "emigration rates follow the economic cycle (as measured by the rate of change of investments or of GNP); declining with prosperity and increasing during slacks . . . some, and maybe most, of this short-run influence is probably *on the timing and not on the decision whether or not to emigrate at all* [emphasis added]."

Thus a driving instructor who had been "dying" to emigrate for years finally does so when the economy falters and driving schools fall on hard times. A *moshavnik* picks the year following a draught in which he sustained great losses, but blithely admits that it was a matter of the "right time" rather than the basic decision to leave which the draught fostered.

In all cases there existed some hint or sign that rather than temporary ups and downs being responded to, it was a matter of lack of faith in the larger enterprise symbolized albeit in the economic sphere. The system somehow did not allow room for certain values without the need to pay what was felt to be an inordinate price, it could not provide a sense of stability and predictability in the face of runaway inflation, or it could not provide a sense of "breathing space" in the economic dimension that could bring in its wake a needed minimal sense of quietude.

Again, we are here dealing with live men and women rather than angels or beings from another planet, so that elements of fantasy, dreams of instant wealth, or just plain greed do no doubt play some role among most leavers. But underlying all this, and notwithstanding the asserted "miracle" of Israel's economy, is a nagging feeling of living in an economic never-never land, suffering from a relative absence of opportunity, and a canvas that both does not reward and does not elicit a sense of challenge. I would assert the primacy of these factors rather than wealth as significant stimuli to the decision to emigrate, although when these factors are alluded to they invariably have a monetary expression. When not monetary, then the factor of "ease" of achievement is raised, or the relative absence of blocks to advancement.

> I started work in a garage in Houston as a mechanic and 11 months later I was the manager.

The above respondent took pains to tell me that being the manager does not hold any promise of particular enrichment but "it is all so much easier in America."

The Russian emigrant previously quoted very plaintively, almost in sadness, noted:

> I don't see America through rose-colored glasses. I expect difficulties. I have some information about the situation there. But maybe with time I will make it, I will be able to advance. Here, what is waiting for me? Another 5 percent, another 10 percent in salary, and that's it.

He concluded, almost shouting about money, but clearly he was reaching beyond:

> I want money! I don't want to be an idealist. I'm not 21 anymore. In America maybe I would have a chance; here, I will be in this apartment, in this hole until my pension. I don't want it.

For another young departee, a dental technician, the very idea of opportunity was equated with being *outside* of Israel:

> *Chutz la'aretz* [abroad] *is* opportunity. It is living in an advanced society. I feel I am a traitor for leaving and I'm just sorry that the Jewish state exists here where it is. I'm sorry we aren't all in America.

Another interviewee—a third generation Israeli who has visited America but does not speak the language, does not have a job waiting for him, and does not have a particularly marketable job skill—responded to my question about opportunities here and there with:

> It is not for nothing that they [the U.S.] are referred to as the land of endless opportunities. There are opportunities in every area of life, everywhere. I don't say that here things are blocked, they're not blocked . . . just smaller, more compact.

An army officer, resigned from the service and about to launch a career in business (the nature of which he would not reveal), sees going to America as a *sine qua non* for merely operating on a decent level let alone success.

> Today I'm changing direction [in life]; I'm going into the area of business and, in my opinion, the way I see things in the future, I see the absolute need to make connection with the American market, and *that,* mainly, is my reason for going.

America is big and without limits to the man of talent and energy. The scale there bespeaks opportunity, while the scale in Israel denotes limitation and a certain crabbedness. A *moshavnik* involved in an industrial enterprise in his community put it thusly:

> The opportunities in Israel are naturally limited. If you produce something good here you can sell it to 200,000 people. If you produce the same thing in America you can sell it to 20,000,000 people. You might be able to get rich here but you can become a millionaire with the same thing in America.

Size, or scale, is without question a matter of importance not only for those with out-size dreams of wealth but for those who seek broad economic, industrial, or business horizons. There is little doubt that the economics of scale do not apply in a country the size of Israel, and that in certain areas opportunity is completely absent or limited due to the lack of an economic hinterland. There are naturally imposed limits to what one can do in a small, relatively impoverished country as opposed to the possibilities in a large and prosperous one. A population of 4 million clearly suggests different dimensions of fortune than one of 40 million or 100 million or more.

But beyond any problem of size that might inhibit achieving the higher reaches of economic achievement, Israelis are saddled with an economic structure that in some ways seems designed to encourage emigration. By design or by tradition Israelis function within a system that tends to absorb capital, tying it up in things like apartments, cars, or goods of one kind or another. Israelis own rather than rent apartments, which in present terms means an overall investment of $50,000, which when compared with an average wage of $6,300 (approximate 1982 end-of-year rate of exchange) must be viewed as exorbitant by any standards. Cars as well are widely owned, and these cost at least double their price in, let us say, the United States, while again the average wage is about one-third that of the United States.

Thus, in view of "costs" as opposed to "income," one can only wonder about the "miracle" of Israel's high standard of living and relative absence of dire poverty. Be that as it may, however, very little, if anything, is left for "trying one's luck" in commercial or business terms. Funds for establishing a business or for expansion are available on a limited and selective basis and at extremely high interest rates. While the standard of living on a daily basis might be quite high, discretionary funding, or money that might be used for a "try" on the upward mobility track tends to be tight or nonexistent.

This in turn leads to a feeling of being stymied, or blocked—without sufficient choice, and ultimately without adequate or sufficient opportunities. This sense of being blocked, of not being able to achieve a desired modicum of mobility and success, can be alleviated when a decision to emigrate is taken and hard assets such as apartment, car, and appliances are turned intto fluid capital, making it possible not only to emigrate but to do so with a considerable nest egg.

Thus, at least for the more settled emigrants—those with families, professions, etc.—the game is being played with loaded dice in favor of the player. Where emigration is generally frought with all sorts of feelings of uncertainty, dislocation, and threat (at least in terms of a certain degree of financial security), a high number of Israeli emigrants begin with a considerable leg up. The system almost cries out to the players to "take a chance," to spin the wheel of fortune given the beneficial starting terms.

For those who after selling apartments and cars arrive in the United States with upwards of $50,000 in cash, who then need not tie up their capital in apartments or exorbitantly priced autos but who can instead invest some and save some, a feeling of giddy freedom, of expansiveness must be the result. Chances can be taken, which would not even be considered in Israel. Risks can be undertaken that in Israel might result in uncorrectable financial disaster, while in the United States the same risk might result in a mere setback of quite correctable proportions.

When massive amounts of effort and affect go to the purchase of basics— like a roof over one's head—it results in a dead end if the individual chooses to stay at home, but can become a bonanza when the decision is made to try elsewhere. This is especially so when various economic set-backs or difficulties crop up. In the following interview, which I will quote at some length, one can see how the achievement of an apartment is seen as a centerpiece to one's economic striving while at the same time proving itself as useless and worse in terms of objective economic positioning.

On the first day after I got to New York, I set my family up, and on the second day I started to work. . . . Success in America is so easy . . . it holds me there, it attracts me. Look, I want to tell you one thing, when people ask me what is the difference for ME to be here or in America, I tell them that there is no difference. What's the difference, I tell them, I define it in a simple manner. Here I was a laboring donkey, and I'm a laboring donkey there also. Here I had a number from Bituach Leumi, and there I have a social security number, that's the only difference But all in all, for me, as a man who supports a family it's much more comfortable. That I have a car that is a bit fancier, or that I have more room to travel around in, that's not what brought me to America.

But here I went to work and there I go to work; I worked hard here, and I work hard there; I eat about the same amount in both places! Clothing? So it's a bit cheaper, or more expensive there. It's not meaningful.

T.V. I have both here and there though here I had black and white and there I have color; that's the only difference. But now everyone buys color here, too.

What changed, you ask? It's simple; look, let me tell you something. I want to be frank with you. I lived here, was born here. I grew up in a slum. I served in the army. Good, very nice. A young man, I could show you my grades, they were fantastic. I was very good, I did my job, I gave my job my best, I thought to make a career of the army; it doesn't matter. I came out into civilian life, very nice, a boy of 20. After all the knocks that I went through, I didn't come out of a house that spoiled me, there wasn't a lot of happiness there, do you understand? And we grew up and we did the best we could and we got to this point—so let's do something *tachles*—so what do you do? You roll up your sleeves and you start to work. Even though I did have an opportunity at that time to go to study, the economic situation didn't permit it, although the army gives you the option to study after the service. Well, I didn't study and I started to work. So you work a year, you work two years, you work hard. When I talk about working hard, I'm not talking about like an American worker; to work hard means to work at certain times, two shifts, and at certain times, 12, 13 hours of work.

I worked in diamonds, but aside from the work in diamonds I had a number of additional jobs. For a time after the army, I worked for the Center on Statistics in Tel-Aviv. So I would go out in the evening and question people. . . . If you want to hear more about what happened after the army, it was a very interesting thing. . . . You find a girl, and you get married and there's no money. Good, so where do you live? I went and looked for a place to rent an apartment, to rent, simply to rent . . . and I didn't have enough money. In the end I found an apartment of 3 rooms, 2 rooms and a small living room, and an old lady lived there and she was willling to rent us a room. A room. There I lived a year and a half with that strange old lady. After a year and a half, at least I permitted myself to live in my own apartment. An apartment consisting of one room, one bedroom and a living room in Bnei Brak. And all that time, from the time of my marriage until . . . a later time, both of us worked. And all the time it was "full job" [sic]. That is to say, a lot of working hours, a great many working hours, a lot of trying to be self-sufficient, and to hold on, to get to a certain apartment, to get to a "normalization" in life. Later on my wife stopped working, because we had to make a kid; that was after 3 $\frac{1}{2}$ years, so I was already 25, 26 and we continued to make an effort, working the same hours, and they were many! We got to the point of owning an apartment; this apartment. After I got to this apartment, we paid off our debts; you get to a certain level, with a car, and then what happened happened in the field of diamonds. My reasons are clear, no? I didn't want to go through the same hard times that I went through, do you understand? And to go back to a situation that I was ONCE in. So I ask you, a simple question, what do you demand from a young man, that was born, that got to Israel as an infant, what more do you demand of him? You can't ask any more of a person that makes all the efforts. Apparently this factor weighed in the balance more than my Zionism in deciding to go to America. I don't call it Zionism, I call it love of the homeland. I don't hold with Zionism.

Here one finds an individual who sees himself as a hard working, moderately ambitious fellow whose horizons are somehow or other summed up in the buying of an apartment (after much struggle) and a few other modest possessions. As soon as his occupation (in this case diamond cutting) suffers a setback he feels his dependency as being total and his field of action as limited in the extreme. An alternative, however, exists and beckons in the form of emigration to America where not only does a job exist (in his case) but his fluidity will be assured through the sale of his apartment and car and the ability to rent rather than buy in the United States. This flexibility is symbolizied by his first comment to me—"on the *first day* . . . I set my family up, and on the *second day* I started to work"— a situation not easily duplicated under Israeli conditions. Thus, he has all the prime conditions waiting for the "right" opportunity to present itself which he can then grasp in a sense of at least relative security; all of which, while not impossible in Israel, is in fact infinitely more difficult to do and frought with much higher risk.

Once again, it seems clear that poverty in any objectively agreed upon sense is not what is motivating the emigration of the majority of Israelis who leave. Indeed, for a variety of reasons, including the price of an air ticket and the standards of receiving countries such as America, the poor just do not leave! Those who leave tend to be those who are dissatisfied with a variety of factors at home, including the economic factors, rather than those who might be said to be suffering measurable want or deprivation.

But deprivation, is, of course, a relative term and in addition does not exhaust its meaning on a purely economic plain, or one involving dollars and cents alone. Deprivation can be found in a sense of one's talents going unused or being underutilized, in minimum satisfaction gained from work and the expenditure of effort, or in the absence of challenge and excitement. And among those leaving the country one finds these complaints placed rather high on the list of motivations or reasons for leaving.

Many Israelis, trained and educated to think of challenge in communal, national, or state-building terms, seem hard-pressed to reformulate this factor in the face of the declining force of ideology and rising individualism. Somehow individualistically focused challenge seems shameful if not a complete betrayal of prior pieties and again we see a tendency to pursue this grail outside rather than in the country, where the same constraints are not seen to hold. Challenge in the Zionist creed meant state building, or inner renewal—never the achievement of personal wealth or comfort. "The challenge for me," said a young Moroccan-born engineer, "was always to live in Israel, to become a part of Israel, to set up a household in Israel. Today people are asking, 'What does this place give me?' And they are concluding that everything can be had much easier and quicker abroad. Maybe the land no longer makes demands upon us."

When I asked him if *he* felt this way he said no, but that others of his acquaintances do: "the sense of challenge is dead."

When I asked another young departee, a computer programmer who worked for a large transport firm, whether he felt a sense of challenge, he answered that he is not "involved with the building of the country." It transpires that being "involved" meant for him the classic formulation of being a kibbutz member or working on reclaiming the land in some other format. But a computer programmer? As he put it, "I'm not doing anything to build the country, to make existence more established, more secure here; I'm not 'conquering' new land."

Another respondent rather dejectedly noted:

> There isn't anything to do! There aren't any pioneers here anymore. The early settlers had to set up a state, to nurture a country, to build it up and today we see the results—we have a nation now . . . it's a matter of preserving what they did.

Challenge in the economy or occupational sphere should, it is widely felt, be channeled in the traditional fashion, which involved pioneering and state building. With the decline of the pioneering ethic and the rise of more individualistically geared motivations, two responses seem to predominate: (1) there is something basically illegitimate about pursuing individual economically motivated ends on, as it were, holy soil, and (2) the horizons provided for this pursuit in Israel are, in any case, restrictive and narrow.

There seems to be much ambivalence in this matter among Israelis resulting in a certain pugnacious affirmation of "doing my own thing, and to hell with everybody else." On the one hand the word "idealism" is infused with an almost impossible aura, and on the other it is sort of "hissed" rather than spoken—and often by the same person. A 28-year-old diamond merchant, one of the few Orthodox interviewees, stated:

> Challenge? Yes, I feel a challenge but with respect to myself and my own achievements in life. I want to grow and develop and for this there is no limit. With respect to Israel—there are definite limits. When I was a kid I was more idealistic and I thought in idealistic terms. Not anymore! I reached the basic conclusion that everyone is for himself.

An efficiency engineer, who has been living in the United States for six years but who returned to arrange his permanent U.S. status ruefully, almost apologetically notes:

> I get the feeling that the challenge factor in Israel has declined. But maybe it has something to do with the fact that I'm not an idealist.

At times, during the course of interviewing I was almost overwhelmed with the feeling that Israel was a society of failed or embittered idealists. Person after person noted either about themselves, others, or both that idealism was no more, and this was almost always noted in sadness and with a sense of loss. And with the decline or disappearance of idealism, went a decline in a sense of challenge in almost all areas. It would appear that a basic challenge for Israelis was seen in the sustaining of a myth of idealism, and the rechanneling of challenge in personalisitic terms has proven difficult to achieve. There appears to exist a rather aggressive sense of guilt—again, consistent with the inability to see Zion in temporal terms, and an insistence on seeing it in abstract, pietistic terms—that leads many to assert that idealism is dead and so is a sense of challenge, but they both died [strangely] because the reward structure is so deficient.

> I still think there is a challenge here but I'll tell you the truth—none of my friends do. Five friends of mine just got out of the army or are about to and none of them knows what to do with their lives. A guy who gets out of the army is a zero. There is no educational challenge and no social challenge and I explain this very simply—no benefits, no rewards. Abroad there is a challenge to work—it pays! Not here!

People "used to know what to do with their lives"; "People were not zeroes in the days of the *yishuv*"; "Reward at one time was in the doing and had nothing to do with measurable return." When to the tarnished or failed idealism and sense of limited challenge one adds the factor of dissatisfaction with work, it becomes easy to see how these elements roll into each other establishing an inexorable movement in the direction of negation and denigration of the society.

People—at least large numbers of people—are unhappy with their lot in life, which includes their daily occupation, all over the world and not just in Israel. I rather suspect that this would be true of people in the Third World, people living at the margins of subsistence as well as the "alienated" of the industrial and postindustrial world. Conventional wisdom suggests that the question of work satisfaction is a luxury of the well-fed—which it no doubt is—but it should not be surprising if dissatisfaction of this kind follows with lightning speed once the more basic satisfactions are answered. Once again the question of work satisfaction, or its absence, is intimately tied to the factor of how the society is perceived from the point of view of opportunities. Here "size" and "history" play a role.

History, in the sense of being dissatisfied with their lot, seems to have achieved a higher level of refinement among Jews than among other peoples from the biblical period forward. A statement of this kind can easily be construed as a grotesque caricature, and, to be sure, observers will easily uncover numerous examples of equal frequency and magnitude among other peoples. Indeed, one might justifiably say that this "dissatisfaction," this tendency to complain, reflects more about the human condition than it does about Jews specifically.

Nevertheless, I would assert that a strong argument can be drawn from history, demonstrating how a Jewish worldview anchored in struggle and contention with God and a repeated rejection of the status quo acted as a sort of patina on Jewish consciousness that has evolved and remained through the ages. Gunther Plaut (Plaut et al. 1981: 1095), commenting on Numbers 11:20 and Numbers 14 wherein the Jews bitterly complain about the desert privation comparing their lot to what it had been in Egypt, notes:

> The cry of the Rebels was for meat and variety, not for food as such, for there was no hunger among the people. Meat was the object of momentary craving; but after this was satisfied—or more than satisfied—the underlying problems which had caused the rebellion still remained. Satiety, boredom, lack of challenge, and the inconveniences of nomad existence were seeds of discontent as potent as want and poverty. A surfeit of manna and meat would not for long cover the lack of inner resources among the people. Long years of slavery had produced a generation that could not adjust its dreams of freedom to reality. Ultimately it was the God of freedom whom the murmurers rejected when they cried, "Oh, why did we ever leave Egypt!" (Num: 11:20).

Jewish religious and secular folklore is replete with numerous tales of heroic figures (from Jacob and the Angel to the victims of Nazi barbarity) who complain to and challenge God with respect not only to the workings of His creation but as to His very credibility as well.

The desert generation asked, "Why manna and not steak," while the present day Israelis ask—jokingly to be sure—why Palestine and not California!

The present essay is not the place to argue a "theology of complaint" as the sociopsychological hallmark of the Jewish people, but there can be little doubt that an almost metaphysical *angst* with regard to "our lot" seems as utterly characteristic of the present day Israeli as it did of his desert forebears. Thus Israelis bitterly complain about the weather in their objectively very temperate climate; about their living conditions though they are demonstratively, on the average, higher than in many more productive and industrially advanced countries; about their government, though it functions at a reasonable level of efficiency when compared with comparable societies; about the quality of goods produced at home in comparison with imports no matter the objective facts of the matter; about each other's public and private behavior, but in tones that suggest the dismemberment of the opposing viewpoint rather than simple disagreement; and more!

Whether performing artists, professionals, business people, or artisans, the interviewees expressed a sense of dissatisfaction with Israel first of all, but more specifically with their "work" situation. This sense of dissatisfaction was often set off against a comparative backdrop—in most cases America—but often was seen as a simple objective failure of Israeli society.

A musician noted that "it is a fact that in America productivity is higher—they work from 9-5, straight through without any siestas." When asked if he worked harder in America than in Israel he answered, "Of course! There, I work 50 hours a week and *I enjoy every minute of it.* It's true that I do the same thing there that I do here, but it's not the same. I play, I teach, I'm in the middle of where things happen. No matter how long I work, every minute is a pleasure."

He expressed resentment over the fact that Israel has a daily siesta that "forces" him to rest whether he wants to or not. But above all he felt that America allows one to measure the value of one's work in terms of visible rewards, which were felt to be absent in Israel.

A very proficient machine technician stated:

> I've gotten to the point where I don't have the possibility of advancement. So I'll reach another level and still another level, but in terms of professional advancement, and until I leave on pension I don't have too much to expect. And that's in another ten years.
>
> I do get some satisfaction from my work although it tends to be repetitive. I get satisfaction, for example, when I fix a tape recorder, a TV, a washing

machine, or a very complicated electronic system. Like last Friday, for example; I fixed a machine that if we had to order parts for it it would have cost a fortune. I took that entire machine apart and turned it inside out, and I used new Israeli parts, and I built a new machine, and it worked. The head of the laboratory came and . . . he couldn't believe it. And that gave me more satisfaction than anything. My satisfaction is that I succeed in fixing something.

But I'm sick of it, listen, all those years in the same place with the same people, no change, so today I fixed this machine and tomorrow that machine, it's like a wheel that keeps going around, the same routine. A little change, something a bit new, a new place with new people, even if they won't be good (people) but at least you get the taste.

Here we see an example of someone seeking change, perhaps recognition, a sense of renewed challenge—all of which he perceives as being unavailable at home. One might well ask if this type of reaction is in any way specific to Israel. Do people elsewhere experience a sense of having reached a dead end, of being bored, or of wanting new horizons? Obviously, the answer is a resounding Yes! But the question here is not whether frustration at work or elsewhere is peculiar to Israel, but rather what are the specific Israeli parameters both in diagnosis of the problem and in projected solutions?

In diagnosis, I sense a willingness or a need to view these reactions to work as sui generis rather than universal responses. Somehow, it is never man's existential position being reviewed, but rather what Israel or even segments of the Israeli reality have done to man.

In most cases Israel is invidiously compared with America and predictably emerges "less efficient," "less rewarding," and "less challenging." At times this is related to the matter of size, as when an aeronautical engineer notes that his specialty is space engineering,which is not a top priority at Israel's only aircraft-producing firm. He tried working there for two years and found it unrewarding. In answer to my question as to what he will do when and if he finds his promised job in Virginia unrewarding he answered unhesitatingly, "I will go to California! And if that is no good to Arizona, and if not there to Washington. The possibilities are almost limitless."

At other times it has little to do with size, as when an administrator in a large firm notes:

The section in which I work could be called a catastrophe! It's a waste; it's throwing money away. The people are no good; the direction of the work is bad, most of the decisions taken are wrong.'

This individual indicated that he had given up, that this sort of thing was endemic to Israel and was near to reflecting an irreversible truth about the society.

Something is seen as being wrong with Israel and Israelis, and the solution most readily and easily proferred is departure rather than a struggle to bring about change. The same administrator quoted above ended his jeremiad with "I know I should at least aspire to be the head of the section so that I could influence things, but I don't think it's my place; I don't think it is where I should make my stand." But why not?

Why are so many individuals willing to try emigration as a device by which to bring about change in various areas of their lives? Does the work motive, the economic factor, provide an adequate causal model for so drastic a step as removal of an entire family from its framework of familiarity?

The work motive or economic causes—as with motives in general—make up a rather hazy and shaky area in studies of migration (Rossi 1955; Pourcher 1970). While undoubtedly important, one is constrained to ask how one uses the same variable to analyze what in one case might be a need for bread and in another a desire for a sail boat. Also, once planted, the economic motive might be said to live a life of its own unrelated to objective considerations, or only peripherally so. In talking of the Italian migrant in the first decades of the twentieth century Robert F. Foerster (1969 [1919]:422) notes:

> The economic principle once so established in his mind, he will often be led to migrate even when his wage at home—in such a region as the Marches for example—is yet sufficient to a comfortable subsistence.

Once a seed of migration is planted—once this device becomes an acceptable mode of dealing with the environment, or answering the drive for upward mobility, or merely fulfilling a sort of migratory itch—the purely economic motive becomes less important.

Indeed, in some cases (and I think the case of Israel fits) migration might be viewed as an attempt to retain or reaffirm values not adequately celebrated or given vent in the society being abandoned. Davydd Greenwood (1976:21) in writing of a Basque migratory movement from rural to urban areas, makes a fascinating argument:

> In contrast to the ideas of most economic development theories, depopulation in Feunterrabia is caused neither by a change in values nor by low profits. The people of Feunterrabia shift from rural to urban employment in order *to retain basic cultural values that are centuries old* [emphasis added].

Can one not suggest that at least part of the underlying motive for *yerida* has to do with an almost unconscious and certainly unarticulated desire to retain or reembrace the values and life style of the *galut?* A high proportion of emigrants from Israel, like the Basque emigrants in Greenwood's study, are clearly not fleeing in the face of economic want. A desire for more? By all means! A sense of gnawing general dissatisfaction? Clearly, yes! A less promising arena with respect to opportunities of all kinds? Without doubt! But also, a certain discomfort with unfamiliar sovereignty, a possible rejection of the "God of freedom," an element of edginess that comes from dashed visions, and upset expectations, and a life style going counter in almost all important respects to the patterns established over 2,000 years of exile in the various dispersions.[1]

An almost cabalistic exercise of *tzimtzum*—of contraction in both a spatial and a sociological sense—has been required of the returnees to Zion and the question of its success or failure remains mute.

Smallness and Its Implications

Lacking a sense of opportunity or being terribly circumscribed has at least two dimensions: (1) the size of the country makes for natural barriers to a sense of expansiveness in all areas, and (2) the system—economic and social—does not encourage a sense of openness and growth possibilities.

There can be little doubt that the sense of "too small a canvas" enhances the previously noted feelings of being "choked," "blocked," or "trapped." In one way or another almost all interview respondees expressed these feelings—some with respect to careers and economic factors, while others were clearly pointing beyond these.

This question must in effect be seen as of great importance in attempting to understand both emigration itself and the concern with emigration. Thus, whatever the importance and essential validity of the position outlined in Chapter 1 with respect to the historical peculiarity of the Jews' relatedness to a temporal Zion, the practical question of how energetic and talented people are to find full outlet in what must be seen to be a narrow and limited physical container is certainly of no less importance.

Repeatedly I was struck by the extent and depth of frustration expressed by a wide range of individuals with respect to this factor of limited opportunities that is tied to a natural and unassailable limitation of smallness—physical and demographic. These, in turn, had qualitative implications that spilled over into areas only remotely connected with the economic category, such as the possibility of achieving high standards of artistic expression where the pool of potential was so narrow. Similarly, these limitations could be felt with respect to using a nonprofessional university degree as a springboard to interesting employment; finding an outlet for an offbeat skill or product; or even finding adequate expression for a marginal, fringe, or underdeveloped, or underrepresented political position or philosophical outlook.

Two of the people interviewed for this study were active feminists, one of whom expressed the latter motif with great vigor, stating: "The possible community of women here is so little that I can count them all on the fingers of two hands and that's just too small a society to live in." In the case of one of the women there was a desire to develop women's studies as an academic field, but she was all too cognizant of how difficult this would be to realize in the Israeli context.

> It's not that the field doesn't exist, but as you know, in the academic community, there's a very conservative view, toward credentials in the first place, to what you have to be and who you have to be. Also you have to behave and all the rest of it, and if you're not a good girl and/or a good boy you can't make it; even if you're good you won't get tenure.

When asked whether she believed that the same thing would happen in the United States she responded:

> Well, it's a much bigger environment, if it doesn't work out you can go to another place. There's an enormous uniformity here, and we're a very small country, which makes us one little community, the academic community in the country. If you burn your bridges in one place it's known all over.

This same woman, in a most poignant fashion, suggested how unfavorable smallness is for any kind of minority or deviant view or behavior pattern.

> I am, you know, a single woman, and not a teenager, a feminist, a lesbian. My field is and should be women's studies and I can't work in my field here; it just doesn't make sense. I've made too much of an issue of myself and I've gotten too little credit for what I've done. There are times when I feel this country is pushing people out. The possible community that I have here is extremely limited, the possibilities that I can grow and do something are extremely limited. And what I've been doing for years is really creating my own environment, putting enormous energy into creating my own environment, and working in it. But I'm tired, I'm extremely tired.

For fringe personalities of all kinds simply making a living in the narrow confines of Israeli society can and does become problematic. Sometimes, however, this can prove a double-edged sword and benefit can be reaped by being the "first" of something or the "only" of something, but more often than not pioneering efforts in the pioneering society require prior legitimation.

One emigrant, a young man of Turkish origin, was interested in developing a new physical therapy process that had been pioneered by one of his

Israeli teachers, who has since left to live in the United States. Neither the message nor the example was lost upon him. In answer to what brought him to the United States to finish his education, he very straightforwardly noted:

> [sighs] It developed during the three years at _____. You see that all your teachers had been in America to finish their degrees, and then they came back to instruct. Why shouldn't you be like them, why shouldn't you go on and develop to a higher level, why should you just stay a teacher? I'd only be a teacher, a gym teacher and that's all.

When asked whether he believed that American degrees were more meaningful than Israeli degrees, he replied:

> My Professor, Prof. X, is the world's leading authority on _____ and he could not go anywhere with it here. Now, he is invited back for very short periods just to demonstrate.

A number of other interviewees also took note of the fact that they first thought of emigration or, more correctly, leaving for awhile in order to get accreditation abroad, as it was infinitely more negotiable than its local equivalent. Usually these people were encouraged to do so by mentors who asserted that because of the smallness of the country, it reflects a corresponding provincial character, which can only be compensated for by some formal training abroad. That this often results in the aspirant staying abroad is considered a marginal question, or an inevitable price to be paid for smallness.

If this is true of academics, engineers, scientists, medical personnel, etc., it tends to be particularly so in the case of performing artists. Here, the smallness of the country and the resultant quantitative and qualitative limitations bring to bear heavy pressures for pursuing a career abroad.

> I'm a musician and I play the clarinet, and that's very important to know because that's the main reason that I went abroad to study. In Israel I got to . . . to a "dead end" with no exit. I appeared with the philharmonic, I played in the Academy (first clarinet). I've played with every orchestra in the country. But I was missing something, something for me, some little push for my self-realization and as it turned out it was in America.

In the case quoted above the respondent continued in almost manic fashion to explain why a serious artist needs a larger canvas, especially if his art is not conventionally popular. I think part of my dialogue with him bears extensive quotation. (I=interviewer, M=musician)

M: Another reason why I had to go and be there, and the reasons that I
left to learn in America . . . I basically don't feel . . . I'm not a concert
player, I've been given opportunities to play in an orchestra here,
various orchestras. I wish that I did enjoy to play in an orchestra,
because then it would be easier for me, even to stay in the country.
There are orchestras and I got offers and so on, but I'm not built to
play in an orchestra, that's all there is to it.

I: That you don't want to be in an orchestra?

M: No, not in an orchestra. As a soloist, or in chamber music; chamber
music is the most important thing for me. So it was even harder for
me, even harder.

I: So you claim that here in the country for a serious musician it's very
very difficult, there's no range, no depth, and that the things that lack
here you find in Europe or America without problem.

M: In quantity, in quantity. In quantity and quality. Now I'll tell you
something; the Israeli Philharmonic Orchestra is one of the best and I
respect it, so it's not true that there aren't great musicians here. Some
of the best in the world in my opinion, but they are orchestra players. I
don't detract from their value, some of the best, some of the top
players are in orchestras. But a lot of the top players leave.

I: Let me ask you something that is not important to the research, but
interests me. If you take people like Zukerman, Barenboim, Mintz
and Perlman . . .

M: They can't manage here.

I: But they go around the world at any rate, why not from here?

M: I can't explain it. I can't explain it, because me, if I, and I'm telling
you the truth now if I'll . . . well with the violin it's different, with the
clarinet the literature is limited, and so is the audience; you have to
build an audience, and that you can do in America where there is a
big audience, a really big one, masses, you can find those interested. I
think it must be the environment, that it's not suitable here, that it's
too limited for musical development.

There is no musician, and I'm also talking of myself, that doesn't need
to "recharge his batteries" consistently. If he appears then he drains
himself, he has to recharge his battery again and I think that the best
surrounding environment is still in America, because of the quantity
as well as the quality, they can potentially find there. I think it goes
together. But not always. That is, whoever wants to will achieve
"quality" but he'll stop somewhere like I did. At some point he needs
the "quantity." "Quality" you have here (90 percent is the "quality"),
but you need the 10 percent "quantity" to be "excellent"!

Indeed, one must recognize the validity of the artist's plight and be
cognizant of the fact that this is and must be the shared affliction of all
small countries no matter how high the level of their local cultural life.
How many symphony conductors can a country of 4 million absorb? How

many concert violinists, or oboists, or percussionists? How large a public exists for the type of crossfertilization and contact so desired, so sought after by talented practitioners of the performing or visual arts? How many concerts can be performed featuring music even slightly off the beaten track, or art shows demonstrating talents not readily saleable?

When I asked the musician whether he thought his chamber music group (which he organized in the United States) could succeed just as well in Israel, his answer was quick and to the point:

> No! Look, you can give a concert four, maybe five times here but the demand is just not there because of the problem of quantity, people. In America, even though at times the quality may falter [he refers to the quality of the audience], the size of the country allows for a freedom just not achievable here.

In answer to why artists of all kinds tend to leave the country, his position, again, was expressed with complete certainty:

> The answer is simple. The University of Tel Aviv has an Academy of Music which is fantastic; it is excellent. There are there, in residence, at any given point in time, two or three clarinet players, while the American university where I studied has a situation whereby 200 clarinetists applied and thirty were accepted. The thirty who were accepted are at the level of excellence and achievement of the Tel Aviv students who are *completing* their studies. Do you understand? So I got to the point where I desperately needed an environment. In music, in art, this is terribly important: it is everything. You need the environment of imagination, and this is to be sure a matter of quality, but also quantity. Here, I played first clarinet from the moment I joined the _____ orchestra, and that just shows how narrow is the competition, how thin the challenge when the numbers just aren't there.

If this situation may be said to be a given of small countries, how much more must it be seen to be problematic for Israel, given its relatively high concentration of artists and performers, who crave above all an audience?

While smallness presumes the absence of bulk, of large or at least sufficient numbers, there is an obverse side of the coin that again can be viewed in negative terms. Smallness brings in its wake a crimp on anonymity, on privacy, on the possibility of escaping from view. A small country tends to display certain aspects of the village—no doubt for good and for ill, but in any event clearly not demonstrating the broad potential for submerging and emerging at choice.

M.B., a fairly well-known journalist of the muckraking tradition, has chosen to leave the country and has found work as a community executive in the United States. His reasons for leaving are rather complex and highly tied into a mosaic involving economic, social, philosophic, and also personality factors. He recognizes the factor of size as being central. "America is big and Israel is small. I can be anonymous there; alone. I don't have to worry that people will stop me on the street and try to get me to write up their case, or expose their hurts. If things don't go well for me in New York, I can get a U-Haul and pack off to Texas. If not in Texas I can continue to California."

Anonymity can be a personal preference but it can also act as a social shield protecting individuals from close scrunity that might result in a lowering of social esteem or even invoke some form of active condemnation.

A 26-year-old, unskilled *sabra* put it this way: "They don't want to work in the country! They simply don't know what work is and everything is beneath their dignity. But in America the same Israeli will do anything, anything to put bread on the table. Why? Because America won't give it to him for nothing and because in America, because it is so big, so wide you can hide."

But while smallness may denote a rather obvious difficulty for artists and certain professionals who depend on an audience or a public, the problem is not perceived to be limited to these categories or some of the others previously noted. Smallness affects more than quality and scope and has impact and importance in a wide-ranging fashion and on people from diverse walks of life.

Distant in standing and different in training from the journalist quoted previously, we see in the following from a hotel desk clerk a very similar—indeed almost exact—sentiment expressed: "The country is not too small from a geographic point of view. But from a point of view of personal development it probably is. There is a natural limit to what you can achieve in a small country. In America you can wander from state to state and come back to where you started from in a totally changed situation—a higher position. Here there is a limit and it is hard to overcome it."

A driving instructor, previously quoted, noted "*Yisrael, he ketana m'dai alei*" (Israel is too small on me), as if referring to an article of clothing. He was expressing a sense of pressing limitations of horizons and opportunities; a suggestion that he had more in him than the country could effectively use or would call upon. In one way or another, a significant proportion of respondees hinted at a similar feeling, although few phrased it so colorfully or anthropomorphically. Smallness led to or implied limited opportunities—but also boredom, to a sense of gray sameness.

A former lieutenant colonel in the air force first said "no" to my questions about smallness and a few moments later agreed: "Yes, perhaps the country is too small. Perhaps it is too confining and perhaps there is much more choice outside which, in the end, I *do* want to be involved with. . . .

"Am I bored? As a matter of fact, yes, I am bored here and I am not bored abroad. Things are closed here and closing in and I need new expression in a new place."

One must be careful in interpreting data of this kind because the factor of placement in the life cycle, career choices or lack of them are very much part of the calculus. But these are not phenomena peculiar to Israel and what is important here is not the feeling of a need for change per se as much as the direction chosen and the *analysis of the underlying causes given*. A technician notes:

> I've been working in the same place for 13 years. . . . Listen, you get up in the morning without the desire to go to work; it gets that bad. I work in the same room with my boss (although the laboratory is exclusively mine) and I have seen that Jew for 13 years—day in and day out—talking with him, working with him. . . . I see him more than I see my wife, do you understand? I'm sick of it, I need a little variation, a change, new air.

In asking respondees whether or not they expect similar reactions to working 13 years in the same job abroad, or getting bored, invariably the answer given is "but there I can easily move, or change when that happens." Others say, "Well, at that point I can always come back to Israel, can't I?"

Thus, once again we must underscore the key point here: the existence of a pervasive body of opinion that holds that Israel's smallness limits opportunity and brings in its wake an overriding sameness—both of which factors can more easily or more successfully be dealt with abroad. This is complicated by a theme previously noted with respect to the heightened competitiveness brought about by the more limited canvas that marks Israel in contradistinction to many Western countries.

An artist, the son of one of the country's leading business personalities, suggests, plainly, that the country is just too small to absorb what he sees as an excess of Jewish "talent."

> Wherever you go in the world you find dominant elites which are Jewish. In France the dominant elite is Jewish, in Germany a dominant elite which *was* Jewish, in the U.S. a dominant Jewish elite in art, science, and literature. If not for the constant wars these pressures brought on by the concentration of too much talent in too small an area would lead to an explosion!

Another explains his leaving on a similar basis, when, after I asked him if in fact all social or personal problems can be handled by packing one's bags and leaving, he responded:

> I'll tell you—it's a typical Jewish problem: It's very hard to succeed among the Jews and it's much easier to do so with the *goyim*. It's easier because there

isn't a broad enough area to succeed in here, and the country just cannot provide adequate opportunities for all.

Frankly, the country is limited: not just economically but professionally as well. Take me as an example! I will be getting a Ph.D. in biomechanics and if I don't find work in what is a very new and very small field, what do I do? Leave my field? Do something that may pay well but will ignore all that I studied and prepared myself for? Well that's possible, if you are more of a Zionist than I am and you must stay in the country. Now in America too not everyone finds his exact niche, but there are so many opportunities to do something at least *close* to what you were trained in. The situation here is limited.

There was considerable agreement among interviewees, expressed in diverse ways, that somehow or other the "fit" between the Jews and their land was not what it should be. Interestingly, and rather surprisingly, very few suggested a relationship between smallness and a physical sense of being closed in. Claustrophobia is, it would appear, not a prominent factor—certainly not consciously—in any decision to seek other places. "Yes, it would be nice to have open borders," or "Yes, I would certainly like to be able to travel abroad more regularly, or more cheaply, but 'suffer'? 'No!'" This feeling was adequately summed up by an interviewee in Haifa who, in answer to my question of how he viewed the smallness of the country, said:

Look, I don't feel crowded, I don't feel crowded. When you travel in the Negev and see all that territory it looks like a big country. It could be that when you *fly* from Haifa to Eilat in an hour and ten minutes [he laughs] *then* you might think it a small country. . . . Look, I'd prefer us to be bigger, but it doesn't bother me. That's not a factor.

A teacher, in answering the same question, said the only thing that bothers her is not so much tied to smallness as to the fact that our borders are closed and in order to get a sense of change you have to pay great sums and expend much time "even for a little vacation." An engineer from Bat Yam noted that even the fact of closed borders did not bother him until he went abroad for the first time and "realized" that things could be different. He added the comment that his sister, who lives on a *moshav* in the Jordan Valley, has never been abroad and does not feel that "anything is missing in her life."

In sum, only eight respondees felt that the "closed-in" aspect, together with physical smallness, was even marginally disturbing. A 21-year-old kibbutznik, just out of the army and leaving to join his father in the United States, summed up this point of view in noting:

The country is too small and I feel it. In Europe you can go, and go, and there's still things to see. Here we are closed in. But if we had peace with the Arab countries Israel could be a fantastic place.

While only a tiny minority of leavers expressed feelings of oppressiveness or discomfort with respect to the physical smallness of the country, many indicated vexation with the aforementioned problem of "fit." Put another way—and remarkably not a few respondents said it or came close to saying it in these terms—the country is viewed as being just too small for a highly energetic, competitive, and talented people like the Jews. It was suggested that the Jews continually "burst the bounds" of the land because the land cannot adequately contain them. It was so in antiquity; it is so today!

> You ask why people don't leave other small countries like Norway or Finland in the same proportions as Israel. I think it has to do with style of life. The Norwegians, for example, live a rather backward existence. They're satisfied. It's their character. We seem to be more on the American wave length, more dynamic, more progressive, and America has the scope which we don't.

The Blocked Society

Even in combination, the issues of smallness of canvas, a sense of highly limited opportunity, and relative economic backwardness cannot fully exhaust what might be called the behavioral-motivation package lying behind the current emigration wave from Israel.

There is unease in Zion and its elements are varied. For many, life in Israel postulates a sense of being "locked-in," of not having an adequate scope of free choice. This ranges from one's body (army service, war) to government (unresponsiveness) to job choice (circumscribed opportunities). Israel, it would appear for thousands among its citizens, represents a "blocked society."

It must be remembered that Israel is not an underdeveloped or rural society and its people are not reflective of an emerging peasantry. But the constraints noted above are those associated with an underdeveloped or even authoritarian structure, while the myths and expectations are otherwise patterned.

Repeatedly and in the case of respondent after respondent, life in Israel was invidiously compared with life abroad. "People are politer over there"; "merchants are more honest over there"; "government is more benign over there"; "the weather is better"; "the quality of goods is higher"; "the opportunities are wider"; and so on.

One can justifiably assert that these responses reflect a legitimizing device for what is essentially viewed as an illegitimate or questionable act. One must, after all, explain ones own side of the matter. It is not a matter of deserting the ship so much as the vessel having proved defective and inadequate!

There exists scant doubt that this legitimizing factor is present. But I am equally persuaded that a preemigration set of perceptions and feelings is present that has played a role in the decision to leave.

Thirty-seven years after the establishment of the Jewish State there exists a wide and deep pool of dissatisfaction with the nature of what has been wrought. This dissatisfaction embraces tangibles like high taxes, reserve duty, the threat of war, the high cost of housing, the absence of civility, the unresponsiveness of government, and many other factors in an almost endless list. There is, in addition, a more inchoate, less tangible, less apprehendable substratum of dissatisfaction that must be seen as at least equally as troubling as some of the "tangibles" cited above.

With respect to the second level of dissatisfaction, we have noted previously that the kind of "disappointment" with Israel expressed by so high a proportion of emigrants raises questions with respect to what kind of society was being sought, or could indeed satisfy. It would seem clear that a putative theme of the classical Zionist design—normalcy—does not, in fact, represent a deep commitment for many. Not normalcy, but a kind of supernormalcy was evidently sought—and not found. Ample signs exist pointing to a struggle between the temporal, here-and-now relativities of normal existence and an illusive perfectability, which has given rise to what I have called the concept of the *conditional homeland*. "Conditional" in the sense of "tentative" rather than as counterpoint to the oft quoted "my country right or wrong, my country." "Conditional" in the rather rare sense—at least rare in terms of most current nationalisms—of the homeland having to undergo constant and repeated testing with respect to a flexible set of variables determining its worth and worthwhileness.

Alternatively, however, one may not lose sight of the existence of the aforementioned tangible, more existentially rooted aspects underpinning the new exile; factors often summed up under the rubric "quality of life," and which can and do range all the way from the aesthetic to the religious-secular conflict and beyond.

Repeatedly one hears it said in Israel (and not only by those who leave or who are contemplating departure) that life is difficult in the country. One hears this from academics who claim an inability to write in Israel, from housewives who assert that the day is never done, and from workers who suggest that they do nothing but work leaving little time for leisure or other activities. When pressed for an explanation, one is told it has something to do with a six-day week, the need to work at more than one job to make ends meet, the relative absence of household machinery such as dryers or dishwashers, and so on. On a purely objective plane, these assertions are weakened by the fact that the work day is not particularly long; Israel in effect works a five and one-half day week and perhaps less. Religious and national holidays do not lag behind any viewable Western norm. Washing machines, mixers, gas or electric stoves, and vacuum cleaners are widely owned.

There exists notwithstanding this perceived notion that the work day never ends, and I would assert that this results from a climate of "nagging," about minor irritations that seem to permeate the atmosphere. Shops are not open at hours convenient to the buying public, government and other offices are not efficient or on the whole marked by a climate of civility, public discipline is low, and suspicion of one's neighbors' intentions seems somehow pervasive. (This last comment becomes palpable in viewing Israelis queued up—one notices that not a millimeter of separation is allowed to intrude between queuers and this not for reasons of desired intimacy but simply for lack of trust that an inch will develop into an opening for line jumping.)   There exists without question an atmosphere of edginess in Israeli society; tempers flare and verbal violence is rampant. A large proportion of those interviewed for this study have been abroad or were born or raised abroad and in almost all cases reference is made to the fact that "people are nicer in *chutz la'aretz*." "Strangers wish you a good day as they make change or pass you on the street, whereas at home you can consider yourself fortunate to receive minimally civil treatment." When asked why she was about to take the drastic step of emigration one woman laughed almost hysterically, shouting: "Why? Why? Because over there [in the United States] I am a child of God, a child of God. I am treated like a human being wherever I go. I am not shouted at or abused. I am not automatically suspect. Washer women in the supermarket don't command me to watch my step. Why?" Another respondee (an immigrant from the United States who had been in Israel for twelve years) broke down and wept repeating over and over the word "garbage"—"People here are garbage, garbage. They're hateful. I hate this place." When asked to explain, a long list of minor cruelties—more lapses of good taste rather than anything profoundly evil—were adduced.

While almost all the emigrants interviewed placed "quality of life" factors high on the list explaining their decision to leave, one cannot avoid the fact that the same complaints and dissatisfactions can be and indeed are heard from Israelis of all walks of life who are not leaving and who in fact have no intention of leaving. Clearly an etiology of migration explaining why one person will leave and one person will stay put based on the exact same variables must be viewed as somewhat problematic at the very least. Problematic though it might be, however, I am nonetheless convinced that these causes are real enough and the search for what separates the leaver from the nonleaver must be sought in other realms. I find J.A. Jackson's (1969:5) comment on what lies behind the decision to migrate compelling if less than totally satisfying when he notes:

This, usually voluntary, decision is rather like the decision to marry. It becomes possible to isolate in a particular environment a variety of predisposing causal factors which lead to the net result. One is left, nevertheless, with a fascinating range of questions regarding the actual factors of selection in the decision-making process which lead some to migrate or marry and particular others to remain as they were.

Thus, we cannot at this stage explain why some people chose one course (emigration) and others who felt very similarly about a wide range of factors chose another (remaining). However, this does not prove the total inadequacy of the causal network. While Taylor and other migration theorists are convinced that there are important differences between migrants and nonmigrants, I remain unpersuaded and, in fact, convinced that those who "stay" and those who "move" as often as not seem to be the same people. The key variable seems to be *opportunity* and the aforementioned "other realms," which are simply inner psychological differences that are not readily or easily probed.[2]

The Role of Travel

Both with respect to opportunity and the psychological realm, leavers seem to be influenced by having experienced something different, such as having had the opportunity to travel or by having faced a need to change their lives in a radical fashion, a need sometimes stimulated by even a passing taste of what lies beyond Israel's borders.

For many, Israel does not fare well in comparison with what is seen abroad. This is true with respect to behavior, geography, aesthetics, and opportunities and it ranges all the way down to the prices for material goods. When the comparison is made—and it always is—Israel is viewed as poor, insignificant, raw, and without horizons in the fullest sense. The post-1967 explosion in travel that has affected a significant proportion of the population has seemingly opened a pandora's box wherein a certain Israeli parochialism has fallen prey to a wide-eyed and somewhat exaggerated and heightened appreciation of all that is foreign. Numerous interviewees have noted with no little sense of wonderment how their first journey abroad "opened their eyes." One might almost think that some of the comments and observations were coming from sequestered Albanians or isolated Tibetans rather than Israelis who, after all is said and done, have from the beginning of their experience of statehood been in deep and unbroken contact with the various countries of the West and the United States. This especially has been the case since the advent of television following the Six-Day War, but even prior to this in literature, films, and personal and family contacts the linkage was far ranging.

Some of the reactions can be attributed to a certain "broadening of horizons" that travel reputedly brings in its wake. But even in comments of this kind one sees the peculiarly Israeli dimension. "After wandering the world—seeing something—I find that my peers here are boring. All they talk about is house, baby, vacation, and so on. Also, I was able to see that Israel was only a point on the map and not the center of the world. I achieved some perspective." This comment by an architect, a bachelor in his midthirties, was not unique on a number of points, including his latter assertion that, while Israel was put into perspective by his travels, he would miss the obverse side of its small-town dimension—a sense of community. But still the key element was the emphasis on the comparative negative— boring, ingrown, and the absence of a certain cosmopolitan flair.

For others, all semblance of balance and objectivity is at least momentarily lost by the ofttimes dazzling encounter with the wide world and its enticements. A driver—member of the country's leading bus co-op—notes:

> When I went to the States for the first time in 1976 I returned in shock! I didn't know things could be so wonderful.

When asked what in fact was so overwhelming, he unhesitatingly answered:

> Everything! Everthing! People's behavior, the bigness of the place, the shops, the variety. It was extraordinary! My eyes fell out of my head. I came back and was ready to leave Israel forever and on the next plane out. In subsequent visits I cooled down a bit and now I see that the U.S. has problems too.

Especially in the case of the United States, the chemistry seems to be very potent and ultimately seductive. When referring to trips to various European countries interviewees generally commented positively with respect to the politeness of people in shops and on the street, and the "distances one could cover without being concerned about hostile borders, the cleanliness and order to be found in public places," But, interestingly and significantly, few were prepared to think in terms of a permanent move to these countries.

One of only a very few exceptions to this rule found his America in England—partially because of background (his parents were immigrants to Israel from South Africa, although he was a *sabra)* and partly because of family circumstances, which promised an easy adjustment in that country.

Here, too, the trip abroad "opened his eyes," and life in Israel appeared less and less desirable. The young man under discussion is a graduate engineer who was growing progressively more restive with a whole bevy of factors involved in living in Israel, primary among these having his life "constantly interrupted" by army reserve duty. After two years of suffering this regime

> I went to Europe and then came the shock of seeing that the grass was greener on the other side. And from every aspect! Things were cleaner, people were nicer and pleasanter. True, in most countries the languages were strange, but when I got to England I suddenly felt at home. I saw signs in England that what was there two years before was still there; everything is permanent, which is to say all the little things which make life good or bad . . . there, it was O.K. Every bank, every secretary one came in contact with, everything that one had to do was O.K. I felt, I felt that I wouldn't have to fight anymore.

Israel is seen in terms of struggle, indeed the word might better be "hassle," and this sense is finally given voice by a revelatory trip abroad. Suddenly it becomes possible to see what was heretofore only viscerally experienced or sensed—that life can be more pleasant, more pacific, and in general more fulfilling. Behavior that had been accepted as normal, as part of the "givens" of one's environment is suddenly found to be mutable indeed. An unskilled, recently discharged soldier on his way to join two brothers in the United States posits that "after being abroad two months I realized that the mentality which characterizes Israelis—noise, aggressiveness, and so on doesn't *have* to be," and it was for him a pleasant though somewhat unsettling shock.

For others, America specifically—but *chutz la'aretz* in general—suddenly presents itself as a sort of visceral, everyman's practicum on how things should be done to the extent that all negative characteristics slide into retreat.

> I think of America as a university. You can learn a lot. I was most impressed on my first visit by how impressive the order was. I was even impressed by public transportation. Even by New York, which everyone says is so awful and dangerous.

Rare indeed would be the native New Yorker or American who would find something positive to say about "order" or the level of public transportation available in his home environment. But for seemingly countless numbers of Israelis who are not after all coming from a primitive backwater, the "eye-opening" experience of contact with the dream acts to short-circuit critical faculties to the extent that a type of Valhalla is seemingly found where others see something considerably less than perfect.

Some harsh conclusions must be reached when so many Israelis from so extensive a crosssection of the population have their "eyes opened" or react "in shock" to phenomena that simply put are nothing more than civil treatment, minimal politeness, acceptable levels of discourse, and decent standards of public service.

A middle-aged small businessman from a Haifa suburb when pressed on his reasons for leaving first said what so many others have said to the effect that his "eyes were opened" by a visit.

> I saw a big world—nice, good, even beautiful—and I thought I would like to have a different life. Everywhere I went I got good treatment, fair treatment, pleasant and comfortable treatment. This was true when I found myself among friends, and true when I was among strangers. I was related to nicely, I was talked to nicely. And it's not the standard of living: I expected that to be high and I was not surprised by anything I saw. It was the *quality* of living which impressed me. Since then I've been thinking—no not thinking—*wanting* to go!

This above informant had during the entire course of an interview lasting more than two-and-a-half hours continuously referred to the eye-opening nature of his trip to the "States," which led him for the first time to a recognition of the underlying causes for a gnawing sense of discomfort that had been afflicting him for years. The trip in effect opened the floodgates and provided the necessary comparative context for giving vent and expression to what had previously been unexpressed or, more correctly, unidentified. In his case (and as he makes it amply clear) the very "pull" of America was not the higher material standard of life, but an almost inexplicable network of events and patterns that were found to be existent there and absent in his homeland.

But while most respondents referred to the behavioral dimension as providing the basic thrust of the "eye-opening" experience, a few did not hesitate in recognizing the role of the material or more physical lures. In some cases the overwhelming dazzle of America seemed to overcome the departee, as in the following story recounted to me by one of the respondents concerning a friend who had emigrated.

> My friend married a tourist guide who had spent time in England and spoke beautiful English. They bought this beautiful four-room apartment—it was really five rooms in American terms—in Shikun Lamed [an upper middle-class neighborhood in Tel-Aviv]. It was furnished lavishly by people who really knew how to live. They had this great big limousine which he used as a business car, and in addition she had her own car. They were members of the Country Club, and she had a maid. They had many friends, lots of parties, a rich social life, and . . . well, they lived very, very well. One day she called up to tell me that they were leaving Israel and going to America. What had happened was they had been in the States the summer before on a visit and her husband just couldn't get America out of his mind once they got back. Because of his work as a tourist guide, he got to meet a lot of big shots among

whom were famous actors and Hollywood types. One of them was X, who plays the lead on [a very popular TV serial] who gave them his house in Hollywood for two weeks and he just couldn't get all that wealth and dazzle out of his head. In less than a year following their return he gave up his tourist guide license, sold his car, sold all the furniture, and rented out the apartment. They went off to America—to Florida—and within a year they owned their own home on a lake-front. He is prospering as a jewelry salesman and she has a part-time job. They both miss Israel; they are both happy and they intend to stay in America.

How do you understand this? Economics?

If seeing the "outside," going abroad proves such a shock or "eye opener," a resultant and related response for many respondents was to assert that a change—a radical change—was now called for in their lives and that this need for change could only be satisfied through departure. Clearly, a sense of something lacking in their lives was experienced by respondents who spoke of their "eyes being opened," but what is of interest here is the expressed feeling that change is synonymous with departure. In almost every case I asked respondents why, if they felt a need for change in their lives, they did not choose to change careers or move to a different town or section of the country. I was repeatedly told that for various reasons—the smallness of the country, the absence of varied opportunities— change meant emigration: "To change one's life style it is necessary to change one's country." This must in the last analysis be viewed as a highly radical solution to a rather extensively distributed and pervasive phenomenon. Somehow a sense of things being set in concrete, of being unresponsive, of deep conservatism has emerged to give many Israelis the decided feeling that the introduction of change into their lives requires the radical step of emigration. Leaving has come to be seen for many as a sort of straining device whereby the deep-rooted parochialism and conservatism felt to be characteristic of Israeli society can be lessened and the broader horizons of the wider world integrated.

We are ten friends who started nursery school together, went to school together, went to the army together. Of the ten, five left the country and five stayed. The five who stayed are OK, but all have copied their parents' lives; their apartments look like their parents'; *they* look like their parents; their interests are to add a little here and a little there—but basically to leave things as they were.

This respondent went on to note that by leaving he managed to save himself from the trap that claimed half of his peer group,, and which would inevitably have gotten him as well had he stayed in Israel. He and others suggested that in addition to an inbuilt social conservatism that characterizes Israeli society, peer group pressure (and parental pressure) to conform is extensive and powerful. Thus, leaving is to be seen as a decided act of fleeing what appears to be unopposable.

For a considerable number of respondents the need to "get out" was expressed in terms reminiscent of those used to describe a need to escape prison or a bad and unsatisfying marriage. A most extreme comment was made by a previously quoted woman about to leave the kibbutz and the country when she said: "I'm dying. You're looking at a dying person who's about to start living in about a week and a half" (her departure date). The same woman indicated that she thought of Israel as rule-bound and rigid, while America represented freedom and flexibility. It was not a matter of changing from kibbutz to city or from one locale to another; it was Israel that was seen as denying, unfulfilling, and, in the last analysis, an impossible choice.

Most respondents were less emotional in their assertion of the need to "get out" and tended to put things in more practical terms, suggesting why and how Israel or staying in Israel was not a practicable alternative for substantial change. Mr. B., a 33-year-old engineer, gave a very different response than the case just quoted. Rather than emotion, he presents an almost cold-blooded view of what things are about.

B: But I thought that if I'm leaving—and I have a good profession, why not go somewhere else entirely; why miss the opportunity of a lifetime? So at first I looked around the country and here in Haifa. There *is* work available but not exactly what I wanted to do. In Tel Aviv there *are* jobs which could interest me but from a psychological point of view going to Tel Aviv or going abroad is pretty much the same thing.

I: What was that? You say that moving to Tel Aviv and moving to another country is pretty much the same thing?

B: It's a move! Maybe it's not a move to a new language but it does mean changing apartments, moving the kid to a new school, a new society, and my wife having to change jobs. It's rather a basic change, is it not?

Mr. B. concluded the comment with the assertion that a reason for the change abroad was not essentially economic. Clearly that problem could be dealt with at home. As he put it, "The main thing is the opportunity to work and live in another country; that's what attracts me." Changing jobs, apartment, and locale within Israel will not suffice. Israel is seen as unidimensional and if change or adventure is sought it must be pursued elsewhere. So much is this thought to be the case that it can be asserted with equanimity that moving abroad and moving from Haifa to Tel Aviv (a distance of 60 miles) is "pretty much the same thing."[3] And in a sense it is, for *true* change—change that involves some sort of dynamic with external forces (as opposed to inner challenges)—the smallness of Israel and the absence of anything like regional differences of significant dimensions raise the emigration choice to heightened attractiveness. As a *moshavnik* put it: "Somehow I want to put some change in my life, to see something different. If I have this opportunity why shouldn't I take it?" When I asked him why he could not go to another Israeli city he responded: "Because I can get there in an hour or a few hours. If we are talking about a change in atmosphere, you have to leave the country."

Mr. B. aptly summed up these feelings by stating:

> I can't say that in general I'm dissatisfied at something specific. Its clear that in some areas I am satisfied and in some I'm not. There are things on the credit side and others on the debit side. My relationships haven't changed as I've seen happen with other people that are about to leave; my relationship to the country has not become more critical, just as it hasn't become more positive; I think that I have remained stable in my relationship to life here—it hasn't changed. Nothing has changed. I just think that it's worthwhile . . . that I want to live in another place. To know at least that I tried to live in another place and it didn't work or it did work and I like it very much, or missing the weather of Israel, or the missing of social life, or the missing of the Hebrew language, or that nothing is lacking and I can manage every place and under all conditions.

For Mr. B. emigrating was a sort of testing of his attachments to Israel and Israeli society: "How do I know I am in the right place until I experience something else?" or "How do I know I am worth a damn until it's demonstrated on a larger more challenging canvas?" Curiously, and given what most outsiders consider to be the heightened challenge of living in Israel, many Israelis seem to view Israel as something of a social and economic hothouse or backwater where "success" does not bear ultimate proof of worth. This must and can only be achieved in the real world of *chutz la'aretz*. Behind the oft-commented upon bluster and "arrogance" of "the Israeli" one finds lying behind these attributes a deep sense of insecurity and inferiority. For something to succeed in Israel it is preferable that it first succeed abroad,[4] for, as a Russian immigrant put it, "the only people who come here are *zug bet*" (second raters). The same informant, a theater person, went on to note more in sadness than grief that Israel had "no culture, no literature, no tradition, and no architecture. Maybe in a few hundred years something will develop, but not now." For him, as for a myriad others, "going abroad" not only "opened one's eyes" but was found necessary for a kind of inner survival as well as a basis for self and societal testing. So deep is the need among some that even the prospect of a lessened economic situation than the one enjoyed in Israel does not daunt the intrepid seeker. The key is to leave, to get out, to go, regardless of the consequences, as can be seen in the following conversation with Mr. K.

K: I was fed up with the economic, political, and the social situation here, also that I saw there was something else abroad. It was everything together.

I: What if someone were to offer you a terrific job here in the country, with goals, I don't know exactly but with challenge, and better money than you get in your present work—would you change your mind and stay here?

K: I would postpone it a bit maybe, but not change it. Postpone it to see what it was all about. When I decided to get out to the U.S. last year we were at the height of the "boom"—I was making great money. Really good, I wasn't lacking anything economically.

I: It might be that your economic situation will be worse in America.

K: It might be.

I: And that doesn't bother you?

K: No, it doesn't bother me.

In most cases, however, the economic factor is not completely absent as a goad and a stimulus to the need to "get out." For many the view from America allowed for a greater degree of symmetry between effort and reward than seemed possible in Israel. The "eye-opening" experience for these emigrants went beyond bigness, freedom, and life style and included a kind of economic justice or fairness that when compared to the situation at home shone as a beacon and a lure, giving no rest to he who had seen or experienced it firsthand. The "choking" feeling pervasive among so many is thought to be correctable or alleviable in America where it is big, expansive, and unlimited. This choking sense often results from a feeling of closed or limited opportunities, as in the following:

> My older brother got married young. He found himself married with a kid and life was merely a matter of work, bills, sleeping, and worrying. He was choking! He decided to go to America, to free himself there; he can travel to Canada and all over. He doesn't expect to be a millionaire, but to have an easier life.

The same choking sensation can come from a need to change or experience change, as can be seen in the following conversation with Mr. L. It emphasizes several themes: a fair day's pay for a fair day's work, and new horizons—both of which seem amply available in America and sadly lacking in Israel.

I: How long have you been thinking of leaving?

L: About a year.

I: Before that you didn't think of leaving?

L: No.

I: Can you put your finger on the main reason?

L: There are several reasons. We'll start with the fact that I've been in America and my eyes were opened, and I saw a new life; I saw that when you work, you also make money. Here when you work, you only work. It's true that you work much harder [there] but you also get more in return; here, you don't even if you work hard. If you're independent you feel it in your hands, that is you value yourself and you get that kind of return. Even though I did get the Effectiveness Prize from the [name of institution], it was for something specific that I did, not for my general efforts and good will all along the line. When you don't see something else than you think then that's the way it is in the whole world. But when you go and you see, say in a factory, you see how the people live, both the good and the bad, those that are miserable and also those that live well—and you see how much they work and how much workers here are willing to work . . . you wonder. So that's one point that affected me. And another thing is that I'm already ten years in the [name of institution] and you want to see something fresh, to taste something different. To see something else, simply to try another place, to change.

What factors can be said to have brought this about? Why does one hear about a choking feeling even when the subject is entertainment or leisure, as when a young departee going off to marry an American girl rather gratuitously notes that there just "isn't a lot in the country if you want to enjoy yourself," or when a Tel Aviv *shuk* [market] stall owner notes that he needs the busy streets of New York for "relief"? Relief from what? Are not the crowds of Tel Aviv of a sufficient viscosity for his needs? Why is there so palpable a sense of disappointment among the leavers—those who have "made it" no less than those still on the make? Why are setbacks and defeats of all kinds met with a hard-nosed resiliency when suffered in New York and a decision to flee when encountered in Tel Aviv?

One simple response may be simply that New York or America represents the pinnacle, the remaining big challenge for the ambitious and self-testers and strivers. But where does one flee to if one fails in New York? And where in Israel can one come up against the challenges and rewards to be found at the very center of the Western world?

Failing Myths

While all this makes sense and no doubt explains a great deal about a great many who choose emigration, one is left with the feeling that the matter has additional facets. It is not enough to note that exposure to the outside brought about a sense of the "eyes being opened," which resulted in shock and a sort of reflex decision to move on. Does every experience of wonderment or difference bring in its wake a desire for the kind of radical upheaval suggested by emigration? Why is it not sufficient to express one's appreciation of different manners and mores in the age-old fashion of emulation, of, as it were, domesticating the experience? Indeed, given the widespread "Americanization" noted in so many aspects of Israeli life, this appears to be the chosen mode of many who have experienced the American model either directly or indirectly. But for tens of thousands of additional Israelis this accommodation is inadequate and a more radical approach is required.

Reasons and explanations abound and they tend to be diffuse and elusive. But if the comments of the emigrants themselves are to be given serious attention, then a quite apprehendable causal network begins to emerge. It begins with a sense of sad and disappointed betrayal and moves on to more refined specifics.

Curiously, *yerida* can in some eccentric fashion be viewed as at least partially the result of a successful system of indoctrination. Rare is the Israeli who has not at some juncture been touched by one of the youth movements, who has not passed through the various state education networks, who has not undergone a course in *Gadna,* or who has not been affected by a myriad still more informal organs of *etatism* where a rather highly defined picture of Israel, Israelis, and Jews is projected. This image is multihued, variegated, and largely directed by the source from which it stems. But whatever the source, a certain unified message is transmitted that can be sketched out without stretching matters to the point of caricature. The next few paragraphs represent an attempt to present the cognitive elements employed in this system of formal and informal socialization that imparts to Israelis a picture of the national undertaking in mythical terms.

Israel is the homeland of the Jewish people and is the only place in the world where a Jew can feel truly comfortable and secure. Jews were forced from the land nearly 2,000 years ago and after many trials, persecutions, and hatreds—culminating in the ultimate crime against Jews, the Holocaust—they have returned to reclaim what was always theirs. The Jews have extended their hand in friendship to the Arabs ever since the return began in earnest at the end of the nineteenth century, but the Arabs have always rejected this and sought to expel the Jews by any and all means, including war, pogroms, and various political weapons. Notwithstanding the benefits reaped by the Arabs by the Jews' presence, Arabs continue to view the Jews as an unwanted, illegal, and immoral intrusion within their body politic. This situation has necessitated the creation of a powerful military arm, which alone assures the Jews' continued existence in their land. This army is in its very nature (and name) defensive and has no designs on the lands, fortunes, or persons of the neighboring states.

The world has stood amazed at Israel's accomplishments and to this day Israel is the subject of perhaps more interest, talk, attack, love, concern, hatred, and envy than any other 8,000 square-mile nation-state on the face of the earth.

Jews have created a just society where a high modicum of security, health, education, and freedom are vouchsafed to all. Finally, it is the duty of all Jews to cast off the fetters of an unwanted minority status and to return home to share in the rebuilding of the Hebrew commonwealth.

The above constitute a rather stylized though fairly comprehensive presentation of key elements which comprise the national myth. All nations have myths and Israel is a nation in many respects like all other nations. Nations are often victims as well as beneficiaries of the national myth structure, as when projected ideals are not able to withstand intensive scrutiny or comparison without serious buffeting and strain. In such cases the successful dissemination of the myth or myths in question can result in the societies being hoisted as it were on their own pitard, where they are bound to fall short in this or that respect. Small deviations in reality from the mythic systems are, of course, always present and tend to be readily absorbable. Trouble begins when a significant and apparently unbridgeable chasm emerges between myth and reality. This can result in a whole range of reactions from personal anomie to real and actual attacks upon central societal institutions. When in the 1960s it became clear that the "American way of life"—predicated on liberty and justice for all, on full freedoms without reference to race, color, or religion—was seriously flawed in practice, a reaction set it. Thousands participated in various political acts, such as marches, sit-ins, voter registration drives, and civil disobedience, in order to bridge the gap. Also in the 1960s, anti-Vietnam war activities again brought tens of thousands of Americans into deep confrontation with their government and this, again, proved instrumental in bringing about change in the direction of mythic ideals. Similar examples can be adduced from history as well as from contemporary events in both Western and non-Western societies, with differences however in the methods used to meet the challenge and relative success in doing so.

The United States in particular seems to be blessed by an inordinate degree of success in "selling" the national myth. In a society marked by two extraordinary historical events—the genocide and near total destruction of the Indians, and slavery, which was the dominant social and economic framework of a significant segment of the society for its first 150 years—it is nothing short of remarkable that the dominant central myth should include freedom, justice, and equality for all.

By some seemingly inexplicable alchemy, generations of Americans absorbed and celebrated a view of U.S. society that was often distant from this elevated standard. "Adjustive outbreaks," such as those adduced above concerning civil rights for Blacks and Indians or American involvement in

Vietnam, have left the overall structure perhaps shaken and bruised, but very much intact. Buildings or whole neighborhoods might be burned, rioters might take over the streets for short periods, a dose of cynicism might be introduced with respect to government and officialdom, but somehow (and still) the basic myth of an America that protects the little man, plays fair, and gives everyone a chance to go as far as his energy and capabilities will take him still manages to rise up out of the smoke. With the exception of a few thousand young people and army deserters who fled America during the Vietnam debacle, Americans—shaken though many might have been by various deviations from the dream or the ideal—do not choose to abandon their country to any notable extent. Flag waving might have declined precipitously, a certain verbal cynicism might characterize the relatedness of many tens of thousands regarding their national symbols and myths, but the basic commitment and faith that Keniston (1965:446) thought to be fading in the 1960s seem to be largely intact.

I am not suggesting that nothing has happened, that the upheavals of the 1960s and 1970s have left American society unscathed and unaffected. There can be no denying that a great deal has transpired bearing diverse implications in myriad large and small matters affecting that society. I do, however, aver that the pervasive response in American society to the factors discussed above is one of a flawed mechanism in need of repair rather than a failed and inadequate vehicle that does not measure up.

This latter response seems prevalent in Israel among leavers and non-leavers alike. Where America can be said to be something of a public relations miracle with respect to its phenomenal success in implanting and sustaining an opulent national myth even in the face of contradictions and partial failures, the Israeli myth structure undergoes a more stringent and less forgiving appraisal on the part of its participants. Where disappointment or disillusionment in America might result in a type of internal exile—a shutting out and a cutting off from the society while remaining in all respects within it—the same dynamic in Israel might result in more basic questioning as to the worthiness or defensibility of the enterprise and in a fairly large number of cases a progressive unravelment leading to departure.

Although citizens going through the American educational system will learn and unlearn the same historical events (such as George Washington's role in the colonial period or whether America has or has not ever started or lost a war) with radical changes transpiring as one moves through the system and the various age groupings, it is rare to hear Americans say in regard to their socialization to citizenship that "they lied to me." It was not rare to hear this said by a considerable number among those interviewed for this study and in various ways, such as: "they exaggerated," "they overblew our strength or our righteousness," or "they enlarged our achievements."

Tied to this was the assertion that "they" overemphasized "duty" as the key element of life in Israel, and underemphasized the possibility that living there could be good in its own right.

For many of those leaving there appears to exist a strong sense of having been betrayed by the exposure and collapse of various collective myths, such as the purity of the army, the complete justice of the cause regarding the Arabs, the superiority of the culture, or even the positive "difference" involved in being Jewish. A skilled mechanic (albeit a college grad), an emigrant from the United States noted:

> As a result of living here I changed my feelings about Jews. I used to think we were superior. I thought we were smarter, cleaner, more energetic, kinder ... but it seems like the dregs of the Jewish people have come here. We found in living here that Judaism is not the bond we thought it was. I'm not impressed with the Jews anymore.

The same informant ventured a comparison with the United States when he noted, "In America we had an image of the success of Americanism. Here there is no image, no idea of what it is to be an Israeli. This is polyglot like America is—but America had direction."

America, he is saying, knew what it was about and by implication Israel does not: it lacks definition and thus it fails to lay any sustaining claim upon its citizenry. It was supposed to be the one thing, but it turned out to be something very different indeed. Should one think that the above-quoted informant's disappointment and sense of betrayal was in some way a function of his coming from the opulence of the United States, it can be matched with the comment of a Russian informant who noted:

> People who came to Israel from Moscow, Leningrad, Siberia ... perhaps for them where they lacked a piece of bread, Israel is something. But for us who lived near the Hungarian border and traveled to Budapest, Israel is nothing special. Nothing new here for us. We expected more.

"We expected more" might almost be a theme shared by all interviewees whether native-born or new immigrant, of Eastern or Western origin, highly educated or relatively simple. "We expected more" and we were taught to expect more, and unlike the Russian emigrant quoted above, not on the material plane. Mrs. M., a highly articulate and thoughtful librarian in her midthirties, native-born, stated that people are leaving "because they were let down by the State. We were brought up on ideals, high ideals ... maybe too much so because these things are hard to achieve. Like, a special state, a special people—everything special. You learn to have expectations."

I: What changed? What happened?

M: Part because of the army, security, wars and things like that. And part is as a result of . . . I'll tell you what my husband said when after complaining about corruption and other unsatisfactory things he would be told by his friends "Well, that's the way the world is. That's the way it is all over." He would then say, "So why am I living here? We should close the State and all go to live in America." [nervous laughter] So you see—here it is supposed to be special or at least so we were told over and over again. It's hard to live here—harder certainly than in America and if it is not special, not better, then everyone comes to the conclusion, "Why bother?"

I: Isn't that a strange way to relate to one's country?

M: Yes! But we are not a normal people. We are not like the Japanese or Greeks who have lived in their lands for thousands of uninterrupted years. There is still much from the *galut* here!

I: But what about people like yourself who were born here and brought up here?

M: But it's things you grew up with . . . the stories from home, the stories from teachers . . . these are things that enter into you. They taught us expectations! Maybe it was a mistake to bring us up to expect that everything should be special; that Israel should be special.

This educational emphasis on "specialness," on unique attributes, tends to set the stage for grave disappointment when confronted by reality, especially, I would assert, in a society such as Israel's. In quiet backwaters, it should be entirely possible to cultivate certain myths where their effectuality is less dependent on outside forces or where the atmosphere is not one of thoroughly unpredictable conflict. But in Israel where these conditions decidedly do not exist, danger and threats to myth maintenance abound. The army and things surrounding the military provide an example of what is meant here.

Every young Israeli with the exception of most Arabs and the ultra-Orthodox Jewish community is expected (and does) serve for a period of three years for males and two years for women in the armed forces. This period of service (again for most) occurs at a highly sensitive juncture of the maturing process for young people in a Western context—18 years of age. It is a time of testing—not only of self but of context, whether family, peer groups, or broader society. It is also a time of judgment with respect to both socializing agents and aims. Young Israelis are brought up to think of Tzahal, the Israel Defense Forces, as sacrosanct: above politics and dispute in this most disputatious of societies. Meeting the reality elicits, as one might predict, a wide range of responses from the young recruits, including indifference. For some, the shock of discovering that armies—all armies, including Tzahal—are comprised of soldiers and that soldiers anywhere share more than they do not is nothing short of jolting. Mr. R., a young departee, three years out of the army, attributes his decision to leave primarily to the shock absorbed during his army service. In response to the interviewer's question as to how long he has been weighing the step of emigration he answered:

> It's a process that took a long time. When I finished high school, I was like all the kids before the army, and I even went to pilot school. I wanted to be a pilot and all those things. During army service I discovered that I was very much against all the militarism, all those things, and I suddenly met another nation that I didn't know. Then all these myths started breaking down, the stories that you hear about the army when you're a child. Then you see what all these things are, what kind of people, what kind of things go on . . . corruption, and all the confusion. I finished the army, and I felt, well, that's all over, that terrible world of the army; it doesn't bother me now; I'm finished with it.

The same respondent continued most poignantly to describe his reactions to the army and the role this played in his sense of relatedness to and anchorage within society.

I: Can you put your finger on a specific incident in the army that made you feel that it's nonsense, or was it a collection of things?

R: There are incidents and there are a collection of small things. You always hear "Israel Defense Force" and for the first time you meet types that are really blood thirsty, that are really just waiting for a war, and there are a lot of them.

I: You're not talking about the ordinary soldiers?

R: It's the commanders. I had an image of them, from the movies, and they're the ones that are shocking, and they're the ones that are setting the example, as it were. Afterwards, after the army, without any connection, I started to understand, as did a lot of people, that in all the past wars, it wasn't exactly the poor Jews against the Arabs who want to eat them. Now it's pretty well known in 1972, that . . . with a little desire, will, it could have been possible to prevent the war in 1973. *That* was the failure, not that they caught us unprepared.

I: What do you do in the army?

R: I was in communications in the air force. And also *samal mivtzaim* [operations sgt.] so I was always walking around the command post rooms and I saw all the things that motivate them, and it wasn't like the character of Dosh, poor ones with a kibbutz hat on. I saw that the situation was entirely different, that there are people who like it. And I didn't.

Mr. R. repeated the plaintive phrase "they lied to me" with respect to other categories of myth but the army was clearly the key element in his almost total disillusionment with his society. With other respondents matters such as social justice, political freedom, and ethnic toleration gave rise to assertions of having been "lied" to.

A 47-year-old physician, native-born, resident in Florida, in a most plaintive tone said, "They told us this was the best country in the world—especially for Jews. But when I saw something of the world I realized that it is not the best country in the world and not even the best for Jews. I feel more Jewish now and I am a better Jew now that I am living in Florida than I ever was in Israel." In most cases it was not a matter of Israel being worse in these respects than other countries, but rather of Israel being no better—and this, it would appear, formed the unassimilable core of disappointment and dissatisfaction. A middle-aged, single woman asserted that "people have committed crimes here," meaning crimes of a political and moral nature that were, she agrees, no worse than those committed elsewhere but "somehow I expected more from this country."

Being "no better" assumes the burden of a curious chemistry whereby Israel does, in the end, come out as being worse. An immigrant from the United States, not socialized or educated in Israel but nevertheless heir to the same pattern of high, if not overblown expectations, notes:

> Somehow I expected more from the country. Maybe that's part of my problem in that I came here expecting that we were going to be different or at least that we were going to be sane. I feel there are no values here, no ethics. As a matter of fact there doesn't even seem to be a word for ethics in Hebrew; everyone says "etica." It's like a foreign word here!

In answer to a question as to whether Israeli society had higher levels of corruption than exist in other Western societies, the answer on the part of almost all respondents was a decided "no," but with an almost collective unified addendum summed up by one respondent who said: "It's the same everywhere except that there is this idea that *here* it's supposed to be different."

It would appear from the responses of a considerable number of departees that "specialness" was not only not readily or easily achieved, but was not considered a desirable goal in the first instance. Respondees tended to suggest in many different fashions that the role of specialness was not only in the last analysis unfulfilled, but was in addition an unsolicited and unwanted burden. A remarkably high proportion of leavers indicated that this misdirected national emphasis led to an accentuation of duty to the exclusion of a sense of sedate satisfaction with life in the country. One respondent noted with a sense of deep sadness that he wanted people to talk him out of leaving but "no one had a positive reason; only negative ones such as the *goyim* will get me out there or I don't know what else. But nobody just tried to tell me it is good here, it is nice here. I spoke to so many people and I waited for an answer—but it never came. Maybe I don't understand things."

But the same respondent did assert that he "understood" when he noted the fact that, as the key element condemning Israel as an unworthy society, its entire appeal as it exists is parochial and without universal dimensions.

> Let's say you're out of the country and you have a friend or acquaintance who's not Jewish and he asks you if you would recommend living in the country [Israel] as a country, not as a Jew. Clearly, if he is not Jewish you would not recommend it. That is to say that putting aside the matter of Jewishness, *no one* would recommend this country as a good place to live!

And this clearly is because of a number of reasons already alluded to and others merely noted in passing, such as military service, the threat and reality of near constant war, and societal tensions resulting therefrom.

Notes

1. As so often happens it remains for literature to enhance and elaborate in a most pithy fashion what sociologists and historians perforce stretch out and whose point is often missed entirely. Dan Jacobsen (1966: 410) in his novel *The Beginners* has his hero Joel attempting to explain to his gentile lover why he left Israel: "I feel guilty to the people there—and to some part of myself—for having left. But I think I might have betrayed some other part by staying. The strange thing is that both parts seem to me to be equally Jewish."
2. This means among other things that any policy assumptions to be adopted by the Israeli authorities regarding emigration will of necessity be rather unreliable.
3. Israelis seem to be inordinately tied to their cities. In a recent poll over 80 percent of Jerusalemites would not consider living anywhere else, and more than 70 percent of Haifaites and 68 percent of Tel Avivians said the same thing with respect to their towns. These very powerful ties to locality on the part of people who have demonstrated at least some ambivalence about the nation-state idea must be seen as a matter of interest for further research.
4. In the academic and professional world, for example, it is preferable to have at least one advanced degree from a university abroad; or if one invents or improves something, it should make it abroad before coming home for local acceptance.

3

Unease in Zion

Tension, War, and Military Service

With respect to reserve duty as an operative factor in people's decisions to emigrate, the picture is far from being entirely one-sided or clear. Some respondents indicated that reserve duty played no role at all in their decision. Others suggested that, in fact, reserve duty could be seen in a positive light as a change of pace, a reliever of boredom, or a bit of time away from the pressures of marriage, family, or the marketplace. For still others it is viewed as a noxious interruption of their life—"always coming at the wrong moment."

Those most opposed to serving tend to be those whose lives and livelihood are most seriously impaired. Foremost among these are small business people, owners of "mom-and-pop" enterprises, and marginal independents of all kinds. For these individuals the regular four or five weeks of annual service can often prove sufficient to put a serious crimp into the profitably and/or competitiveness of their enterprise. In times of emergency when the call-up can extend to 60, 90, or even more days per year the results can be nothing short of catastrophic. For people on salary, on the other hand, or for nonindependent professionals, the more positive view of reserve duty is often held. For example, a lab technician observes:

> I enjoy going to reserve duty. Each time I enjoy it. I like the army; I like the responsibility [he is a company commander]. When I have responsibility I feel good.

A physicist notes that given the flexibility apparent in this unit he does not find serving at all onerous.

> They let me plan my reserve duty more or less in advance so that it's comfortable for *me* rather than for *them*. So from that point of view I don't have any trouble. If they think they need me for a month, or a month and a half—then I'm all for it. I am not against reserve duty.

Others suggest that a little service to one's country is not much to give when all is said and done. A mathematician suggests that "that's the way it is; that's what we have to do in this country; it's the price we pay for being citizens of a certain state."

For many Israeli men, *miluim* (reserve duty) performs an at least partially positive role in their lives. It is on an obvious plane a societally sanctioned release from routine, providing the possibility for the youthful camaraderie associated with everybody's "good old days." What could be jollier than a bunch of middle-aged men coming together to do their own cooking, tell smutty jokes, engage in endless banter, and perform virile tasks such a night patrol and guard duty—and all bearing the stamp of societal approval? It can function as a constant renewal or reaffirmation of youth and vitality pushing into middle age and beyond a sense of control and challenge that might be in somewhat short supply in a more conventional world.

Another latent spin-off of yearly army service may be seen in its leveling properties. It tends to provide a superb antidote to the increasing non-equalitarianism and heightened stratification of Israeli society relieving the build-up and accumulation of pressure and extending the life span of a declining central myth. It is still eminently possible for the professor to be commanded by his students, and for the "boss" to taste the bitter ashes that are the lot of the common soldier everywhere—oftimes at the hands of his erstwhile employees, who might be his superior officers. The fact that this upside down world is only temporary and that the proper order of things will be returned to in due course allows the phenomenon to be seen as ideal in many ways, and to the relief, I suspect, of all sides.

Furthermore military service provides the opportunity of meeting and mingling with (in a rather structured format) segments of the population with which one does not ordinarily come into contact in everyday life, at least not at the same level of intimacy and intensity. Thus the Ashkenazic school teacher will talk with the Sephardic shop keeper, the German journalist with the off-handed American, the exotic Soviet Georgian with the sophisticated Parisian finding as often as not that a common core of feelings and reactions (and certainly interests in terms of the army and their service is concerned) exists and binds them together. It is, in some ways, a chance for yearly reaffirmation of an otherwise abstracted and markedly sloganistic sense of oneness or at least "common cause."

The role that the army plays in inculcating a sense of Israeliness or in the socialization and growth patterns of Israeli young people cannot be too strongly emphasized. Service in the army and what kind of service one performed is of the highest importance in social placement of the individual. So central is this ability to serve that even in many cases of physical disability (sometimes of a rather remarkable gravity), strings will be pulled and pressure placed to have the individual accepted for service. Not serving is viewed as the ultimate loss of status as an Israeli.

Thus even among departees, those leaving the country in most cases permanently, service in the army tends to be seen as the main link with the otherwise rejected past and nonservice is viewed as a more serious departure from acceptable norms than the act of leaving itself. Recently, hundreds of ex-Israeli residents in New York petitioned the visiting Israeli chief of staff to make provision whereby they might return to Israel each year in order to continue to do their annual stint of reserve duty. When the children of emigrants were recently included in a program to encourage return it was not as farmers, building workers, nurses, or computer programmers that they came to spend the summer in Israel, but as participants in a special *Gadna* or paramilitary program specially developed for them.

Even in attempts at humorous rejection of military service, one can detect a sense of opposite intent as when one respondent said: "One great advantage of being in America is not having to go to *miluim*. We *yordim* joke about it and say that instead of *miluim* we promise to visit Israel for one or two months every year." A moment later the same person assured me that "*miluim* was no problem," as if the very act of joking about so serious a matter placed him beyond the pale.

Still, for a proportion (about 25 percent of the respondents) rejection of the whole system or how it was carried out was asserted by them to have played a role—though not a central role—in their decision to leave. Most of these were people who suffered direct and persistent losses from being called up. A few were students or recent graduates in technical subjects where absence from classes tended to set them back, unlike the case with humanities or social science students who tended to take a lighter view of the interruption. A recent electrical engineering graduate observed:

> I was two years into my studies when the trouble started [thoughts of emigration]. Those two years were terribly difficult for me and according to Murphy's Law I always got called up at the worst possible time—and for a full month at a time. It made me angry; I had done my three years and I was trying to get on with my life and was having a hard time doing so. Then I would get a whole month—or more correctly 45 days and *that* is something terrible. Then there was the matter of the treatment you got in the army. They treat you like a demented child. You can't say what you want or do what you want. They were forcing me into the dungeons for 45 days each year where you are treated like a worm and commanded to come, go, stop, and so on.
>
> When I was doing my regular service the commanders were at least older than I was. But now it doesn't matter how old I am or what I am outside— there [in the army] they do with you as they like.

Clearly, for this respondent the army was not viewed as a breaker of dull routine or as a social leveller, but rather as an unwelcome and destructive intrusion into his life. This view, while a decidedly minority one does, however, represent feelings experienced by at least some of the leavers.

For another small group the intrusive factor is not so much unwelcome as is the fact that the army is seen as ineffective and essentially a time waster:

> The basic idea of being called to reserve duty doesn't bother me. But what I do there bothers me very much: the way things are conducted, the lack of justice involved in who is called and for how long, and most important the fact that what they do with you once you're there is generally a waste of time. It's truly awful!

> It's not that I think my talents aren't being properly used—it's simply that I don't do anything! Just loaf around and do work that is really make-work in order to keep us occupied. The organization of reserve duty—of the army—is really pathetic.

But if the general opinion regarding *miluim* is positive, albeit with the hesitations (and more) of a minority as outlined above, feelings with respect to war and the threat of war tend to occupy a much more serious place in the decision-making process involved in emigration. Any romantic notions that might be associated with a military change-of-pace once a year while doing reserve duty tend to recede when confronted by the pain and fear that most normal human beings associate with war itself. And, as one might expect, the closer the individual involvement with actual combat and the older one becomes still seeing "no light at the end of the tunnel," the more upsetting and dislocating the prospect of "more war."

Nevertheless, researching the question of war as a motive for deciding to leave the country has proven a most difficult task. While almost everyone interviewed responded rather conventionally to the effect that "Yes, war is awful," "Yes, peace is a priority objective for Israelis," "Yes, the fact of one war leading inevitably to a follow-up war was taking a toll," "Yes, we cannot afford to let our guard down for a moment or lose even one war," etc., very few were willing to state blatantly and without caveat that fear of war was a significant factor in their decision to emigrate. But the sum total of responses decidedly indicated the presence of a widespread and pervasive sense of concern and apprehension on both a personal and a communal level. Some respondents brushed the question aside with bravado comments to the effect that one is more likely to get hit by a car on Israel's highways than killed in war or at the hands of a terrorist. A few respondents did not even have recourse to probability games of this sort and simply stated a variant of what a middle-aged, middle-class departee noted with no little aggressiveness: "I feel safer here—I just feel safer here than any place else in the world."

A few respondents suggested that while they themselves were able to handle the threat and the actuality of war, this was not the case with their spouse or other members of the family, which might or might not be a convenient device for displacing a personally unacceptable or uncomfortable response to the phenomenon. In these cases the respondents noted that leaving the country was "for the wife," "for the kids," or "for Mom" rather than resulting from personal fear or concern.

Researching this question is difficult for a variety of reasons. Israel, for one thing, is probably one of the last outposts of unvarnished machismo in the Western world. The virile physical enthusiast who volunteers for arduous duty, combat, parachute jumping, underwater demolition, and other wild things not previously countenanced by Jewish tradition is seemingly preeminent. Bravery and *chutzpa*, especially the physical varieties, are highly valued and widely celebrated. Neither the *yeshiva bucher* nor the "bookworm" are likely holders of an elevated status or any particular social honor. (The combination, however, of intellectual virtuosity, even poetic sensitivity and physical courage and prowess is highly valued.) Thus for Israelis socialized within this type of framework admissions of being influenced by elements of fear, perhaps even cowardice, do not come easily.

Additionally, the person leaving is already in violation of an important norm that demands *aliyah* not *yerida*—staying in the country, not leaving it. To admit to breaking one norm (leaving) because of an inability to fulfill another (physical courage) is a difficult matter indeed.

Thirdly, the myth of Israel's military invincibility has been so widely reenforced since 1967 that thinking defeat, widespread destruction, or about possibilities of large numbers of casualties places the thinker in a context of perversity. Notwithstanding the shock and upset of the 1973 war, rare is the Israeli who would suggest the possibility of serious defeat in future wars—at least aloud. And here is the difficulty! While not in most cases admitting to deep feelings of fear functioning as a goad to get out while the getting is good, a majority of informants skirted this position making it unmistakably clear that war and insecurity were in fact potent elements in the decision-making process.

A minority of respondents were nonetheless rather straightforward in their evaluation of this variable sometimes expressing their position with great poignancy. A young physician, a resident in orthopedic surgery already living in America, talked at length about his leaving, asserting that there was in fact only one cause and that was war. He was involved in the Yom Kippur War and remarked:

> I was in a trench and watching an enemy plane come over again and again to strafe. I had an Uzi [an Israeli submachine gun] and I remember feeling as completely helpless as a human being could feel. I remember thinking that he [the enemy pilot] wanted nothing so much as to kill *me* and it was absurd, absurd. I decided then and there that if I got out I would leave and go anywhere—anywhere where there was no war.

The speaker was so typically an Israeli that he appeared almost as a stereotype. In his American persona he was clearly a most unlikely and uncomfortable figure. Not only was this so to the observer but he himself noted that he found nothing about America particularly attractive and he missed home terribly. When asked, "Why don't you come back to Israel?" he answered, "When you can promise me no more war I will come back. I cannot, I will not go through another war." A secretary weighing but undecided about emigration, the mother of a six-year-old boy proclaimed, "I will stay here [in Israel] until my son is 16 and if by that time the cycle of war after war has not ended I will take him and leave—with or without my husband. I am not going to offer him up as a human sacrifice."

Only one informant had suffered the loss of an immediate family member in war, but in this case he asserts that this was one of the main though not the only causes for his leaving the country.

> My brother was killed in the Yom Kippur War. He was a lieutenant in the army and his death brought turmoil into my life. I was 18 when he died and just going into the army. He was a wonderful person, only 28 when he died, leaving behind a wife and two children. The usual tragedy in the land of Israel! [said bitterly] His death gave me a push telling me I will live life, such a full life, such a wonderful life that it will be enough for two . . . and I feel that in America I can do it. One life for me and one for my brother.

It becomes clear after talking to so many Israelis representing differing segments of the population and differing worldviews and political configurations that the image of a Spartan Israel able to absorb in blithe fashion war after war with near stoic indifference is rather far from the mark. The effect of war seems progressive and cumulative with each succeeding chapter of the ongoing conflict exacting an escalating price in terms of personal fear and dislocation and societal anomie. The "first war" is, at least for those who do the actual fighting, bad enough, but succeeding conflicts become progressively more difficult. The wife of a soldier who has fought in two wars notes:

> My husband started to think of leaving after the Yom Kippur War. He saw all the dead and wounded and decided he wanted out. Before this war he used to sort of look forward to *miluim*. After, he feared and hated it.

The same woman noted her own changing response to what she conceived of as constant war.

> To tell you the truth I worry about my son [age 10]. This is a country which kills its young men. Any mother who tells you she doesn't have this worry is lying. What's going to be with this constant blooding of the generations? I hope in America I won't have this worry.

In the case of war, as with other matters previously noted, exposure to "another way" through a trip or visit abroad often acts as a precipitant for a changing of attitudes and perceptions. Trite and self-evident as the thought might be, it still strikes one as amazing how easily humankind accepts any conditions as immutable givens of nature in the absence of contrary evidence or experience. Israelis are brought up with the notion of war being a fixed given of their national existence. When the former chief of staff of the Israeli Army, Lt. Gen. Rafael Eitan promised the nation a hundred years of war as he did in 1983, only the more liberal newspapers editorialized against the portentious projection, while popular reaction was significant in its quiescence. For Israelis, as for other societies, rites of passage mark significant way stations in the life process. For Israelis, unlike most other Western nations, the eighteenth birthday and the departure for long years of army service is nearly unquestioned as the leap from adolescence to adulthood, from light-heartedness to ultimate responsibility and ultimate danger. It is, when all is said and done, the way things are! It is a given of the collective existence.

Somehow one begins to forget that it can be otherwise, at least elsewhere. Just as childhood blends into adolescence and blossoms into adulthood, so one moves from the things of childhood to the deadly games and devices of war. It is, seemingly and apparently, thusly ordained. For some it even begins to assume the trappings of a sort of deadly backdrop to everyday life. One young couple in a northern border development town report that "we hear the guns all the time . . . and the *katyushas*. Just a few weeks ago a few *katyushas* whizzed overhead on their way to _____ . And sometimes there are fire exchanges which you can see in the distance."

The husband of the couple assured me that this situation was definitely not a factor in his decision to emigrate except insofar as he occasionally feared for his wife. She in turn assured me that she was not overly concerned by the element of terror or war. On the contrary, they both emphasized that "the situation" tended to have a cohesive effect regarding a sense of community for "in _____ when the *katyushas* fall you are part of things, part of the glorious [said ironically] experience here." The above comes from people living in a settlement that is constantly threatened but only rarely hit. Another perspective is reflected in the comments of a previously quoted engineer living in a northern community that has been hit with some frequency over the years. Here the *katyusha* attacks and terrorist acts are not seen as in any way harmless, or normal, or as a social cohesive. They are viewed quite realistically as a threat to life and limb, and a disruptive factor in communal and personal life.

> We have been suffering from this problem [*katyusha* shellings] since 1970. What can I tell you? People are fed up and they can't take much more. What's been happening here in the last few weeks is criminal. They [the government] built security rooms which were added to existent apartments and it turns out that the security rooms aren't so reliable. The shells go through the concrete and for a simple reason: to stop a *katyusha* you need about ½ meter thick concrete. The concrete in the security rooms is maybe 20 centimeters thick. So you see what I mean when I say security is the most pressing problem here?

The same community witnessed a mass exodus of the population due to *katyusha* shellings, which reached a high of some dozens of shells falling on and around them for days on end. People could not stand the constant and long periods spent in inadequate shelters and claims were made to the effect that there were not enough shelters to harbor the entire population, perhaps resulting in the unfelicitous but deeply felt reaction of my informant when he asked, "What does this place give me which would justify my staying?" He went on to note with much enthusiasm that "without *katyushas* I don't think anything could get me out of here—and in this I think I would be joined by everybody who lives here."

For people living under these particular conditions no "eye-opening" trip abroad is required in order to convince them that a change is desired. No comparative framework is needed in response to shells showering down on one. But for others, the deeply imbedded conviction with respect to the inevitability and unescapable nature of danger and war and even of their country's total rightness and purity of intent in these matters can be shaken by exposure to other views and other contexts.

A practical engineer, born in Romania but brought up in Israel, appeared to be speaking in a state of unrelieved shock when he told me: "It's only when you go abroad that you realize what the war thing is. The attacks, the *katyushas*, frogmen on the beaches, bombs on the buses—it's frightening, it's upsetting." Another departee noted: "I guess the main effect of my living in Texas of all places was to realize that I'm scared of war—although it's subconscious. On the surface I don't admit it; but it's there."

A graphic artist talked about his disillusionment with the country in general terms but specifically with respect to war:

I'm not a pacifist! I agree that in the first years of the State wars were thrust upon us; they were unavoidable. We *did* have to wrest this country from the Arabs to make it our own.

But recently, at least since the Six-Day War, and even more recently, with the coming to power of the Begin government wars if they come will be at least as much our fault, if not more so. We have demonstrated an aggressiveness, a willingness to go to the gun as much if not more than the Arabs.

And I feel—for the first time—a sense of physical threat. I don't know about coming back for the next war.

The 1973 War more than any other conflict in Israel's history must be seen as instrumental in the unravelling of a societal consensus. This conflict marks the end of innocence with respect not only to a consensual evaluation of Israel's basic security needs, but also with regard to a certain black-white interpretation of the seemingly endless conflict with the Arabs wherein Israel was seen as all "good" and the other side as all "bad." For the first time a growing minority of the public wondered aloud if in fact "our side" has done everything possible to achieve peace and if in fact "there was nobody to talk to" among Israel's adversaries. This is not to suggest that a reversal occurred or that a broadly agreed upon societal "definition of the situation" was destroyed or replaced. But that it was shaken cannot be denied. I am personally unaware of Israelis living or travelling abroad lined up at embassies or fighting each other to board El Al planes in order to get home and join up for the Peace for Galilee campaign or Lebanon War in the summer of 1982. In 1967 and 1973 they did and in the thousands! The Yom Kippur War of 1973 was no less a watershed in modern Israeli history than was the Six-Day War of 1967, but clearly and understandably manifesting a decidedly different threat. The Six-Day War led to a certain closure with respect to old myths and a corresponding and not unrelated expansion of horizons—to the extent in some instances of the creation of phantasmagoria unanchored in hard reality. The 1973 war led to the rise of feelings of doubt with respect to the long-term survivability of the enterprise, to the development of a certain morbidity, a kind of societal growth of intimations of mortality. For the first time one was privy to conversations in which young Israelis despaired of ever knowing peace. A notable minority announced this as the last war in the sense that they would leave the country rather than fight again. Indeed the highest number of emigrants to leave the country since the early 1950s did so in 1974 following the war and my evidence suggests support for the obvious—the two are not unrelated. This was the first Israeli war that at least a strong minority of Israelis sensed "need not have been" had step *x, y,* or *z* been taken. One interviewee put it thusly when referring to the Yom Kippur War:

> It's almost like buying back Karma. In other words—it's not that there wasn't justification for both the 1967 war and the Yom Kippur War, but underneath there was something more . . . and that is that there were people like Nachum Goldman and others like him who were looking for solutions, peaceful solutions but who didn't have a chance. Every suggestion was turned aside because people were making a lot of money. It was like they had too much to drink, they were drunk with the present and they couldn't see the future at all. So we got war and war takes its toll on people. Aggression takes its toll on people—and on their souls.

Other respondents, without trying to apportion culpability, do nonetheless "sense" that something basic has been altered in the national configuration. For the first time following the Yom Kippur War large numbers of Israelis could tell of someone they knew who had left or was contemplating departure as a direct result of the war. Sad stories of young men who had been "broken" by the experience made the rounds—"the friend of a brother," the "uncle of a girl," or the "brother-in-law of an acquaintance." Typical of these reports was one recounted to me by a young married woman who was intrigued by her own ambivalence and that of other *yordim*.

> I think that the majority of *yordim* don't hate Israel or feel any animosity toward the country. In many cases it's a matter of the shock of war. I personally know of a couple who left after the Yom Kippur War—they just left cold. The man is a brother of a neighbor and he, his wife, and their two children went to live in Iran until that blew up. They came back to Israel, but only long enough to leave again. I think they are in America or somewhere. He just had a shock and he refuses to fight anymore; he refuses to have anything to do with war. He is frightened.

Other tales were recounted of a similar character but interestingly most were second- or third-hand, which has a significance of its own. Equally significant, however, and the obverse of the above noted phenomenon was the relative absence of a personal and direct linkage made by the emigrant himself between the decision to emigrate and the factor of war. For most respondents it was clear that the factor of war now played a heightened role in any personal or familial calculus from what it had or would have prior to the "shocks" of Yom Kippur 1973, but it remains extremely difficult to adequately assign weight in the matter. The evidence points to a growing and heightened importance for this factor as a strong item of concern and one of increasing significance in the general "package" of elements that play a role in the decision-making process, but in the final analysis, Israelis, including those who have chosen to leave the country, continue to mirror the classic image of "true grit" in their attitude to the challenges of war.

Perhaps it was best summed up by Mrs. Y., a mother of two small children leaving a small settlement in the Galilee for the United States, feeling a mixture of guilt and a certain diffidence.

Y: At the time of the Yom Kippur War I had two children—one six months old and one two years. When I think back to it I remember how tense I was then; I was not myself. I did exactly what I had to do; I had things in the shelter for the kids and I had a bag ready, before I went to sleep, with bottles and diapers. I slept in my clothes, and everything went well. I watched the TV and the news. I took care of the kids. I laughed with them and played with them. After the war was over, and after my husband was home and after the cease-fire I said to myself, "How did I live through this?" And I don't know . . . I guess under stress I stand up very well. [small laugh]

I: And if it should happen again?

Y: If it should happen the way it happened the last. . . . Look, I'm not prowar, and I don't like the idea of war, but war in Israel will not drive me away. I mean somebody has to be here. Look, of course I'm afraid when there's a war, I'm afraid a bomb will fall on me, I'm afraid my husband will get killed, I'm afraid the kids will get killed, I'm afraid that maybe this country will go to the Arabs. Of course I'm afraid, and what would happen if, God forbid, if this territory was conquered? But I believe in Israelis, I believe in the strength and the wits of the generals of the army; I have a lot of faith in them. From that point of view I wasn't worried. Of course I was worried that an Arab plane could infiltrate and drop a bomb on us—that bothers me; but that wouldn't be something that would drive me away from Israel.

Tied to, but not synonymous with war is the question of tension and what role it might play in lessening the attractiveness of staying and enhancing that of moving to another country. Again, as in the case with the question of reserve duty, a small but visible and audible proportion of respondents saw tension in Israeli society as fulfilling certain positive integrative functions—at least on the societal if not the personal level. Of the 117 people interviewed for the study, 21 felt that tension in everyday life was not only not an upsetting factor but it fulfilled something of a positive role; 13 saw it as both positive and negative. The remaining respondees indicated in one way or another that it acted as an irritant and that in the majority of cases they were willing and anxious to trade any excitement deriving from tension for the boredom and satisfactions of its opposite.

In the first camp comment ranged from a mere salute to the salubriousness of tension to those who felt it would be among the cultural artifacts most sorely missed while living in a new country.

What will I miss most? I will miss the pressure. It will be too easy. Here you live under psychological and material pressure while there [the United States] it doesn't exist. People don't think there at all! They live their own lives and that's it.

Another respondent noted:

> I think the Jews like to worry, to be under pressure, and in the long run we will not be satisfied unless we live that way. For example, we went on a trip abroad with some friends a few years back and at one point my friend asked "How can they [the foreigners] live that way? They have plans for a year, for two years ahead while we make plans from month to month at the best. We live with pressures, and fears that any day something can happen—a war, a terror attack, reserve duty, devaluation of the currency. . . ." And the tension referred to? They actually missed it, they couldn't live without it. Being so calm was too close to being dead.

In an interview participated in by both man and wife, we have an example of rather differing views of the issue on the part of the spouses. The husband (H) is a small independent businessman and the wife (W) is a speech teacher.

H: We're used to living with the worries of security, the economic situation, party worries, otherwise it's not worth it. Without national worries, strikes, security, Arabs, terrorists, it's true that it's a pleasure when you don't have them, but I think if we don't have them, somewhere we'll miss them.

I: Do you agree? [addressing the wife]

W: I don't think that I agree. A couple of years ago there wasn't a problem of terrorists and we lived very well. I don't agree that we need what is bad, because it's bad.

H: I didn't say that it was good that it exists, but a world that is *all* good, a world without security problems, you know, someone once said that the way to destroy the Jews is with peace.

I: Do you agree?

H: No, I don't agree with it, but there's something in it. If there aren't problems of security, and we wouldn't live under a load, under pressure, just to work and not to worry. . . .

W: So, what would be so terrible about that, what's wrong with Switzerland? What's wrong with Holland, where they don't have all these things? They're suffering? I think that they're very happy.

H: They're used to something different.

W: It's not any harder to get used to good than it is to get used to bad.

H: I'm not saying that war is good, worries are good; someday there won't be any. Let's say that from tomorrow there'll be peace, and that everyone has enough money to buy what he wants, there's no inflation, no corruption, everyone says "good morning" to his neighbor, a real Garden of Eden. I think very quickly something will happen here. The lack of a load, a burden, pressure. . . .

For the majority of departees the element of tension is not viewed so philosophically or benignly. Tension, a general air of edginess, and red tape combined with a pattern of public behavior and casual interpersonal relationships that do not seem to stand comparison successfully with perceived patterns abroad are, in fact, seen as weighty elements in any calculus of departure. Most respondents felt that their decision to emigrate was to some extent stimulated by the "difficulty of life here" or the "poor quality of life in the country," which to a marked extent was synonymous with the factor of tension and the unacceptable mode of public behavior resulting from tension.

I asked interviewees if they could distinguish clearly how they tended to feel upon awakening in the morning here or abroad. A few said that this was entirely dependent on circumstances, but most who had the experience of living abroad said *chutz la'aretz*. A couple, the husband a former high-ranking army officer and the wife a grade school teacher (he native born, she born abroad but raised in Israel) made it clear that stress of a constant and inordinately intense nature made life in Israel unattractive—once an alternative had been experienced. Another emigrant, a former American, returned to the United States for a period of time in order to test her feelings about America and then returned to Israel to see how "it" stacked up. She emphasized that her stint in America had "given her different skills, skills of quiet, of peace" that were out of place and "essentially useless" in the tense and combative atmosphere of Israel. The same respondent noted that the need to "live and act heroically" took a tremendous toll from men and women in Israel, robbing them of all tranquility and lending a patina of roughness to collective and individual life. "This country," she sighed, "is full of anger. . . . I feel the stress from the parents who are screaming and from the way people drive their cars and push in markets. It is relentless." A young bulldozer operator notes:

> You ask why I and other Israelis have to go abroad to "freshen" ourselves (*l'hitavrer*), to change our lives, to travel? It's because of the pressure we live under constantly. I just spent three years in the army and fought in the Litani campaign and it has been a matter of orders, orders, orders—whether you like it or not, whether you agree or not: one needs release from these things!

He adds, "Americans don't need this because they don't know what trouble is."

The above might be thought of as an example of obvious and incontestable forms of pressure or an example of tension associated with life in a war-afflicted society. It should be neither surprising nor arguable that young people would find the demands of long years in an often dangerous military framework tension-producing and a source of pressure. As both a release from the above and a sort of self-awarded prize for having "lived through" the experience many Israeli youngsters promise themselves a trip abroad immediately following conclusion of army service and before the main "agenda" of postarmy life unfolds. This should not be seen as a particularly remarkable response in view of a variety of objective factors. The term used to explain the need for such a voyage, however, is significant and revealing. It is a term used by a high proportion of departees as well in an effort to explain their leaving Israel: *l'hitavrer*—literally, to air oneself or freshen oneself. An opening of blocked pores, a release from built-up tensions, an escape from pressure—all are intended in the term *l'hitavrer*. Note that the term used is not *l'shanot* (to change one's life) or *l'shaper* (to improve one's life), but *l'hitavrer*—suggesting a different order of causality from that to be found in the etiology of other immigrant groups in the modern context. The term bespeaks a sense of constrictiveness that chains one and must be broken through in order to achieve not change but liberation.[1] What are the factors that lead to an expressed need of this kind? What are the underlying reasons for a high proportion of interviewees embracing the notion that waking up in America leaves one "feeling good," while the opposite is true at home in Israel?

There was no hesitancy expressed on the part of departees in filling out the picture with numerous personal observations suggesting the heavy toll taken by stress and tension in Israeli life.[2] Put as plainly and as simply as possible, large numbers of people who are leaving the country find life in almost all its ramifications and dimensions preferable abroad. Whether it be called quality of life, the persistent aura of tension, pressure, stress, public behavior, or whatever, thousands of Israelis make their positions clear using the oldest referendum technique known to man—they choose with their feet; they leave.

> This is a pressure cooker. You feel it all around you in every issue. In America I feel easy and unpressured. I'm not affected by anything except that which concerns me directly.

Clearly a bit more than the existence of pressure is implied by the above quotation from a former nurse. For this individual as for so many others "abroad" meant the chance to free oneself of macro-concerns, as it were, and concentrate on a narrower, presumably more handleable context. A more handleable context would of course be one's own life style, which for many is seen as circumscribed by convention and both parental and environmental pressure. Interestingly, almost all the nonmarrieds interviewed, both men and women used the term *l'hitavrer* to mean a release from the parental and environmental pressures that are seemingly escapable in tiny Israel only by emigrating.

> I feel social pressure here. The pressure to live a certain way is heavy here and it constantly suprises me anew when I come into contact with it. The pressure for example to invest your money in four walls, rather than invest it in a business. Pushing to get married and so on, while in America I can live as I want. Here I have to be "in order." All my friends without exception, are married, children, apartment—in short, *m'sudar.*

Others less affected by these pressures simply appear to be "broken" or personally devastated by the atmosphere of tension they see as pervasive.

> The quality of life lacks for me, the quiet. . . . I haven't got the peace here, I haven't got any rest here—they make my life bitter here all the time. There's a strike here, a strike there: you call and they don't answer the phone—the switchboard doesn't work. Today a doctors' strike, tomorrow a teachers' strike. If I want to buy something today it costs a lira and tomorrow it costs two lira. Why? I can't . . . I just can't. . . . If I want to buy a simple appliance, I do a little research and it costs a thousand pounds. I get the money together— a week or two goes by and it costs double or if not double, at least 30 to 40 percent more.

> Stress and competition at every turn, everywhere, wherever I find myself— stress and competition. I got tired!

The above plea—for in effect it is a plea—was stated not by an immigrant or poorly acclimatized newcomer from the efficient West but by a 42-year-old native-born bank clerk who after a short visit to America "discovered" what had been disturbing his peace of mind but had heretofore eluded definition. America gave him a sense of peace and surety that Israel did not. America projected an aura of continuity and predictability that Israel did not. America appeared loose; Israel was tight and inflexible. A 26-year-old graduate student in the social sciences comments in a fashion more to be expected from a 62-year-old in a calmer atmosphere than Israel's when he states that he cannot explain either his own departure or that of others other than by noting that

> there is always some tension in the country, some situation where tension fills the air. And the more time passes, the more the tension increases. In the beginning at least there was the feeling that something new was being created—at long last and after 2000 years a Jewish State was being formed. Now, after 37 years where the State is fairly highly developed we see that maybe it wasn't quite what we expected, what we wanted, and that maybe living somewhere else you can live a quiet life, a life without tension, a good life. I'm not talking about those who live in Harlem, or Brooklyn, or in Queens. I'm

talking about living in a house in a small town where you can find a quiet life. In this country even if you live in a kibbutz you still feel the tension. You pick up a newspaper and you read just about every day that the Arab countries have decided this or that about the fate of Israel, or suddenly you read about an agreement between Saudi Arabia and the U.S. where they are sending them AWACs and other of their most advanced equipment, or an agreement with Egypt. It's as if everyone is pressing on Israel from all directions and you're in the middle of this uproar and *that* makes it very hard to live here.

As noted earlier, the atmosphere of tension is seen to have behavioral implications so that Israel—especially when compared with experiences abroad—is seen as uncivil, impolite, aggressive, rough, and in general in unfavorable terms. For those leavers who were themselves immigrants to Israel, especially from Western countries, these comparisons are both sharper and have something of a different tone. In noting a change of attitudes over the years (13 years in Israel) a woman notes both changes in herself and in the environment as operative. After commenting that Israelis demonstrate "an enormous amount of aggression . . . reflecting a vast amount of frustration and anger which people seem to take out on one another at every opportunity," she notes that her attitudes have changed from acceptance to a feeling of "being worn down by it all." In answer to my question concerning what has brought about this change, she notes:

Well, I think I was very naive! Part of it was having come here from the U.S. with its fake politeness and plastic smiles. I said to myself, "Well, this is real, people aren't afraid to bump into each other, or to yell at each other." But I think also that the country has changed. When I first came, it was right after the Six-Day War, and for several years thereafter, there was a kind of community which was created by the war situation. That disappeared and was not renewed by the 1973 war. That war had a more intense effect. Part of it also was that in the early years I just didn't see things for what they were—I mean I didn't *want* to either. It never occurred to me to think anything critical of this country. I really wanted it to be great and perfect and rosy and in fact it was that way for me for quite some time. Only very gradually did the other reality show itself.

While, as noted above, immigrants to Israel reacted more sharply, the key variable seems to be a comparative context—either recent or long-standing—wherein Israeli patterns of behavior and the general atmosphere compare unfavorably with what is available abroad. Few matters aroused such intense response among almost all respondents as the matter of public behavior and its resulting influence on "the quality of life." Negative comments and feelings covered the ground from politics to parent-child relationships and just about everything in between.

There is no culture in Israel. In Russia no child would tell an adult to shut his mouth. Even my own child is beginning to behave that way and I can't accept it. We are going downhill here! I can't take this.

The same informant designated behavior in the Knesset on the part of Israeli parliamentarians as "disgusting," and as more suited to either a *shuk* (market) or a *shul* (synagogue) than to a civilized forum. Many informants comment on the element of aggression in all its ramifications. Four (all women, two active feminists and two nonfeminists) talked about pervasive sexual aggression in the country. A nonfeminist observed that the Israeli male is absolutely and incomparably relentless in his pursuit of casual liaisons and will not (unlike American men) be put off even by the threat of calling the police. "The American," she notes "might try twice but if rejected will leave the field." Not so for the Israeli, who will pursue the matter mercilessly. Another respondent, in this case an active feminist, sees behavior in this country toward women as being particularly brutal. She notes:

This kind of brutal treatment of me and other women when we would go out to speak and so on in the early days of the feminist movement . . . this was extremely shocking, extremely shocking. And it wasn't until I went to speak about similarly unpopular matters in other places in the world that I realized that there was a big difference: the reaction could be hostile, anti-, but nothing like what the rules of etiquette allowed for here. Here, you can say or do anything: there seem to be . . . you know, no limits!

This "brutality," it is avered, has its root cause in a type of anger fomented by the society.

There are kinds of angers that can be created by a society that is constantly failing to satisfy the needs of the people who comprise that society. Like having time—time not devoted to running all over the place to pay bills or nail down some official. Anger at the emergence of the idea that the individual exists to serve the country . . . this sort of thing makes for aggressiveness. And it is *this* more than anything else which is hard to take.

Most informants, I think, would reject the criticism levelled by the activist quoted above. Few women even raised the question of women as such, but I do nevertheless suspect that some of the points underscored in the general broadside such as a general "nudginess" or aggressiveness in the atmosphere would be easily and widely embraced. As might have been predicted almost all respondents found the American context of civility admirable and desirable and thoroughly worthy of emulation, although few thought it possible in the Israeli context:

> Behavior in this country is terrible! There are no manners. Pushing, shoving, refusal to line up for buses . . . people are barbarians.

> The culture here is weak—shouting, pushing, terrible behavior.

> The Israelis have a lot of room for improvement. The Israelis have a lot to learn.

> People abroad are willing to go out of their way to help you. Here they think they are doing you a favor.

> Here, everybody treats you like dirt! In the supermarket you're treated like dirt. In the street you're treated like dirt. In offices you're treated like dirt. There's no relatedness. In America though all these things were wonderful—people are helpful.

In the interview situation a certain interesting pattern emerged wherein almost all respondents castigated Israeli behavior and praised American or foreign behaviors. In numerous instances the interviewee literally gushed about Americans who were helpful, nice, kind, or went out of their way for the visitor. Stories were related about being helped when stuck with an empty gas tank, or with directions, or with a myriad other forms of assistance. When asked if similar treatment had not befallen them at home in Israel from time to time, the near universal response was "No." Here again, one cannot lose sight of a certain legitimating tendency—why after all leave home if one is satisfied?—which is no doubt fueled by a very selective vision, but still, one cannot but be shocked at the vehemence and near universality of the negative responses concerning not only public behavior but life in general in Israel.

Aside from any legitimating devices or needs, it seems utterly clear that the vast majority of leavers have—whatever their personal ambitions or aims that are thought to be more readily satisfiable abroad—a serious "argument" with the State of Israel, a certain failure of affect. In Dan Jacobson's *The Beginners* (1966:410) the hero explains his reasons for leaving Israel as deriving from shock, discomfort, restlessness, and so on, finally adding what could be seen as the crux of the matter when he says, "I suppose I just didn't like the place enough, basically." The matter is of course not quite so simple. Ambivalence is deep, obtuse, and far-ranging for most. The same person who will recite a litany of complaints about boorish and uncivil behavior will attempt to place it in some kind of explanatory context. Thus, after noting that Israelis are rude one might try to explain it as a continuation of army-learned behavior ("it's a roughness that you learn and can't unlearn so easily") or another might say of his countrymen that their behavior is barbaric—but it is after all only a surface phenomenon and underneath they have hearts of gold and "can truly be depended upon in a pinch."

Not a few respondents emphasized this latter tack in noting that while they liked the general atmosphere of civil behavior they enjoyed abroad they also distrusted its depth and its dependability. "Israelis," it is asserted, "may be many things but they have courage and they care." I was treated to dozens of stories indicating that the vaunted (and appreciated) American politeness and civility was only skin deep. One respondent told of being impressed and pleased with the check-out clerk in the supermarket who always asked, "How are you today?" and when once she was told "terrible" and still responded with "That's nice." This was seen as a demonstration of the "mechanical" nature of things in the United States. Americans are viewed as mechanical, even robot-like in their human relations, whereas Israelis are seen as earthy, "real" people who do not manufacture emotions or respond like automatons. But still and nevertheless the very same individual who told the story of the supermarket clerk added a hope that "we could bring American human relations methods here." What was wanted, of course, was the improved version—"kindness, but deeply felt."

For many there was a belief that things were improving, or would improve as time passed—but they were unprepared to wait. Too much in their environment had disappointed. With respect to another "new-old nation," V.S. Naipaul (1977:151) put it: "For so many people India seemed to have gone wrong; so many people in independent India had become fugitives or sought that status." "Fugitives" is Naipaul's term for *yordim*—and one must admit that the word offers intriguing possibilities: fugitives from themselves, fugitives from communal responsibility, fugitives from a dream gone sour, fugitives from binding links, and above all a volitional and yet nonvolitional distancing from what should have constituted a natural center.

Some leavers saw the dissatisfaction as deriving from an essential rawness characteristic of Israeli society that can be explained or understood, but they were unwilling to wait out the process.

> There are things [like behavior] which annoy, disturb, and anger. I think there's a lot to be improved and I understand that it will take a long time and that there is no other way. The only solution is time and patience.

But "time and patience" are exactly what the above respondent was ultimately unwilling to embrace as models of personal behavior. He, at least, was moving on. Understanding was one thing, acquiescence another.

It became clear in the course of the interviews that it was not environmental tension or uncivil behavior that stimulated a feeling of unease.

There was something perhaps inadequately subsumed under the rubric "quality of life" that was experienced as deficient or lagging. Israel was experienced as a sort of "nagging" society where people are just not left alone. They are pursued constantly with threats emanating from the television screen that they will lose their set if they do not pay the user tax, from the army about advising on a change of address, from the house committee about paying their dues. There are constant threats of war, impending economic disaster, looming genocide, draconic income tax measures, repeated strikes, and dire results from failing to complete matriculation. There is the burden of aggressive language ranging from the Knesset to the marketplace; of highly polluted air, rivers, and beaches; of taxes on everything from travel to eating; and of overbearing bureaucrats and unresponsive politicians.

The problem arises as more and more people find these patterns unacceptable. At some point along the line—probably again as a by-product of the insatiable travel-passion of Israelis—a considerable number of them learned that these tension-producing aspects of their lives were not preordained or written in stone. Life could be different. Indeed, life was different and by extension preferable in a large number of alternative societies.[3] One respondent noted that even in Italy, which is climatically and characterologically close to Israel, "things were different, things were better, from the behavior of people to each other to the physical aesthetic of the country." Another informant recounted the behavioral conversion of her husband with surprise and what seemed like pride in his ability to "lift" their standards to those found abroad.

> A few years ago my husband went to America and stayed for three months. He couldn't get over the treatment he got. Everybody was so nice and polite. Please and thank you! Don't raise your voice! He loved it! When he got back he heard me yell from the balcony to our son to come upstairs and he said, "shush—don't yell; what kind of behavior is that?" I had to walk down three flights to get him. Before that—he yelled as good as I did.

The above is somewhat reminiscent of the sort of "immigrant" literature one so often finds showing how the benighted product of a lesser civilization is elevated through accommodation to higher forms of behavior.[4] Perhaps this is reflective of the fact that Israel is in reality so young an enterprise, so unformed in many respects, or it might be simply a reflection of Israelis' penchant for imitative behavior on a grand scale—the latter perhaps resulting from the former. In any event one is able to discern their readiness to "adopt" and "adapt" in diverse areas ranging from fashion in all its manifestations, to infiltration of the language with foreign additions, from educational patterns to popular music. Many Israelis are either unsure of or unsatisfied by the prevalent life-style of the country and in many cases see matters deteriorating rather than improving. One thoughtful respondent tried to place the matter in a broader context when he noted:

> It's hard to define criteria to compare the quality of life. I think that what's happened to us is the standard of living has gone up, but that we weren't prepared to keep up the quality of life, in order to adapt ourselves to the changes in the standard of living . . . I have some feeling that the quality of life is going down, but I think that it's a result of a raising of the standard of living, and a lack of thought, of the means, of the awareness, that could plan and prevent the consequences.

The above represents an attempt at balance and moderation: a readiness to see a dynamic at work and to draw relevant if possibly mistaken conclusions. Rather shocking was the widespread unwillingness or inability to remember positive human encounters that had to have befallen interviewees in the course of their experience in Israel. Notwithstanding the previously noted need to legitimate the act of migration with its resultant selective vision and memory, one is still nonplussed at the widespread willingness to see only bad in Israel and among Israelis and only good among foreigners and abroad. With only seven or eight notable exceptions, all the departees viewed behaviors and the general quality of life in Israel in negative terms. Among the exceptions was a convert to scientology who thought that "the problem here was simply a matter of faulty communication," and another who felt that the work day began too late in America leaving little time for "the important things in life." Still another thought childbirth a happier experience in Israel. A few, as previously noted, also commented to the effect that polite and civil behavior abroad tended to be skin-deep while when you *did* get humane treatment in Israel you could be assured that it came from the deeper recesses and was quite real.

On the whole departees demonstrated a sort of short-circuiting process[5] whereby high-quality human experiences at home just could not or did not occur or if they did could not be compared in any positive light with what could and did happen to them abroad. Thus one couple went on at considerble length (two and a half pages of transcript) describing how a cheese merchant in Holland insisted that they taste everything before they buy and how such a thing never had nor ever could happen in Israel. When the interviewer suggested that in fact similar treatment on the part of grocers had been his lot in Israel on numerous and diverse occasions he was told: "Here there is no such thing; here everything is very hard and when you see the quality of life there and how pleasant it is to live that way—then it becomes very hard to put up with things here." In some respects the decision to emigrate brings in its wake a sort of conversionary aura and fervor wherein the preconversion life in all its dimensions is held in contempt and more importantly introduces a miasma of forgetfulness with respect to "how it really was." It is clear that a web or structure for accommodating the new status and explaining the rejection of the old (to oneself as well as to others) is being constructed. In the process the old must be denigrated, castigated, and rejected, while the new must be praised and embraced as the embodiment of good, truth, and beauty. There are indeed objective dimensions to categories such as the quality of life in Israel, style of personal interaction, or levels of tension and stress (the latter much harder to measure and objectivize admittedly), but what was effectively transmitted in the interview situation was a near parody of factors that do unmistakably exist and not only in the inflamed minds of departees. Just as a convert might be said to "fall in love" with the new or renewed object of his faith, the emigrant—at least in our context—seems to be busily engaged in falling out of love. And as such, all the warts, all the defects and shortcomings of the formerly beloved stand out in gross profusion and the boldest of relief. Thus, Israel and Israelis are brought to task for any and all shortcomings, leading at times to the evolvement of a grotesque burlesque or caricature of culture and personality in the society. Factors that can just as easily be interpreted in a positive light are seen as only negative, while situations and behaviors that would pass unnoticed abroad are held up for examination, comment, and ultimately condemnation in Israel. Thus one is not surprised to hear rather repeatedly the assertion that "it is easier to live in America than in Israel." Insofar as quality of life is measured by the ease with which goods are accumulated, wealth achieved, or bureaucratic problems overcome, Israel does not compare well with other Western countries. One is prepared to accept at face value the assertion of departees that tension and pressure are considerably higher in Israel than abroad and that certain behaviors possibly resulting or at least tied to these factors tend to add to the negative side of the scale determining whether to remain or emigrate.

But another dimension is broached when certain undesirable personality traits are seen as more prevalent among Israelis than among others—traits such as irresponsibility, an inordinate dependence on influence and who one knows rather that what one knows, a tendency to haggle and deal at every turn, a high degree of intolerance, and a refusal to allow the "other" both psychological and real space. A number of departees referred directly or obliquely to what they perceived as a sort of pincers behavior on the part of fellow Israelis with which they could not make their peace. Not only Israel but also Israelis gave them a "closed-in" feeling that is reflective more of a difference in life style or cultural differences than deficiencies in the quality of life.

Did you ever notice Israelis talking to each other in the street? If you have you would have noticed that their heads are always close together . . . they always talk close to me . . . they deny me space.

The speaker, a son of the kibbutz, went on to note that "America was different," noting that there "they let you feel relaxed, at ease, there one gets the feeling that 'I' exist, that I'm worth something." When the interviewer suggested the possibility that physical closeness might not indicate lack of respect for the individual—perhaps even the opposite—he was told "No, no it is a wish to dominate, to overcome the other." The same interviewee indicated the existence of a streak in the Israeli character that might be termed the *"über Chochum* syndrome"—an innate need to outsmart the smart, and outexpert the expert. "Israelis always know better than anybody else how to do things."

Many took note of intolerance on the part of fellow Israelis, although interestingly few found reason for complaint in what to outsiders might appear the most obvious arena of intolerance—reputed religious coercion in Israeli society. Comments tended to be concerned with insistence on the part of family and neighbor that the individual tow the line in terms of "keeping up with the Joneses." This was especially felt by single males and females who had reached their late twenties or early thirties and who were not yet *m'sudar* (i.e., married, childed, apartmented, jobbed, and carred). For them (as noted previously) escape abroad promised perhaps the only solution to what was perceived of as relentless, indeed merciless family and peer pressures. Many expressed chagrin at what was perceived of as interference in utterly personal aspects of life by broader societal or communal forces. Others commented about imperiousness on the part of almost everybody at every layer of hierarchy who was in a position of authority. In explaining his emigration a young academic noted that his main expectation with regard to life abroad would consist of being "left alone to lead my own life in peace and quiet without fearing that all sorts of 'officials' will lord it over me or give me the run around."

Most of the interviewed commented in one way or another about the nefariousness of "influence" or "favoritism" (*protektsia*) in Israeli society. Numerous examples were volunteered (the interview schedule or guide did not mention the term) demonstrating how things moved only on the basis of who one knew—in business, government, the army, or education.

In a society in which so much that is basic is unsure—physical survival, continued cultural autonomy, economic viability, intracommunal understanding and stability—the need for solid anchorage is understandably great. Uncertainty rather than certainty is the characteristic hallmark of Israeli society, leaving a residue whose importance cannot be gainsaid. One of the results, I would aver, is the often observed and commented upon conservatism that seemingly pervades all levels and dimensions of Israeli society. It is as if in an attempt to exercise control, at least in those areas over which individuals see some realistic chance of influencing events, Israelis are pushed back upon the narrow, essentially personal and individualistic confines and recesses of behavior as an arena of action and intervention. Thus, while one may not be able to seriously influence the questions of war or peace, demographic balance between Jew and Arab, or economic independence as a guppy in a sea of sharks and whales, one can assure oneself that some things are forever. What things? Matters such as family relationships, acceptable neighborly relations, and private property (whether collectively or individually owned). The world may be cosmically unstable, but at least mothers should keep their children's heads covered in the hot Mediterranean sun, young people should marry and raise a family, furniture should be purchased as suites, the main meal of the day should be taken at midday, and supper should be a slightly altered repeat of breakfast.

Now these behavioral artifacts are representative of a particular culture and as such are neither particularly remarkable nor more or less outrageous or lovely than other, similar cultural patterns in other societies. What should be of interest is the valence achieved by these and other behavioral "quirks" that are guarded and often defended to the point of offense to at least the outside observer, and increasingly to those caught within its web. Clearly, what is being so assiduously defended here are not key elements of a value system such as love, honor, mercy, and so on, but relatively narrow and marginal pieties that should occupy secondary and tertiary positions of importance. But violation of these norms and others like them bring forth a type of condemnation and often attendant sanctions of some weight that must be explained in order to reach any requisite understanding not only of the etiology of *yerida* and dissociation with the society but of the society in question itself. It appears to me that two possible avenues of exploration exist: either these tendencies are explainable in cultural terms (i.e., a certain interventionist comprehensive type of Jewish cultural pattern developed in or transported to Israel), or this represents an attempt to gain "control" in the only areas promising some degree of responsiveness and surety as a direct outgrowth of personal intervention.

I would suggest that both avenues of explanation are apt. Again, one must keep in mind the fact that the majority of Israelis are heir to either the East European *shtetl* tradition or the North African *mellah*—both of which were essentially geared to the intrusive and the controlling in terms of personal behavior. What has emerged in Israel might be seen as a sort of secular *shulchan aruch*, or book of laws whereby "the way" in almost all dimensions of behavior is set forth and rather highly articulated. Proper dress and proper modes of conversation, contact, disputation, play, and religion are all rather mechanically and solidly set forth. Deviations from the widely accepted norms are seen as personally and communally threatening. Sanctions while objectively mild (i.e., criticism or social distancing from the repeated offender) tend to be widely and easily applied.

Though heir to and based upon a multipronged tradition, modern Israel was also in many respects a revolutionary undertaking and like other exemplars demonstrates a sort of radical conservatism. Much like the puritans of New England who also legislated dress codes, modes of public discourse, kinds of marital and personal relations, so too did the *yishuv* and its inheritors, the State of Israel, and for similar reasons of uncertainty and insecurity. Alex Weingrad (1966) titled a book on Moroccan Jewish farmers in Israel *Reluctant Pioneers*—a title both felicitous and compelling in many respects, not least the suspicion that in the end all pioneers are reluctant, all experimenters are unsure, all nay-sayers contain within themselves the seed of an embracing yea, and vice versa.

When added to the general context that might be seen as the handmaiden of a radical or revolutionary path, the aforementioned factors of objective insecurity in key areas of life that afflict Israeli society, one need not stretch matters to absurd lengths in order to understand the need for control, for order over those areas lending themselves willy nilly to this type of intervention. And clearly this need for control leads to the creation of a type of societal atmosphere that in its positive dimension is warm and sustaining and in its negative dimension is intrusive—and for some personally devastating.

Thus added to, and as a related element to the tension and stress objectively a part of the current Israeli reality, one must be cognizant of cultural, situational, and historico-sociological irritants, all of which act as factors of some complexity in evolving the type of environmental atmospherics that characterize Israeli society. What specific weight should be assigned these atmospherics as factors in deciding to emigrate constitutes a difficult if not unsolvable problem—but insofar as the evidence seems to indicate widespread and deep dissatisfaction with the "quality of life" in Israel, and a much higher level of satisfaction with life abroad or a desire to seek change by going abroad, it does not seem too sharp a departure from the hard facts to suggest that the role played is significant indeed.

Politics and the Political System

One area very much tied to the matter of atmosphere is that of politics, with which Israelis seem to be at one and the same time both overinvolved and without faith in its efficacy either to affect desired change or to express a broad concensus. Observers have often noted the very high degree of politicization that seems so characteristic of Israeli society, wherein intrinsically apolitical activities and services such as sports, medicine, banking, religion, cultural events, housing, and other functions assume a political mantle of one kind or another. Thus Israelis might play football under the aegis of *Maccabee* (General Zionist-Liberal), be x-rayed by *Kupat Cholim* (Labor-Histadrut), bank at *Mizrachi* (National Religious Party), and pray with the Gerer Rebbe (Agudat Yisrael). To a marked extent this pattern merely reflects a holdover from the prestate organization of the *yishuv* and does not reflect a truly realistic measure of partisanship or of compartmentalization. Its significance is in large measure more symbolic than anything else, while its real import is on the structural level wherein the parties retain a central role in the disbursement of services of a kind that tends to be depoliticized, and either privately or governmentally controlled in most other Western societies. Thus parties in Israel often have interests to defend or issues to push that are above and beyond what would be acceptable (or even understandable) in most other Western countries. This can and often does lead to confusion when, for example, an enterprise controlled by the labor-dominated Histadrut finds itself in a dispute with its workers. Does party ideology or do objective economic determinants decide the matter? Similar instances reflecting conflicts or dilemmas can be adduced for most other political parties, with the interesting result being somewhat the reverse of what might have been predicted. Rather than resulting in a high level of political involvement and a heightened sense of what might be called "political efficacy," Israelis appear largely uninvolved and display signs of feeling politically powerless.

In a country whose citizens are so often faulted for being aggressive on the individual plain, it is of interest to note the high level of passivity visible on the public or political level. Israelis accept with almost sheep-like equanimity vexations that would result in a storming of the halls of authority elsewhere. Taxes, as noted earlier, are near confiscatory; retroactive legislation is not unknown; civil treatment on the part of government bureaucrats and officials leaves, on the whole, much to be desired; mail delivery is a sometime thing at best; police services are inadequate and uneven; the courts, while on the whole fair, are slow; most hospitals tend to be overcrowded and understaffed; schools show repeated instances of slap-dash conceptualization and underprepared teachers; strikes involving basic services are suffered in silence; pollution of air and water progresses at a Third World rate; and there is governmental and political interference in the most personal of matters, such as marriage, even how one chooses to identify oneself, or what one chooses to eat. This acceptance defies understanding—at least when utilizing Western European or American standards.[6]

Lest one be led to believe from the above that Israelis are a beaten down, sodden, frightened population of broken souls who either do not care or who are indifferent to various issues that confront them, let me state most vigorously that for this there is ample contrary evidence. Israelis are still quite capable of vigorous reactions over matters such as the personality of Menachem Begin, settlements in the West Bank, the future of the Golan Heights, and other such burning issues of the day. Israelis still go to the polls (voluntarily) on election days in great (though declining) numbers. One's political "identity" in Israel is still a matter of considerable weight and seriousness.

I am not suggesting that Israelis do not have strong feelings about many issues. I do suggest that with the exception of what might be called foreign policy and security issues the vast and overwhelming majority of Israelis demonstrate a palpable passivity somewhat out of synch with other dimensions of national character and societal behavior. This is interesting inasmuch as foreign policy is probably the area least susceptible to public action, given the array of forces and players involved that lie totally outside the Israeli spectrum of control. One would think that regular mail delivery and civil service on the part of civil servants was decidedly within the realm of citizen intervention.

This makes sense, however, when one recognizes the preeminence of two pervasive elements: the political system is not geared to being responsive to any demands emanating from the public rather than the political structure itself, and the issues that above all else animate and disturb the average Israeli are in fact those associated with "foreign policy" because it is these that are perceived as holding the keys to the ultimate survival or demise of the society.

Why this sense of powerlessness? Why this perception of unresponsiveness? Again I would assert that it reflects a valid response to existent structure. There is no constituency system in Israel. The whole country is a single electoral district. A member of the Knesset from Tel Aviv no more nor less represents a Jerusalemite than a member from Beersheba. When one votes in Israeli national elections one votes for a party list *en toto* rather than for this or that individual. The citizen can reject the list but not *x* or *y* politician. Similarly *x* or *y* politician is aware that he does not hold a personal mandate and is thus not personally or regionally responsible to any constituency other than the party faithful. He is responsible to the party—not the electorate. It is the party that decides which slot he will occupy on the list—not the average voter.

In view of this type of structure it should not be surprising if Israelis choose to exercise their passions on broad issues above the nitty gritty rather than waste their energies in a miasma of indifference. In effect, it is as if Israelis choose to give voice to the larger issue rather than seek visible change on issues that fail to gain the attention of politicians and decision makers. Thus Israelis are faced with a sense of futility with regard to local, bread-and-butter issues, and a recognition of ineffectuality with respect to the "larger" issues of foreign policy—both leading understandably and inevitably to a recognition of impotence and political powerlessness. Not only can average citizens not effect change regarding the "Americans," the "Russians," or the "Arabs," but he is also unable to gain a response on relatively minor issues affecting his person or the quality of life. In Israel's highly overpoliticized society one quickly comes to the realization that neither the world at large nor the immediate environment will prove responsive to efforts to bring about change along the lines of one's choosing.

Thus the "passive" Israeli will accept, bend, adjust, and complain until (for some) the decision is reached that "I've had it" (*nishbar li*) and rather than work for change in areas that have left him unfulfilled or dissatisfied he will undertake radical action of a once-and-for-all nature, which for some means leaving the country.[7] But who leaves? Victims of active political wars who have failed? The right? The left? The unaffiliated? The evidence available to me suggests all of the above. Interviewees seemed to reflect to an almost perfect extent the political configuration of the country at the time the research took place. About 40 percent were Likud sympathizers, about 40 percent were Labor, and the rest were to the right and left or apathetic. The one correction possibly necessary is that the Labor sympathizers seemed largely to reflect the more hawkish rather than dovish views within the party. Thus the upsurge in emigration in recent years cannot be attributed to dissatisfaction with the Begin government, or unhappiness with settlement policy, or a desire for liberalization regarding the Arabs. It is not even reflective of any particular dissatisfaction with coalition government or the enhanced role of Orthodox religion in Israeli political and social life that the coalition dynamic has brought about. Where the political issue plays a role it is generally not in regard to specifics but rather with respect to a sort of floating dissatisfaction with the political process and a growing unhappiness with its unresponsiveness.[8]

This was especially, but not exclusively, the case with the small group of leavers who were politically active and/or who reflected a radical perspective on matters such as feminism, gay rights, separation of religion and state, full Arab rights, or a Palestinian state. For these individuals despair seems to be the pervasive response to the political atmosphere current in the country. One activist summed it up thusly:

Let me tell you about the political situation not in terms of what *is* but of what lacks. The fact is that there isn't any background for Arab politics; no confrontation politics, no background, and no beginning as such for organizing outside the existing frameworks of the system to bring about change. That kind of social and political activity is not part of the Israeli scene and is not understood in Israel. Among other effects, this lack makes the country very dull . . . there is no involvement, there is an enormous apathy which is well earned considering party politics as they are. The whole thing is [for me] very alienating.

The same individual suggested that the smallness of the country may have an effect on the poverty of its politics in that one sees the same small group of interlocked and intermarried elites at every juncture leading to "a sort of city-state atmosphere."

Others at this end of the political spectrum take note of high levels of intolerance for the deviant view manifest in Israel. One activist after denigrating the possibilities inherent in the Peace Now Movement—a rather mild protest movement by contemporary Western standards—asserted that "Israel is definitely not going to listen to any of this." The same informant noted an experience that demonstrated rather "conclusively" the "close-mindedness and narrowness of the political scene."

I find it shocking sometimes. People just don't take a stand here even though they don't like what is going on. All I hear is "What can you do?" One of the things still fresh in my memory is what happened just after Holocaust Day at the University (no, it wasn't right after—it was June, I think). The Arab students asked for a room to mark the anniversary of the Six-Day War and they were refused. A number of them were milling around and were real angry and this guy walked past and said "Ah, they're lifting their heads up again." I didn't want to get involved but I couldn't help myself and I said to him, "Holocaust Day wasn't so far away and you've already forgotten. What is this country all about? Are we taking the place of the Germans?" He went wild; that's one of the things you are never supposed to say in this country. He screamed and he yelled and I just wanted to escape; to escape him and to escape the country.

Needless to say the above incident did not trigger the desire to leave Israel. That decision had already been made, and according to the informant the political atmosphere of the country played a key if not decisive role.

For most interviewees, however, the political factor although often expressed in strong terms was clearly not determinative. Rare was the leaver who claimed total or even partial satisfaction with the political behavior or structure of the country. But even in cases where fairly strong language was used in describing the perceived reality one could somehow sense that "politics" played a secondary or even tertiary role in the decision-making process. For example, a Likud supporter, a political hawk who presumably could find satisfaction in the present government's performance, noted that "the political situation in this country is intolerable. Nobody cares and nobody represents the citizen. It's merely a matter of 120 idiots [120 members of Knesset] yelling at each other—at public expense."

A more left-leaning sympathizer of the Labor party notes that "the general political situation bothers me, it really disgusts me." The same person listed "clean politics and a clean society in the State of Israel" as some of the things that might make him change his mind about emigrating. (But the first listed factor had to do with career possibilities.)

During the course of the interviews very few did not avail themselves of the opportunity to state that politics in Israel "bothered" them. But the answers, with the exception of those from the political far left and the highly active, tended to be either a very general feeling of malaise or of the hobby-horse kind. Thus some noted that in this as in other matters Israel gets "worse and worse" year by year and as in so many things it is a matter of personalities.

> It's *tohu v'vohu* [empty and void] in this area. I say it is a matter of the players in the field with the field being the State of Israel and the players being those who operate the State. Those players are not suited to this field. Every year it gets worse and worse to the point where I feel that I need a vacation from it.

For Labor party stalwarts, it is a matter of the Likud being in power that has soured things. For right-of-center voters, the Labor-dominated Histadrut was often faulted for having brought the country to the point of ruin: "Why do we have over 100 percent inflation? Because of the Histadrut and its poison; it is the poison of the State" or "Since the Likud, our situation has never been so bad. Even if people make more money everything costs double and triple and we are worse off."

Others refer to the fact that "for a tiny country we have too many political parties, so that I can't make out who represents what." Others note that "parties come and parties go but you still see the same faces." The politically inactive or unaffiliated seek unity governments and the bridging of gaps, while partisans cast curses and perdition upon the opposition.

Surprisingly, not a few respondents demonstrated remarkable ignorance of the political situation in this most politicized of countries. Two respondents (both of fairly high educational attainment) identified voting Likud with voting left. They later explained that in one case Likud was to the left of their real choice and in the other voting Likud meant a change from his previous affiliation and that was viewed as a left-like move. Others attributed secret agendas and inclinations to political groupings, such as one is more "Jewish," another is more "aware" of economic realities, or still another "understands the Americans."

Two-thirds of the respondents—a figure crossing stated political loyalties—were not in favor of significant territorial compromise. They were in favor of staying on the West Bank, the Golan, and the Gaza strip, while many expressed serious reservations about the Sinai pullback.

In matters such as full rights for Israel's Arab citizens and relations between church and state—once again the conservative view was dominant. Similar views were expressed with respect to government involvement in the economy and to economic matters in general.

Large-scale agreement existed among interviewees to the effect that all politics was dirty, and that politicians were, on the whole, untrustworthy. Most thought these propositions universally applicable rather than limited to Israel, although with respect to excessive diversity of opinion, Israel was seen to be preeminent.

Most also expressed in one way or another a sense of powerlessness, not only with respect to the ability to affect matters of prosaic or everyday interest but with respect to the very destiny of the collective enterprise. An emigrating political scientist stated:

> It's all a game between the superpowers and for them Israel is just another dot on the map—a game-toy. Every war we have fought, every security problem we have faced for more than 30 years . . . is all a result of the larger plans of the superpowers and that's all. It doesn't matter if we have a strong army or a weak one . . . if the powers want Israel to exist, it will and if they don't want Israel to exist, we won't—no matter what *we* do.

A general trend among those queried was to assert that America was considerably more promising a society than Israel in that the American political system was marked by responsiveness whereas the Israeli system was opaque: "Here you can try to change things . . . but not to the same extent as in America." One of the most thoughtful and articulate interviewees put the matter of America versus Israel in terms of political atmosphere and behavior in a most forceful manner. After suggesting that America has undergone significant political change in a progressive direction in recent years and being challenged by the interviewer with the question as to whether the election of President Reagan is to be seen as a reflection of this, Ms. M. parried:

M: But that's if you look at High Politics. If you look at how people are living over the years, over the decades, there's been a change to what is more, what I would call Low Politics, and this is much more important basically, than the structure staying the same. I don't think that America is a radical place, a utopia; I don't think that there's any possibility of major changes coming about politically in the United States, but it certainly is a pluralistic society, and we're obviously the opposite of a pluralistic society. Here, the pressures of conformity certainly are high and while I don't like to use the word "fascist" I think that they are crude in some ways. I mean if you take a look at the educational system, people are being systematically trained not to think too much, not to ask too many questions.

I: Where do you see this?

M: In the schools. In the schools.

I: Systematically?

M: I think very much so, I do. Yes, I do. I was very pleased that my daughter could go to an experimental school for the first 11 years of her life. I wasn't instrumental in setting it up for that reason, but it's that kind of creation of an educational system that I'd want my kids educated in. But then when she did change over it was very clear to me *and* to her what was happening. You know, here are the books, here's the information, and repeat it and don't ask too many questions.

I: Does that not reflect an incapacity or a lack of training on part of the instructional staff as much as it could represent fascism?

M: But you know what socialization is like. [in a bored tone] You create one generation in the kind of mold that you would like them to create the second generation in, so you could go on as long as you can. I really don't want to call it fascist, it's certainly not a fascist country, or a fascist educational system, but it has many of the characteristics of one and its effect. I find people here very oppressed intellectually, and politically and economically as well, without the tools for any kind of resistance other than getting up and leaving.

I: That's an interesting point. You said at the beginning of your comments a few minutes ago that people are voting with their feet, they're getting up and leaving. One could almost assume from that that these people who are getting up and leaving are in some form or another potential activists and they're going to take up the fight when they go abroad, but they don't seem to do that. Why do people here opt for leaving and people who want change elsewhere try to join or organize a movement?

M: Well, I think that people here have the feeling that "What can be done, there's no choice." You know there are no movements to join, really. You know you can't expect everyone who would like change to organize their own group. I think that it's even worse than that; I think that they don't even think in those terms.

I: What terms, organizing?

M: Yes, organize, make change. I think one thing, my sense of people's reaction to activism is this total sense of hopelessness, that no matter what one does it will be impossible. And to a large extent that's right;

I've given over ten years to activism, but that is to a large extent correct.

I: That things can't be changed?

M: That control is that centralized, and that the access to power is that narrow, power itself being so small that you really can't do very much to make change: ah, little bits here and there and you have to be very, very satisfied with a slow, slow pace. And being very pleased with any small changes that occur over the years.

But when all is said and done one should not be as surprised at the unresponsiveness of the Israeli political system as at the growing, somewhat inarticulate sense among so many that they want and expect more. Again, one dare not lose sight of where the great majority of Israelis are coming from—not from the tradition of the French or American Revolutions, or the Magna Carta—but from the authoritarian contexts of Eastern and Central Europe and the quasi-medieval framework of North Africa and the Arab world. Political activity of an evolutionary nature on the part of the citizenry was not exactly the model dominant in these societies. Israel's political structure is somewhat Byzantine in its hue and flavor as well as its syncretistic nature involving as it does a melding of two Eastern cultures. Thus, the fact that so many expressed dissatisfaction with local politics—at least in broad terms—is to be seen as reflective of the weight and influence of exposure to new and seductive outside forces. For the Israelis true politics is first and foremost ideological, which means that politics is a matter of the "big issues" rather than the nitty gritty. This no doubt reflects an additional reason for the aforementioned "passivity" visible among Israelis and their involvement with matters of ultimate import rather than daily problems with abysmal telephone service or inadequate mail delivery. Nonideological politics is viewed as being somehow illegitimate or at the very least lacking in seriousness. This tendency is of course aided and abetted by the almost total implosive nature of the war-peace issue that consumes all within its path. There is no room and no time for much of lesser import—and everything else, it must be admitted, is of lesser import.

The Religious Factor

In matters of religion as well as in politics one might be misled by a surface overview of the Israeli reality. Just as in the fact that Israeli society is so politicized one might have thought that Israelis would have a strong and highly developed sense of what I have called political efficacy, so given the fact that the majority of Israelis (at least in behavioral terms) are secularists or nonobservant one might have expected serious and deep-seated reservations expressed about the dominant role enjoyed by religion and the religious establishment over so many key and central aspects of life in the Jewish State.[9] In fact, a proportion of leavers did express negative feelings in this regard, but most either found the status quo entirely acceptable or at least livable. Still others thought religion did not enjoy sufficient power and influence.

In the latter camp were to be found people from all ends of the political, educational, and ethnic spectrum. A Moroccan academic voted Likud, as he put it "for several reasons, one being that they are more Jewish." A former air force officer notes that "rather than religious coercion existing in this country, I maintain that there is not enough religion—our kids don't learn about their religion in our schools." The same informant drew a parallel with the United States where he felt that "Judaism was seriously taught to Jewish youngsters." (Let it be noted that he was affiliated while working for the Israeli government in the United States with a southeastern suburban reform congregation where the level of Judaica taught could not be excessively high and certainly by any objective standards below what was taught his children even in the most secular of Israel's public schools.)

Another informant felt that the strength of the religious establishment acted as a preserver of Judaism and Jewish values for the generations to come. He was in favor of *halachah* determining practices associated with marriage and Jewish identity, as were approximately one-half of all interviewees.

One might have expected that in a group expressing so much dissatisfaction with so much in Israeli life and in fact taking the radical step of leaving the country, this matter of religion would have come under serious criticism. (It should be noted that I am clearly not including the few people in my sample who were Orthodox or religiously observant. I am referring only to those who according to all external factors are considered part of the nonreligious camp.[10])

For most religion was a matter of indifference, or more correctly it was accepted in its present form as a given of Israeli life and society, much as three years in the army, the Histadrut as the behemoth of the marketplace, or the existence of banks on every street corner are accepted—as part of the landscape.

Although Israelis cannot marry or divorce civilly, must observe *kashrut* in public places, are defined religiously whether they like it or not or whether they believe or do not believe, have their children instructed in *yahadut* (Judaism) even in secular public schools, can only marry within the faith and only after certain categories of nonmarriageability are checked (*mamzerut* and *agunot*), cannot travel on buses or attend cinemas on the Sabbath or Jewish holy days—few find any of these sufficiently onerous as to create a fuss of any kind. Neither do many seem unduly upset by the allocation of large sums of public funds to religious institutions or by the fact that most Orthodox women and many Orthodox men do not serve in the armed forces (or do alternative service).

Even when hundreds of religious zealots create weekly disturbances by throwing stones at private autos that are violating the Sabbath in Jerusalem or Bnai Brak (and in some cases causing casualties including at least one death), when the national flag is burned in Mea Shearim on Lag B'Omer, when a performance of Handel's Messiah is nearly broken up by yeshivah students, or when secular residents in religious neighborhoods are terrorized because of their "life style" we tend not to hear of outrage or even serious upset on the part of the "secular" majority. Complaints of a "tsk, tsk" nature are heard; few secular Israelis approve of the above behaviors; some thoughtful Israelis are in fact fearful with respect to the implications of much of the above, but nothing like a significant welling-up of negative reactions is experienced.

In this as in matters of a broader quality of life or of a political nature, it has something, I feel, to do with the "overrunning cup syndrome"—there is just too much threat of a life-and-death nature confronting Israelis on a day-to-day basis to leave much reaction for matters that can only be viewed as secondary in import. In some ways the absence of reaction on the part of the secular majority to what should objectively be viewed as the excesses of the religious minority should be seen in prophylactic terms as a sort of mental-health measure whereby the essential and the nonessential are sifted and sorted.

One could view the matter differently, however. The refusal to adopt too critical a position concerning the religious establishment might be seen as an act of filial piety whereby the Jews' cruelly uprooted and ravaged past, which was largely religiously traditional, is reaffirmed at least symbolically by respecting its legitimacy as a centerpiece for national existence.

Attendant upon this is the additional factor of a young society searching for its own cultural legitimacy and expression; looking for certainty, continuity, and tradition and finding little other than the faith of the fathers to tie matters together. What after all binds a Moroccan tailor, a Yemenite jeweler, a Polish farmer, and a German dentist other than a fragile but existent common faith? If this structure be undermined what in fact will serve as a cultural binder among the diverse strands of the House of Israel?

Thus we confront a most curious situation in contemporary Israel: A largely secular population willingly (or at least unprotestingly) gives significant powers over a great many central affairs of considerable weight to a religious minority who enjoy not only disproportionate political power but who in addition have access to a highly disproportionate percentage of the public treasury.

But is the Israeli public largely secular as I have thus far asserted? Insofar as behavior is concerned, or observance of basic *mitzvot*, such as strict adherence to rules of *kashrut*, family purity, prayer, observance of the Sabbath, and religious study, one would have to agree that the majority are not observant and in that sense secular. But if by secular one means a certain commitment to two realms and their separateness and integrity—the sacred and the profane, the religious and the irreligious, the god-believer and the god-rejector—then the Israeli public largely tends to fall into another category. This could be summed up by that old saw of the lapsed Catholic who avers "I don't believe in God but Mary was His mother." In the Jews' case, "I don't observe the *mitzvot*, but if I were to, then the religious [Orthodox] pattern is the correct one, the legitimate one. The Orthodox are the keepers of the flame which I could not or would not maintain. The least I can do is not to disturb their efforts."

This could also represent a sort of visceral response to the effect that true separation of political and religious power at home in *Eretz Yisrael* is impossible in the context of Judaism and that the combination of the two always and inevitably disappoints. In the *galut* we could and often did demand (where possible) this separation but how could this be justified in the organic context of *Mamlechet Yisrael*?

Also, as noted in other contexts, Israelis are great respecters of ideals, ideology, and deeply held beliefs. When these are demonstrated in seeming sincerity and with unbounded commitment and enthusiasm, most believe that these stalwarts should not be interfered with; indeed, they deserve encouragement. Thus, when so many emigrants stated their acceptance of the role and behavior of a religious establishment in Israel they were reflecting a largely current Israeli attitude, as were those who thought that religion should occupy a still larger role.

Again, one cannot assume from the above discussion that issues of religion and state, religion and society, and religious "coercion" occupy no role in the consciousness of large numbers of thoughtful Israelis. From responses on the part of departees as well as comments from Israelis who are not contemplating emigration one cannot but be impressed by the feeling that something portentious is going on. What exactly it is is difficult to isolate at this juncture largely because of the aforementioned pious embrace of "traditionalism" on the part of so many, a refusal to spit on the graves of the ancestors, as it were. In most interviews where people tended to assert that the "religious issue" was not for them a disturbing one, some discomfort over the matter was generally evinced following some active probing. Thus a number of women—and not only active feminists—indicated some chagrin over the "chattel" role of females in *halachah* "which has so much power over my life." Others, including one subject who asserted that religion had insufficient influence over life in Israel, had complaints about things like having two chief rabbis instead of one unifying figure, the degrading of practices like *kashrut* with "money" interests or involvement, or the introduction of party politics into the "religious realm." Some questioned religious interference in matters like medical autopsy and transplants wondering why "they" have the power to "legislate . . . in this area." Still others indicated a modicum of discomfort over violence perpetrated by certain elements among religious zealots as with "fanaticism" in general.

Thus, for many if not most interviewees serious deficiencies in the religious realm were recognized and while one must accept at face value the majority view that these did not play a role in their decision to leave, one must at the same time assume that these factors do act in some subliminal fashion toward the construction of the web that ultimately results in emigration.

The Arab Minority

Less surprising than the generally accepting response one was privy to on the part of *yordim* in religious matters was the tenor of response with respect to feelings with regard to the Arabs in their midst.[11] Here, two types of response were seen to be unequally present: fear and guilt, with emphasis on the former. Both were arched over with what must be viewed as a sense of despair with respect to the future, although the nature of the despair felt was different among the differing political hues. The more "liberal" felt that the country was moving toward nondemocratic forms while the more "conservative" expressed fear of the Jewish majority losing its "grip" on the country and its institutions.

Without making invidious and thus wrong-headed and simplistic comparisons between two quite different countries—Israel and the United States—one is nevertheless struck by the at least surface parallels between White attitudes toward Blacks and Jewish attitudes toward Arabs. In fact, one need not limit the comparison to Jew-Arab, White-Black in that the similarities are those one sees in diverse social contexts involving ethnic or social superordination and subordination. The dominant group—in this case the Jews—seems largely convinced that its culture is under threat from the subordinate group and thus limitations are placed on the aspiring group's freedom. Assurance is posited to the effect that a "decent" level of compromise in meeting the minority group's demands will not suffice and that a "whole loaf" will be demanded. Evidence is brought to bear demonstrating good will and high-minded acts on the part of the majority that are only met with sullen ingratitude and sometimes treachery on the part of the minority. Readiness either on the part of the minority or in some cases the majority (or both) for assimilating change is oft raised to explain the need for slow progress of an evolutionary (modest) rather than revolutionary kind. Doubts concerning the "character" of the minority group's members and their ability or desire to adapt to the lofty standards of the majority are put forth. Overstimulating appetites within the minority by the injudicious or premature raising of expectations through the opening of educational or opportunity channels is often questioned.

Again, it must be emphasized that while similarities exist with other minority-majority contact situations, so there are dissimilarities. One can never wander too far from the fact that an ongoing war is in progress over very real flesh-and-blood issues, such as ownership and dominance of a particular piece of land wherein the categories "majority" and "minority" became enfeebled and perhaps irrelevant. This possible irrelevance is perhaps best demonstrated by the fact that while Jews are a numerical majority in Israel, they represent an almost infinitesimal minority in the geographic area wherein Israel is located. Playing with the dial of a radio in Israel can be an instructive experience in this regard when it soon becomes apparent that for every word of Hebrew one hears on one's set in Tel Aviv ten words of Arabic can be heard. While one station in the area provides television in a mix of Arabic-Hebrew-English, five or six can be picked up in differing areas of the country broadcasting in Arabic.

Arabs were never subordinate to a Jewish polity and have no deadening national memories of such dominance. It seems needless to add that Israelis do not confront an ordinary situation of weakness-strength, dominance-subordination, or superiority-inferiority. Arabs do not experience their culture as inferior to that of the dominant political groups, and in fact there is ample basis for the assertion that their "slumbering" culture and society are in the ascendancy and will at the very least survive if not prevail. In any event it is entirely intact and functioning, rather than in any way endangered—at least not from the majority culture.

Thus, the drawing of any simplistic parallel with the United States or South Africa will not stand the test of relevance, although one cannot escape the existence of some blatant similarities on the behavioral-attitudinal level. One such similarity is to be seen in the relative invisibility of the minority member at the same time as his physical presence is pervasive. Arabs build buildings, drive trucks and cabs, wait tables, repair plumbing, remove trash, and in short are obsessively visible in all phases of manual, unskilled, and increasingly artisan tasks in Israeli society. One would be hard pressed getting through a day almost anywhere in Israel without coming into at least some minimal contact with an Arab.

Yet rare (and getting rarer) is the Israeli Jew who speaks Arabic with any degree of fluency, has Arab friends, knows a bit about Arab culture, has an appreciation for Arab music or art or religions, has any sense of Arab history—ancient or modern—or even the slightest inkling of respect for any of these. Arabs—as other invisible men in other contexts—tend not to be Mohammed, Ali, Rashid, or Alia but simply "the Arab." Thus one hears about "them" or "the Arabs" rather than about specific people with traceable histories and visible attributes.

This invisibility is so strong an element of the relationship that in a country of 8,000 square miles and about 4 million people, of which about 600,000 are Arabs, it is possible to come across myriads who have never "met" an Arab fellow citizen. They have seen "them," heard "them," rubbed elbows with "them"—but never met "him."

In asking leavers about their attitudes toward and experiences with Arab fellow citizens one of the factors that achieved prominance was the way in which Arabs were viewed *en bloc*:

> I work with them and I like them although they have very strange practices (the person was referring to sexual perversions).

> I like to buy from them in the shuk; they have better produce than the Jews.

> I study with them at _____ and I have a very positive relationship to them.

The above sampling might be said to reflect a fairly positive attitude but again one sees a marked inability to see the Arab in individual terms. Interviewees were asked to tell about relationships they had had with Arabs other than as employers or coworkers and there were almost none, although opinions about Arabs were profusely volunteered. One exception—and almost the only one in the entire sample[12]—stated:

> I want to say something about the Arabs and that is that aside from giving birth with Arab women in a full hospital, I've had no contact with Arabs. Other than like I said in a full hospital, or sitting next to an Arab on a bus. I have never gone into an Arab store, I have never had Arab friends, I have never had an Arab neighbor, I've never met an Arab doctor, until I came to _____ . And there I had Arab classmates. And I want you to know that this experience has enriched my life, it has certainly helped to improve my outlook on the Arabs, because my outlook on the Arabs was the outlook of most Israelis; that's all I knew about Arabs.

When asked to characterize that outlook, she replied:

> That they're enemies to the State, that they're enemies to the Country, they're traitors, and be careful of them, and never believe them. They'll smile at you, and they'll stab you in the back . . . but that's true about a lot of Jews as well. I think that people should be valued on the basis of a personal relationship with them. . . . I don't know, maybe it's because my relationship at _____ was with Arab girls and not with men. Maybe Arab men are different, I don't know.

In the above example we see some movement in the direction of individuation, but even here a fairly high degree of tentativeness: "Maybe Arab men are different." Tentativeness perhaps, but also visibility, a readiness to engage individual Arabs on a level of mutual recognition and, presumably, respect.

Invisibility is both a product of and a cause of widespread stereotyping. The less contact there is of a personal, reciprocal nature the more recourse there is to a process of group categorization. This together with the existence of a very real conflict between Arabs and Jews brings to the fore what might in fact be expected: fear, suspicion, doubts as to what path should be chosen, disdain, confusion, and (among a minority) a touch of hatred.

Some resort to complex and highy fanciful constructs manifesting curious distinctions that upon closer observation, make a certain sense. For example, a number of interviewees sensed an important change had taken place in and among Israel's own Arab minority since the 1967 war.

> The Arabs from 1948 till 1967 didn't bother me at all. It didn't bother them either; it was comfortable for them to have been under Israeli rule or at least they had gotten used to it. The Arabs *since* 1967 bother me.

In this and other interviews it was recognized that the Arabs of Israel had entered upon a new phase of militancy since 1967 and this was clearly thought of as an unwelcome development. For the first time Arabs were consciously being viewed in terms of competition and not only on the cosmic level of two opposing nationalisms. Among the "new factors" pointed to were assertions that the minority had taken over this or that segment of the economy (building trades, herding, cattle feed production, iron mongering, and automobile repair were those cited most often); that unfair competition was being practiced by Arab professionals and university graduates who had a head start on the Jews because they did not serve in the army for three years; that the PLO was underwriting all sorts of projects, from scholarships to medical training, and providing services for Israeli Arabs that were not available to Jews; and so on.

This new atmosphere was often compared to the rather pacific and highly domesticated position of the minority prior to 1967 where they "would not dare to lift their heads." Now their demands were felt to be excessive even when mixed with a modicum of sympathy for their situation.

> They [the Arabs] *do* suffer from discrimination but the more rights we give them the more they'll wake up and want more . . . they will want equal rights with us. You see, if we give them more they will ask for more. So how do we deal with this . . . this giving of rights. It's beyond me.

The person quoted above—born abroad in a Middle Eastern country but brought to Israel at the age of 14—indicated perplexity with respect to how one should treat the Arabs: on the one hand there should be no desire to harm but on the other there should be a strong reluctance to acquiesce to parity or even proximity. "A lot of us don't want to see the Arabs." When asked what this meant he added, "We don't want integration—we may have to give them rights, but we don't want to live with them."

Highly conflicted and somewhat aggressive attitudes toward Arabs were to be found among those departees coming from countries of the Middle East or born to parents who had emigrated from those lands. Within this group there was almost universal agreement that Arabs could not be trusted, that they were devious and disloyal, and that they were treated much better by Jews than was the reverse in Arab lands.

> I personally know the Bedouins that live in our area, and they get all the benefits, like social security, and the hospitals and all the things that they need. I don't know, what can I tell you? I have a problem. When I get to America and get all the rights, I'm happy about it. But with them here, I don't know, it's a problem. Let me tell you, we came here, a minority from an Arab land, and we didn't live as well as they lived. We ourselves said that the Jewish State will be for the Jews and you can't ask them to be part of Israel. They want our benefits, but they'll kick us about all the same. I came here as a minority, and we didn't have any rights where we came from and we didn't get what they had, and we were scared . . . so why do we give to them?

One can hear in the above a certain reverberation of scores to be settled and of fears that have never quite been laid to rest: "Now we are in the saddle and there is no reason not to give as good as we got." Another respondent, when asked whether she was satisfied with the treatment accorded to Arabs, answered:

> I would like to see a Jewish State without so many Arabs. We have a lot of Arabs at work—they work at the factory mainly—and I don't have anything against them. Most of them are very nice and while I don't have anything against them on principle I want an Israeli-Jewish State without an Arab minority.

> Look, I accept that there are Arabs here because I have no choice, but frankly we should not give them full rights of citizenship. They should be limited for all sorts of reasons including security, economics, and everything else.

While heavily concentrated and perhaps somewhat sharper among emigrants from Arab lands, such responses were clearly not limited to them. In response to a question as to whether he saw any problem with Israel's Arab minority, a former professional soldier of impeccable Ashkenazic background stated:

> The problem is that I would be happy not to see a single Arab here. I think that it would be much more comfortable for this nation if we were only Jews here: we don't need any additions. While I don't like it however, I think the present situation is a workable one which doesn't require an immediate or radical solution.

Almost all respondents expressed fear with respect to the emergence of a Palestinian state on the grounds of security but also because of possible threat to legitimacy. There was widespread conviction—one might call it a national consensus—that was being expressed to the effect that any Palestinian State alongside Israel was merely the first step in the ultimate dismantling or delegitimation of Israel.

> While I don't think we need the territories (how can we absorb another million Arabs?) we do need them for security reasons. I certainly don't think that we should allow a Palestinian entity to grow into something that has a private army and everything . . . that won't prove anything and will only threaten us.

The question of legitimacy came to the fore in numerous comments to the effect that if Israel relinquished their claim over Nablus and Hebron what rights would they have in Haifa or Jaffa? Thus while most respondents rejected the possibility of enlarging Israel's Arab minority by incorporating the heavily populated West Bank, few were willing to relinquish claims to sovereignty—mostly based on historical rights wherein the Jews are vouchsafed the entire "Land of Israel." Some respondents claimed a status as Palestinians no less authentic than that which was being claimed by many among Israel's Arab minority.

> I'm a Palestinian! I was born in Palestine—right here! Why don't I have the right which they are demanding? If the Arabs demand something why not us? I don't know what they want.

As noted earlier in this section, there was a heavy weighting among departees toward a rather conservative, indeed regressive attitude with respect to the Arab minority. There were fears with respect to a delegitimation of Jewish nationhood; fears of a physical, threatening nature; as well as fears with respect to competition in the economic sphere. Only a small minority were able to express much sympathy for the plight of the Arab minority and these tended to be concentrated among the political left, the highly educated, professionals, and, overwhelmingly, Ashkenazim. One such respondent noted that the only thing that might change her decision to emigrate would be "the creation of a Palestinian State on the West Bank and in Gaza, plus real peace and a situation where Jews and Arabs learned to live with each other without feelings of superiority and inferiority. And there isn't the slightest possibility of that happening . . . it is pure fantasy. You see, I really like it here—I like the landscape, the sky, the light, the climate. I really belong *here* physically! But there is no way to change things!"

Some respondees noted that the lack of symmetry in the relationship between the Jewish majority and the Arab minority was unproductive and undesirable. One interviewee noted that she felt uninvolved—at least insofar as any presumed allocation of guilt was concerned but "I don't applaud it [attitudes and behaviors toward Arabs]—I condemn it! I condemn a lot of the attitudes of Israelis which are against the minorities. I feel that . . . I mean how many Jews know how to speak Arabic? Just take that for an example! How many Jews know about Arab culture? The Arab religion? But there *are* Arabs who know about Jewish culture and Jewish religion making this a very one-sided relationship. It seems to me to be unfair!"

A few among the more left-leaning departees saw the intercommunal scene in Israel as one of missed opportunities and lessening options. The key feature among these respondents was not the analysis as it was a feeling that the die has been irreversibly cast, leaving *them* with an overriding sense of hopelessness with respect to the future of the collective enterprise and their own personal destiny. Again the post-Six-Day War period is seen as crucial.

> What's happening today is a continuation of what's been going on for quite a while now and that is this insensitivity, this total insensitivity, to the demands of what was earlier [pre-1967] the more radical elements of the Arab population. Their demand then was simply for recognition as equal citizens of the State of Israel; for economic, social, and political rights. This insensitivity has created a much more radical stand among the Arabs—but you know the Arabs are not the only population ready to explode. The Sephardic Jews are primed to blow as well. Irresponsiveness to modest demands is creating a situation where the response from these groups is going to be much more

radical than it would have been otherwise. But it will take time: you know there is still very heavy control being exercised with these groups.

The above interviewee was sure that the future of the country as a whole was bleak and ultimately unpromising. While comments of others who saw things similarly were somewhat less "honed" and precise, the overall feeling was a desire to leave before the final expected collapse would engulf them. But, as noted earlier, pessimism with respect to the Arab-Jewish relationship was overarching and pervasive. It included the educated and uneducated, people of Eastern origin and Western origin, of left and right. While the more liberal were concerned with the "soul" of the nation, and the more conservative with the threat to continued Jewish dominance, both felt the future to be unpromising and threatening. A native-born technician in his early thirties notes that even the partial peace with Egypt has not brought more hope, but, in fact, the opposite:

I'm very pessimistic! The situation is much worse than it was four years ago [before peace with Egypt] because the local Arabs, the Israeli Arabs didn't behave the way they are behaving now. They wouldn't have dared to talk the way they do now.

Another respondee, again leaning to the conservative side of the political spectrum, summed up the feelings of most when he said:

The problem with the Arabs is dirt [literally "mud," *botz*]. And I think that it is a problem without a solution. You can look at someone like Rabbi Kahane [a radical rightist preaching violence against the Arab minority who has recently been elected to the Knesset] and say that this man is right; that we should bloc them up and not give them anything because soon they will take over Parliament. On the other hand you can say that they are people and that we must give them freedom—this is after all a democratic state based on democratic ideals. But this is mud too because you can't know where this will lead. There *is* no solution in my opinion.

It should not be necessary to add that when large numbers of people in a given population feel that a central concern is "hopeless" or without a "solution" a serious threat to societal stability is evident.

Most departees would (and did) claim that this "hopelessness" with respect to the Arab issue plays a miniscule or nonexistent role in the decision-making process. On a conscious level there is no question but that this is indeed the case. But here as in so many other areas or dimensions of social existence in Israel the persistence of a layer of subliminal or subsurface threat or instability cannot but add to the general context of stress that is part and parcel of daily existence in the society and from which large numbers of people seek redress and release. Some continue to struggle day in and day out. Others opt for a forum of privatism that involves the cultivation of one's own personal world—inner and outer. Still others— whether in full understanding of the processes at work or not—opt for departure from the country and the pursuit of greener pastures in other places.

The Intracommunal Factor

Keniston (1965:387) has observed that "any social order in which a goodly proportion of its citizens do not fit is in that measure a society whose demands have outpaced its ability to prepare men to meet them." There is at this stage of Israeli development scant doubt even in the minds of the simplest observers that a gulf—of status, power, and wealth— exists between those Jews who stem from Europe and the West and those from North Africa and Asia. As with relationships between Arab and Jew, a substantial scientific literature exists in this area, but our present concern is less with the detailed picture than it is with the placement of this factor in the etiology and dynamics of emigration from Israel.[13] Thus, rather than discuss how this intracommunal gulf developed or what its objective dimensions consist of, it must be sufficient to note as above that we are dealing with a society where "a goodly proportion of . . . citizens do not fit" and they experience various degrees of hurt, anger, and resentment that inevitably have behavioral implications of one kind or another.

Two factors seemed to emerge with great clarity from the interviews: (1) a marked tendency on the part of *yordim* of Eastern origin to initially deny that a sense of being discriminated against played a role in the decision to leave or that they personally had suffered discrimination, and (2) a mixed sense among non-Easterners that the problem was exaggerated and that eastern culture and behavior left something to be desired, the latter leading to a feeling of dissociation with the common enterprise.

When one comes across a rich, well-established fruit stall owner in mid-life making in excess of $1,000 per week who decides to give it all up and move to America, one must ask why. The answer at first is *nishbar li* (I was "broken" by high taxes), but the man has successfully evaded taxes and continues to do so. A second layer of defense was breached when he asserted it was to "assure a better life for my children," which upon further probing resulted in a very clear statement (and understanding) to the effect that "here, no matter how much I earn I will always be a Moroccan while in *chutz la'aretz* I'm just another Jew." In effect his departure for America is a throwing off of ethnic disabilities, which is not felt to be possible in Israel. "In America," as was noted by numerous respondents, "neither the Jews nor the *goyim* know these *kunzim* [tricks] about Sephardim or Ash-kenazim. There, we are all Jews or Israelis with no distinction made." Ironically, full Israeliness is sometimes achieved by Jews of North African or Asian background only after leaving Israel and taking up residence in foreign parts. What American would be able to distinguish between the accent of a Moroccan and that of a Pole? More importantly, who would care? An Israeli of whatever prior background is, for the overwhelmingly majority of non-Israelis, simply an Israeli. Thus emigration is a means of reaching an unhyphenated and weightless status that otherwise might have taken generations to achieve at home.

Once the wall of denial is breached it becomes crystal clear that a power-ful factor among the large number of Eastern Jews who leave (35 percent of the present sample)[14] is that they do so partially because of their "objec-tive" position within Israeli Jewish society. "I have been called *kushi* or nigger not once here. I've been called *schwartzer* too—but this only by the older generation." The above from an Iraqi-born salesman who went on to note that "the whole establishment in this country is Ashkenazi and the Sephardim are under their control in all things." Almost all respondents of Eastern background argued that the establishment of the country, the elites in all areas of social, political, and economic life, were Ashkenazim. The only disagreement was between a minority who claimed this pattern was consciously fabricated by the majority for dominance whereas the majority tended to look at the matter as somewhat more flaccid and less premedi-tated. Whether premeditated or not, consciousness of inferior status—if not inferiority itself—is pervasive among the full range of Eastern Jews, from the relatively high-status Yemenites to those stemming from low-status Morocco. Notwithstanding, and as noted above, there exists alongside this consciousness a persistent need to deny its usage or effect on oneself. A young Yemenite departee noted, "I haven't really suffered from discrimination as a Yemenite. Generally Yemenites are liked in Israel. But when you get on a bus sometimes and maybe get a little boisterous they look at you as *edot hamizrach,* as an Easterner, etc., not pleasant."

A respondent from Turkey, when asked whether or not he has suffered from discrimination, just stated, "Well, I'm dark you know," but then went on to say, "No, no I haven't suffered from it [discrimination] at all—although I know it exists. It disturbs me *greatly* [said with deep emphasis] that it exists in this country at all—but I, personally, have not had any contact with it."

A Moroccan clothing shop owner in Tel Aviv when asked about discrimi-nation said, "*Nu, meeleh,*" (never mind) as if to indicate that "these things do happen, you know, but one cannot become too overwrought by it." He did, however, note that he voted Likud for among other reasons the fact that "as *edot hamizrach* I can identify more with them than I can with Labor." The same respondent felt that the ethnic coloration to class in Israel was considerably harder to bear than what he presumed to be the more objective basis that exists in America. In Israel he saw matters as "us" and "them" with "us" being poorly dealt with and "them" getting it all on the basis of where they came from and "speaking Yiddish," rather than deriving from skill, energy, or talent. He as well as a number of other respondents tended to see class as open-ended and fluid in America, while being closed and ethnically "stacked" in Israel. "In America I buy in the same store as millionaires, whereas here I don't even *see* the rich."

Many respondents while denying any personal pain did emphasize a sort of collective or "Jewish" pain they experienced due to the very existence of "ethnic prejudice" in Israel. "It disturbs me terribly—especially when we Jews expect to be able to live together here in peace and instead we eat each other up alive."

Some interviewees bounced back and forth between identity with the ethnic subgroup and the dominant Ashkenazim. These tended to come from higher status Eastern groups such as Turks or Iraqis rather than from among the lower status Moroccans or other North Africans, and were generally second rather than first generation Israelis. Some indicated that prejudice against Easterners was "earned" by certain unfortunate behavior such as rowdiness, lack of emphasis on education, and unstable family structure, which was avered to be preeminent among the Eastern groups. A few were rather pleased that they "didn't look like Easterners" and were able to "pass" as Ashkenazim.

But again, for most the status of Eastern Jewry in the state of Israel was clearly a heavy burden to be borne and though it might be asserted time and again that "I never experienced prejudice personally," this was invariably followed by examples demonstrating the opposite.

> I'll tell you, I haven't felt discrimination at all. I've seen that it exists; I've seen it but it wasn't directed at me! For example, I saw it in the army where at a base I was on instructors got to stay on because of *protektzia,* whereas I couldn't use that route. I don't have any *protektzia* but I stayed anyway simply because I was an excellent soldier and they couldn't very well leave someone with lesser qualities there while rejecting me. They did however leave _____ the son of _____ [the owner of one of the country's leading business establishments] because he was rich and Ashkenazi. Of all those serving with me there wasn't one other fellow from the Eastern cultures. I was the only one. But at work I don't see or feel discrimination. I hear about it, people talk about it—but I don't see it clearly.

> On the other hand the town I live in is 80 percent Moroccan. How do you explain that a government committed to integration would allow such a

situation to develop? Why were the North Africans all concentrated in border towns? How come you don't see Russians and Americans where I live?

The connection between this sense of discrimination and leaving Israel is almost never made consciously and verbally. Only one interviewee—whose comments will be dealt with at great length—stated clearly and unequivocally that prejudice was a prime element in his departure.[15]

Emotion was clearly evident while this question was being discussed. Agitation was visible among many as they related their "stories" with regard to this specific; the palpable pain and disappointment that such could be their fate among their brethren in the Jewish State was at all times present. Use of the very words "hurt," "pain," "disappointment," and "regret" were extensively resorted to in discussing elements associated with this dimension of Israeli life.

> It hurts me when I hear jokes about Easterners.
>
> I am hurt when they laugh at the weaker among us instead of extending protection.
>
> I felt it [discrimination] when I came here as a little child and I've felt it all my life.
>
> Our shame as a nation is seen in our refusal to value people for their behavior and achievements—and not from where they come.
>
> We were willing to learn from the Europeans: we came from less-developed countries. But that doesn't mean that we are less than them.
>
> We were willing to learn to receive from the Ashkenazim, from the kibbutznikim. But they didn't want us—except as workers.
>
> I'm not saying we didn't have faults—but you can learn, you can learn. No one was born "knowing." We are not without intelligence.
>
> You know it was bad enough when the Ashkenazim didn't want the Sephardim. Now—you have brought it to the point where the *Sephardim* don't want the Sephardim.

The one interviewee who in fact did place the factor of discrimination against Eastern Jews at the top of the causal chain resulting in his emigration was in fact more a member of this subgroup by self-definition, personal identity, and perhaps verbal flimflam than anything else. He is of Bulgarian origin, which is indeed Sephardi, but hardly part and parcel of the dynamic of low status-low achievement that is the assigned fate of, say, the Moroccan Jews who might be said to epitomize the term *"edot hamizrach."* His bitterness—and bitter he is—perhaps has its roots in other causes than a presumed sense of ethnic pique but his chosen vehicle for its expression is the ethnic case and one emerges with the unmistakable impression that not withstanding his perhaps questionable credentials on technical grounds he is nonetheless a most potent and articulate spokesman for positions I felt to be present among a large majority of *edot hamizrach* departees. While they tended to deny and be defensive—even apologetic—he chose to speak openly and freely. What follows is part of a lengthy interview conducted with Mr. R., with the major emphasis and thrust bearing on the issue of the *edot hamizrach.* I began by asking him why he chose to leave Israel.

R: [pause] Well, I didn't want to leave. I left against my will.

I: What do you mean?

R: At that time in the country there were conditions that forced one into a certain situation and gave one certain expectations. . . . They educate you to a certain thing and then you see that the reality is the opposite of your expectations, different than what they've been brainwashing you to all this time and you see that there is no way to change it here, and the only way to succeed in what you have wanted to do is outside the country.

I: Excuse me, but what do you mean, it's too telegraphic?

R: There's an education for materialism in the country. Also, we're living in the Middle East and they teach us to respect the West so there exists some duality between our existence here and the fact that we are expected to create a subculture like the Americans. For example . . . and then you say, wait a minute if this is the way it is, that the American system and the Western way is so much better, then why should I copy it here, and not go to the source? And then you arrive at the conclusion that all the Israelis have arrived at—that is those that are galloping there.

I: When you first started to think about going there was career uppermost in your thoughts?

R: No, no, not when I left . . . I'm also Sephardic, and a Sephardic who people say is talented, but I didn't have the opportunity to get ahead in terms of my talents in this country. Here I had gotten to the limits of my possibilities for success and I knew that in a place where my Sephardicness wouldn't be an obstacle I would be able to go further.

I: As a Bulgarian you consider yourself a Sephardic? That's not exactly Eastern culture.

R: I consider myself as part of the Eastern culture [*edot hamizrach*].

I: But . . .

R: If I were to go to America it would become blurred there, but here I have to deal with the reality of the Middle East, and not with the Westernness of America.

I: Yes, but about this point that you see yourself as part of the Eastern culture, the Bulgarians in the country are considered as part of the elite; I think for example that the highest percentage of doctors, in respect to numbers, is among the Bulgarians.

R: About what you said that the Bulgarians are considered part of the elite, I don't know where you made that up; maybe you should ask them yourself, maybe there's a tendency to associate with the ruling class, because in this country every group of people has that tendency; because that's where the money is and the power. It might be true that among Bulgarians there might be a higher percentage of doctors than among other groups, but still, if you go to Yaffo, or the Lubinski market, there you'll find the poor Bulgarians, the porters, the workers, the carpenters, the mechanics like all the Eastern culture peoples. There's a difference between the Bulgarians and the rest of the Eastern culture peoples; it's a fact that we're from Europe, so sometimes there's a blurring of areas. But the Bulgarians, their habits, traditions, and even in the discrimination toward us, we're considered Easterners—especially me since I'm even darker than the average Bulgarian.

I: Do you think that you personally suffered from this?

R: Yes [his immediate response].

I: How did you feel this?

R: In all areas, in all areas, in all the areas of life.

I: As discrimination against you, as . . .

R: [here he cuts in] . . . as discrimination.

I: In getting a job?

R: In getting a job, in the army.

I: In the army as well?

R: Also in the army, yes. In the army there was very serious discrimination against Sephardim.

I: Against Sephardics yes, but again I differentiate between the Moroccans and the Bulgarians . . .

R: No, no, people don't go and give you a test of what type of Sephardic you are, they discriminate. They see that you are darker, that you identify with the Sephardics, that your culture isn't exactly of Vienna and Berlin, or . . . or Moscow or Warsaw. There is very serious discrimination, that isn't only on a racist basis, but also the *protektzia* you wield—who does it go to? All those that have the connections, and those that have friends among the high officers, and these are usually the Ashkenazim. The Sephardim don't usually have the *protektzia.* So we pretty much suffer from this in all walks of life. I have suffered from it in the army, in school and education, and also in closing the theater to me. I was prevented from advancing in the theater mainly because they didn't want a Sephardic with independent views in such a sensitive field like the communications network, and I stress the point of "independent views" because I know that this was the fear. Whereas if it was an Ashkenazi with independent views I think that the obstacles would have been fewer than those laid in front of me. But the discrimination is not only felt in this area, it's also in the very image of the State. You turn on the radio, the TV and all that they show, all that you see, are Ashkenazim; the main culture, the dominating culture that you see, is Western, and eventually you get to feel like surrendering emotionally, you begin to realize, to feel, to see that though you're part of the majority here, you're not wanted. Perhaps many people have not spoken to you this way, but when you know them well, when you sit for a couple of hours and talk with them, a lot of those that left will tell you that that's why they left. It's not pleasant to talk about but there it is; there's a tendency to not talk about it. But I'm sure that you've interviewed a lot of people, that if you go deeper you would find that that's the real reason that they left, but they'll give you a thousand and one other reasons; they won't express themselves in this fashion . . . it has a psychological cause, it's psychological.

I: You claim that this is your main reason for leaving?

R: I think that it's a reason for a lot of *yordim.*

I: But for you?

R: For me, it's mostly because of it, and also I say that it's the main reason for a lot of the Eastern culture peoples. I'd say that it's about 80 percent of the real reasons of these people. Even though there is a tendency not to show it in public, not to talk about it. It's part of the indoctrination that you go through in the country. It's one of the things that you don't talk about, and also they're ashamed. They've gotten us to a state where the Eastern culture peoples are ashamed that they are part of the Eastern culture, and therefore we don't want to bring it up as a reason, because as soon as you do bring it up people start saying "What really, there's discrimination?" [This last said in a derogatory tone.] People suffer in quiet and don't talk about it. But when I met people outside of the country and talked to them, after you get to the personal level (and the Sephardics have a different thought procedure than the Europeans, than the Westerners. With us, as soon as you're on the personal level we reveal ourselves, but if you come to us with questions we won't usually tell you all the real reasons for what we think.) So as soon as you sit with them and know them well, they'll say listen, I'll tell you the truth, this is the reason why I left. That's the reason that a lot of the research done on the Sephardic population is so often wrong and inaccurate. Because it is done with the standards and the thought patterns of the West and you [plural] try to do with the Sephardics what you do with the Westerners and it's not appropriate. You're not aware that we think in a different manner—less analogical [*mufshat*] and more with the spirit.

I: More emotionally maybe?

R: More emotionally [agreeing]. For example, with the public opinion polls. I remember that they had an opinion poll on how people voted, and they always came out with the thought that the Sephardics aren't interested in their own representation. Now the Sephardics are educationally at a lower level, so that they don't take seriously something like an opinion poll. For example the person will go to someone more educated, say with ten years of education, so you'll look for the one who is more educated, in the community or in the family, and then you have slanted the data, because the more educated person is going to have opinions that are closer to those of the Ashkenazim. This, you see, is because of his identification with them. If I really wanted to make an honest appraisal and do honest research work, I would have to be more balanced in asking. . . .

I: We try, we try.

R: But there's a problem because it's much easier to get clear answers from the educated man, than going to the person who works all day or does dishes; the less educated person, the poor one, that it'll take you three hours to interview when you want to finish it in 15 minutes. That's why I think that in your work especially that justice will not be done on the ethnic issue.

I: But that's only if you're correct. I'll tell you later . . .

R: [he cuts interviewer off] If you'll go deeper you'll see that it has to be correct, it can't be that in this country the Sephardics aren't discriminated against. And if a man will tell you that he left because he couldn't get an apartment, or because he couldn't get work, then ask. But *why* can't he get an apartment, or why can't he get work? You have to go to the roots of the problem, and I, simply by coincidence, have worked on these matters and I arrived at these conclusions.

I: When did you start feeling this identification with the Eastern culture peoples, especially the problem of ethnic discrimination?

R: From six years old [immediate answer].

I: From six years of age?!

R: From the age of six, but until the age of 26 it was under the surface, I pushed it away, but at the age of 26, how do you say, I had my fill of it [*mayim ad nafesh*] and that was the beginning of the Black Panthers in the country and I started translating it from inarticulate feelings into political terminology . . . to understand it politically.

I: Would you define yourself as a leftist politically?

R: No, I don't know what a leftist is.

I: According to the standards of the country, I would say that someone who is Shelli, Rakah, and left of these is a leftist.

R: If Shelli, Rakah, and Mapam is left for you then I'm not. I hate them with a deathly hatred [small laugh]; them, I don't consider left. The only chance that I see for the left in this country is the Sephardic left, that will come up out of the Eastern culture peoples as they are the working peoples. What do the kibbutzim have to do with the left? They just call themselves that you see, and the Hashomer Hatzair buy a bank in Chicago with all their money.

I: What exactly happened at the age of 26? What changed?

R: Well, it was . . .

I: Something must have happened . . .

R: It was a progression of things. I had at that time a theater, and they put obstacles in front of me ["they put a 'foot' in front of me"], the theater succeeded from a professional point; culturally it was a very successful theater, an underground theater as it's called. But in every instance that I had to have dealings with the municipalities they would fail me; the city hall, the law, the police. It got to real physical violence so that the police really beat me . . . .

I: Why, I don't understand . . . .

R: Because they didn't want there to be such a tool that would have effect on public opinion, in my hands, not only because I'm a Sephardic, but because I'm an independent Sephardic, and I had a very radical approach to the establishment. I didn't do anything against the law, but apparently for the democratic rulers of this country it was enough. And then I started to think—if they aren't going to let me express myself in a democratic fashion, because they don't like me, and that's the reason that they bother me, and hit me, and all those things, and at the same time I started to hear what the Black Panthers were saying, I said to myself well, maybe there's a connection. And I started to think, and I came to the conclusion that they wouldn't have done it to someone who is an Ashkenazi but they permitted themselves to do it to someone who is Sephardic. And that brought me along in the chain, link after link, along this chain to identify with all these problems.

And one thing led to another so that I began to see links in the chain. For example, our policy toward the Arabs. I'm against our policy, I'm against our governing another people and that we don't do them justice. I think that Zionism is bankrupting itself as long as it is being realized at the expense of another nation of people, instead of realizing itself by compromising with the interests of another nation. I'm also against the fact of Israel becoming a trailer being pulled by the United States. I think that both the United States and Israel are participating in a mistaken partnership; the relationship between the rulers in America and the Ashkenazi rulers in Israel will result in tragedy for both sides. I believe that within several years, here in this country, they'll be a very deep feeling of "Yankees go home" [this last said in English] and a request and a demand, like there was in Iran to throw out all those people, because people are becoming more aware of the advantages being taken and the relationship between their rulers and rulers of another country.

I: What about things that aren't attached to politics or connected to your inner feelings about discrimination, what about simple things like *challenge,* here in the country do you feel that you lack challenge, personally, and is that something that you find or expect to find in America?

R: There are professional goals here, but it's a choking situation, you understand. Those secretaries from Russia and Poland are sitting there, and have everything that you need. But we won't give it to you. You want to be a worker? Yes. Well, you see then they tell you, "Why do you want all these problems? Come and be a worker [laborer] in the municipality." They offered me work in the municipality [this said in an amused and surprised tone]. You see it's not that they prevented me from working, but I said, wait a minute, if you're talking about challenge why do they prevent me from doing the work that I'm talented in? If my talents are in the theater and cultural areas, positive areas, why should I become a worker? Why should they give it to Herzl, or Rubinstein? You see, why in a State where they claim that you're equal? Where they say that you're a Jew among Jews? And then after a decade of years they say no, why should you work according to your talents? Work, work so that you'll have enough to live on. I'm interested in challenge in life, and there are enough challenges here for me to attempt them. Why do they prevent me . . . .

I: You're not bored here in the country?

R: Bored? . . . No . . . well, yes and no, yes and no, the challenges exist in unlimited number in this country. I would even say there are more challenges here than in America, but here they also choke you, that is if you're part of a certain social sector—I would even say specific ethnic group, they prevent you from attaining those goals that you want to achieve and in a vulgar manner at that. They don't even do it gently; they prevent you, saying, we are the rulers, we are the judges.

I: O.K. You don't think that it's changing, that it's getting better?

R: No, I think that it's getting worse and worse. It's gotten to the point that the Ashkenazic group has become an interest group, that isn't interested in giving up its interests, and they developed an insulation to the cries of the people as you could say in pictorial language. Look, listen to the radio, you can't hear the music that we like—everything is Elvis Presley, Cliff Richards, and rock and disco and all that. . . .

I: That's Ashkenazi?

R: It's Western. . . .

I: Do you think that the Ashkenazic kid has more connections with it than you?

R: Of course, of course. Maybe you can't be objective but you don't know our culture. There are hundreds of Israeli artists from the Eastern culture and hundreds of records and cassettes have been printed in Buchari, Parsi, Moroccan, Algerian, Egyptian—all sorts, even in Hebrew. It's being created here with singers like Izmo, and Rachmo, and Shimi Tavori and tens of others who create songs and music. Do you know the story of Nisim Sarusi?

I: No.

R: Well, that's another story for *yerida*. He was one of the most popular singers in Israel and he had to leave because the Broadcasting Company simply blacklisted him; they wouldn't broadcast him.

I: What happened? Where did he go?

R: I think he's in France. But he was a number one singer in terms of selling records and cassettes, but couldn't be heard on Israeli radio— Why? He would sing the songs of the communities [the Eastern communities] and he would sing in an Eastern manner, with Hebrew words, so they wouldn't broadcast him. One day Yaron London humiliated him on some TV program, and after that he declared that he was leaving the country. It was an instance that shocked people, but in general there's an insulation to these things. And this insulation can only be changed by drastic measures.

I: What about those that leave for this reason and go to a place like America? Do they have more room for expression in America?

R: Let me explain. In America you don't have this choking. I've lived in America so I can answer you. When you get fed up here, in all the areas, economically, job wise, socially it chokes you entirely and the State itself is in seige and isolated, and it's a small nation geographically. People want to get out a bit to get refreshed. And here there's no chance. I go to the communities to talk to the people. "What, you come from America? Tell us how to get there, help us get there," I say why we have the most beautiful nation here, "What beautiful," they say, "can you make a living here? You can't."

I: But people make a living.

R: I tell you that people don't make a living, we've got ll percent jobless today [small bitter laugh], and where do you find the unemployment? In the poor communities. In the richer neighborhoods of the Ashkenazim you'll only find l percent unemployment, and in the kibbutzim you won't find any unemployment, but if you'll go to the poor communities you'll find 25 percent out of work, the joblessness divides itself. . . .

I: According to the government there isn't ll percent unemployment.

R: Why isn't there ll percent?

I: They talk of 6 percent, but anyway we won't argue the issue.

R: And now there's a lot of letting off [of workers], but I don't know about the percentages, I know that the statistics they get are the ones that suit their theories [small laugh], so that I don't depend too much on the numbers that they give, I always multiply them by two or three.

I: But you said, and justifiably I think, that the country is little, and there are certain difficulties, and people go to America. In America you don't hear the beautiful Eastern songs that they wanted to hear on the radio, they don't live within a Sephardic framework, they can't develop from a cultural aspect . . . there's also joblessness in America. . . .

R: First of all, when a Sephardic Jew goes to America, his chances of succeeding there are ten times more than here. Because there isn't discrimination because he's Sephardic, except for the few Ashkenazic Jews there that are aware of it, and they are the minority on the American social scene. For example, take me, I went to America, and within a month I had sold percentages of paper of $110,000. I went into the designing of dresses, and within a year I had a turnover of a million dollars. In this country I wouldn't have been able to do it.

I: Because you're Sephardic, or because. . . .

R: Because I'm Sephardic! I'm telling you that I couldn't have done it.

In point after point the comments of Mr. R. have about them the ring of acuteness and of being on target—albeit oft reflecting a strong and sometimes distorting aura of bitterness.

In interviewing people of Eastern background I was indeed often impressed with a certain circumlocution at work around issues of prejudice and discrimination against them—a certain reluctance to level with the clearly Ashkenazi interviewer on this point. Mr. R. is correct, I think, to attribute this at least partially to shame, to a reluctance to accept that a possibly "earned" measure of second-classedness was driving them from the land. "You taught us to be ashamed of ourselves and of our culture. You taught us to identify the 'good' with you and the 'bad' with ourselves." Recently many Israelis were appalled when a member of parliament of Eastern origin observed that "gefilte fish made him sick." They correctly surmised that this observation had very little to do with fish and in fact represented a perhaps misaimed (certainly trivial) blow for cultural emancipation from the Eastern European dominated establishment. Both Ashkenazim and Sephardim understood the telegraphy invoked and reacted accordingly: one on the level of chagrin and pained hurt, the other with no little measure of glee! A blow had been struck—even a low blow—redeeming a chit of cultural autonomy, twisting the lion's tail, and lessening an overriding sense of meek shame in face of a dominating *über-kulture*.

That Sephardim "think differently" than Europeans as Mr. R. asserts is again an effort to suggest cultural differences between the two broad groups, a point which has been made ad nauseam and with which one can have little argument, if the point is one of emphasis and style rather than process. Clearly, different groups manifest differing approaches and attitudes to a wide range of matters including those such as "emotionalism," "intimacy," and "abstraction." That this leads to error in interpretation and at times to an inability to communicate is clear, but here the objective truth of the assertion—you don't understand us—is less salient than its professed existence. There is a widespread feeling among *edot hamizrach* that in fact a stylistic barrier between themselves and the "others" reflects a kind of characterological barrier that has and will have grave and important consequences for the future of the collective enterprise. For example, one is often informed that Easterners think more with their hearts than their heads, or that *edot hamizrach* manifest greater tolerance for difference than Europeans, or that Easterners are warmer and more hospitable than their Western counterparts. Many of these stereotypes come to the fore in the course of interviews on the part of both *edot hamizrach* and Europeans demonstrating their rather widespread dispersal within the population. The important element here however is that both groups seem to accept the dominant group's essential ranking of these patterns with cerebration being better than emotion, analytic precision better than warmth, and tolerance a poor substitute for commitment. The second-ranking qualities are not viewed as totally negative—merely as second best.

When Mr. R. asserts with great vehemence that Easterners whatever they might say are really leaving because of discrimination, again a strong supportive argument can be adduced. No one argues with the facts of the matter that show *edot hamizrach* lagging in education, jobs, skills, power, shelter, and almost any other measurable variable. But here our interviews seem to indicate that *edot hamizrach* leavers are no poorer or more poorly sheltered or less skilled than leavers of European background. What is clear, however—more from hints and general tone than outright assertions—is a perceived body of barriers against advancement and success in all areas of endeavor because of membership in one ethnic bloc rather than another.

In a variety of ways one is being told what Mr. R. asserts most forthrightly—I am leaving because here I am seen as less than I am really capable of being or becoming; here I am being kept down and there the "complexes" of intra-Jewish relationships will not be operative allowing one to achieve one's natural level.

While Mr. R.'s rhetoric to the effect that the usual political groupings do not apply to the Eastern communities must not be taken too seriously, it certainly does seem to reflect the current feelings of at least 50,000 Israelis who voted for the blatantly ethnic party known as Tami, placing three people in the Tenth Knesset.[16] A firmly held desideratum of Israeli politics heretofore had been that "ethnic politics does not work here." This clearly is no longer entirely true and while it still appears somewhat wide of the mark and indeed presumptuous to conclude (with Mr. R.) that "left and right" do not apply to *edot hamizrach* there exists scant doubt that the "ethnic factor" is in fact emerging to assume a position of prominence on the political landscape. Thus I would aver that he is at least correct in terms of psychosymbolic impact in noting a further sense of anomie, of unconnectedness to the societal process on the part of large numbers of *edot hamizrach* people that logic suggests cannot but play a role in deciding to pick up stakes and move elsewhere.

Mr. R.'s use of the names "Herzl" and "Rubinstein" is telling and is suggestive of the open code utilized by both camps—East and West—to identify and focus on the "other." It is Herzl and Rubinstein who get the perks distributed by the society, who get the leg-up in career. It is the Bitons and Alyakims who are expected to be hewers of wood and drawers of water. Easterners are expected to fill the manual roles leaving the creative and supervisory tasks to their more advanced brethren among the Ashkenazim.

And lest one think that this process is merely fortuitous, an historical and sociological accident as it were, observe how "they" (Ashkenazim) are attempting to control culture. Eastern songs must (as Mr. R. asserts) live an underground existence on cheap tape cassettes while the "official" air waves are full of "Western" rock and roll.

Finally, as to why America: Will America solve these problems of cultural deprivation? Will America honor and uplift what Israel has denigrated and suppressed? Perhaps not, but in America there is elbow room in both a psychological and physical sense, thus providing at least the illusion of autonomy. America is the great leveller where as noted earlier there may be Jews and non-Jews but certainly no distinction made within the Jewish camp. There, it is the familiar pattern of "us" and "them," Jews and *goyim* with none of the status anxiety invoked in the intra-Jewish battle in Israel. In Israel status anxiety is even further enhanced rather than dissolved or alleviated through the addition of the Arab factor. While it is certainly true that the addition of tens of thousands of Arabs from the territories to the Israeli work force—most in low-skill, low-status jobs—has in some measure "lifted" Jews on the social ladder and these primarily from among the *edot hamizrach*, it would appear that both a dollop of competition and an aura of uncertainty remain. Competition on the lowest level is brought about by the fact that employers of unskilled labor *prefer* Arabs from the territories to Jews because one does not "lose" them to reserve duty, national insurance rates can often be avoided, and base pay and working conditions can be manipulated to fall below par. Thus, for a certain number of Jews competition remains a factor. Uncertainty is brought to the fore by the fear that the structure could collapse. The territories could be "returned" and sealed off catapulting those who had only recently been elevated through the addition of a new and foreign underclass back into their old slots at the bottom of the socioeconomic heap.[17]

Here again it must be emphasized that the majority of those emigrating are not from the lowest rungs of the socioeconomic ladder. But insofar as the factor of ethnicity is *the* undifferentiated tar brush throwing into one container the barber and the barrister, the doctor and the dustman sharing a label and an ascribed identity more than any realistic semblance of objective interests, these factors must be viewed as key elements in the causative chain.

This applies not only to the subordinate groups. *Edot hamizrach* might attempt to flee a perceived negative valuation of "Jewish Arabs" ascribed to them by their Ashkenazi brethren. Askenazi Jews might experience a sense of status threat by the existence of a group of fellow Jews who are perceived as having the disdained characteristics and low standards of the enemy. And the result can be a choice for eliminating the threat by leaving.

The seeds of levantinization are perceived as being borne by their natural bearers—the *edot hamizrach* who over the centuries have been "Arabized" just as European Jewry has been "Westernized."

> The country is levantine and of course it's only natural. The majority of the population is levantine and just as if one lived in Japan one would become Japanese so when one lives in Israel one comes levantine. Japaneseness will overcome you and you will become Japanese in your food, your dress, your outlook.

Although the use of Japan as a model might be rather unfelicitous, the point being made by this interviewee is that the "locals" hold the keys to the future as it were, and, as he noted, this prospect was not entirely welcome on his part.

Other Ashkenazic departees either directly or indirectly indicated in their majority that levantinization or even large-scale visibility of *edot hamizrach* was disturbing and negative.

> The typical Israeli for me is a black [Sephardi], an animal. The Ashkenazi is weak and is not a typical Israeli who is the opposite of weak: he is strong and you cannot break him.

Lest one think that the above represented a positive though backhanded valuation it should be observed that it was followed by the thought that "Ashkenazim are worth much more than Sephardim. . . . I feel much closer to them."

A number of departees recounted experiences with people from *edot hamizrach* and again one was put in mind of Whites talking about Blacks in the United States or gentiles talking about Jews.

> The Sephardim are doing themselves damage here. They constantly yell discrimination and identify themselves as the poor victims. They are causing a schism in Israeli society.

> I think the Sephardim shout discrimination because it is beneficial for them. Deprivation and discrimination exist in the country, but they are shouting about things *I* am deprived of as well—only *I* don't shout when I'm deprived that it's because I am an Ashkenazic or don't have a pretty face.

"Special privilege" for reputed or real deprivation was widely condemned by most Ashkenazic interviewees. Compensatory programs or acts established to offset reputed discrimination tended to be viewed negatively by almost all Ashkenazic respondees, but also by quite a few from the *edot hamizrach* who saw it as either Ashkenazic patronage or an admission of inferiority or need on the part of Sephardim.

While admitting to some "signs" of prejudice against *edot hamizrach*, very few Ashkenazim with the exception of the few on the left of the political spectrum thought that actual discrimination was practiced. Among some there existed genuine bewilderment; among a larger group there were signs of growing anger over what was considered to be unjustified demands being made (and responded to) by one section of the Jewish population.

> I think that they've blown it [discrimination] bigger than it is. It could be that 20 years ago there really was this problem, but today it seems to me that from every molehill they're making a mountain. For example, you'll say about someone that he is Moroccan and straight away he'll run to the TV and to the papers, what's this discrimination? It's possible that it exists, that people always have a bit of racism toward each other. For example in America toward the blacks, or the Puerto Ricans. In this country it can be toward the Arabs or . . . there are people in the country that have racist feelings with respect to Moroccans, the Iraqis. In my opinion it's not justified, and it shouldn't be like that.

> The army was the place that I saw it least. It's integrated. I was in the artillery, and there, there was everyone, Moroccans, Iraqis, Ashkenazim, and my commander was also of Eastern origin. My battalion commander was a Yemenite and so you see, there was integration, very positive integration, and in my opinion it should be done in the entire State.

> What is a mistake in my opinion is to take an Eastern origin person and on that basis put him in a key position . . . just because of his origins. In my opinion that's a negative move because it makes the other side bitter. Like what they did in America in the universities, when they decided that the blacks should have an advantage over the whites. In this country, someone told me that in the Mechina [college preparatory course], for example, that if there is one place and the competition is between an Ashkenazi and an Eastern origin person . . . the latter will get it, because they're giving the advantage now to the Eastern origin people. In my opinion that's not the best way to do it; everyone should be equal. In my opinion it shouldn't be like that.

As noted earlier, there was a significant body of opinion among Ashkenazic leavers to the effect that the country was becoming "levantinized" and the unmistakable meaning here was as a result Israel was becoming a less desirable place. Some respondees saw things as simply a matter of "our" type of people versus "their" type of people with theirs lowering the quality of life. "They" are "dirty," "criminally inclined," "primitive," "aggressive," "loud," and so on.

Others were less inclined to blanket condemnation or sloganistic stereotyped appraisals but nevertheless arrived more or less at the same point that *edot hamizrach* have introduced a different, "foreign," and less acceptable or desirable dimension to Israeli life. One such respondent was a rather thoughtful student who noted:

> Most of the people who made my life miserable in the army were of Eastern origin. They were the sergeant-majors, the quartermasters, the armorers, the gate-guards, the drivers and what bothers me was the way they related to people—as things, as objects. I accuse the Eastern origin people of introducing a great deal of what's bad in this country. Hard as it is to say . . . it seems to me that values and behaviors were different among the dominant majority in the early days of the State.

The respondent went on to note that time might bring about change in a positive more "cultured" direction but that for the present "they" had turned Israel into a nation of people who "spit sunflower seeds on the street and roll bottles down the aisles of the cinema."

He and many other Ashkenazic respondents of high and low educational attainment, native and immigrant, thought that in one way or another the country was being "taken" from them. People of different habits, background, accent, and sometimes skin were assuming more and more visibility in Israeli life. The familiar East and Central European flavor, which was viewed as autochthonous, is now seen as threatened. The ability to identify fully with the total community, the *yishuv*, the family is seen as being undermined through the introduction of an exotic "otherness," leading to a higher degree of identity with the specific subgroup and a lessened identity with the collectivity.

Not all characterizations of *edot hamizrach* by Ashkenazim are mean-spirited or negative. Any number of respondents commented fondly about "their" warmth, humor, joyousness, and salubriousness. But at the same time it was at all times clear that a breach or tear in the psychoemotional national fabric was being sensed and expressed, again making Israel *into a place more and more like anyplace else.* In America one could expect to feel a sense of insider-outsider, and in Israel one felt such a sense. In America, however, the pattern represented a continuation of a culturally and historically sanctioned—one might almost say sanctified—model. In Israel it signified both a failure and a threat to the vaunted unity of the Jewish people, indeed to the very notion of nationhood.

Caring Too Much

However much certain developments might tend to make Israel a place "more and more like anyplace else," Israelis relate to their state somewhat differently. Perhaps because of the relative newness of the experience of national autonomy or perhaps due to the continuation of a minority syndrome of hoary antiquity there exists among many a sense of inordinate burden or responsibility for any signs of the untoward, unfavorable, or deviant attaching to the national enterprise. It's a burden and responsibility assumed, seemingly in a most reluctant fashion, and shed with a stochastic sense of relief.

It was put best, I think, by the wife of a successful businessman who observed that "the people who leave the country are the people who care too much and the people who care too little." She concluded, with a nervous outburst of laughter, that "the people who are staying are the people in the middle—the normal ones." Needless to add, "normal ones" leave as well, but her emphasizing the factor of intense caring as a strong element in the departees' causative chain was, I believe, very much to the point.

In virtually all the interviews, I was struck by the near unanimity of the response to a simple juxtaposition of two questions. Respondents were asked how they felt about reports of crime and corruption that they were invariably treated to by the Israeli press and media. Responses were predictable (who after all is in favor of crime and corruption?), but what was less predictable was the veritable hand wringing (literal rather than figurative as often as not), the expressions of pain and disappointment, and the cries of "what have we come to?" that accompanied their comments. Respondents were then asked to project how they *think* they would react to press reports of crime and corruption in America if they had not yet put in any serious time there or how they *did* react if they had already been there in the past. Again there was near unanimity, with the thrust being "Here I care—there I couldn't care less." (The one caveat noted by more than two-thirds of the respondents was "unless it concerns me personally in which case I do care there as well.) Person after person noted the fact that they viewed a key social variable quite differently when seen in terms of "mine" and what must ultimately be considered "theirs."

> When I read about crime here it disturbs me greatly. This didn't happen in Iraq. That sort of thing was the business of the *goyim*.

I think the fact that we have murder here—that one Jew kills another is even worse than *yerida*. If I see it in America, however, it won't concern me particularly.

It [crime] bothers me here. It stands out . . . reading about it, hearing about it. When I was there [Boston] and I read or heard about awful things like murders I didn't really care, but when I heard something bad happened in Israel I jumped and right away ran off to get more details.

Corruption in other places I don't care about—it's not mine and I'm not part of it.

I don't know if corruption exists in places other than Israel—I haven't interested myself in the problem. But here things are threaded with it.

These are a small but representative sample of the tone of responses received. A higher number of respondents asked, "How could Jews do this or behave in such and such a fashion?" Strongly indicated was the thought that if this be "normalcy" we want nothing to do with it. A few thought that this reflected an "overconcern" on the part of Israelis for what in fact exists among all people.

We have hot blood. Others operate on much lower temperatures than the Jews. Everything concerns us. We take everything to heart—what happens in Tel Aviv or Nahariya. In America I doubt whether a New Yorker cares about what happens in Los Angeles.

For most, however, the fact that life might have gone sour in Israel or that a degree of rot had infused itself into the body social was decidedly *not* seen as overconcern or a result of "hot blood." It was seen rather as a sign of the onerousness of sovereignty, the burden of a normalcy that was in some deep sense probably not being sought at all. As noted earlier in the present work, the embracing warmth of a marginal existence that allows for the growth and development of a comforting feeling of "us" and "them" was, for many among the leavers, being resought in the *galut*. There is in this seeking a strong skein of irresponsibility or more precisely a desire to shirk off an overburdening sense of responsibility for that which inevitably must emerge from a "normal" context bearing a "normal" distribution of deviance as well as achievement. The abnormal context of *galut* allows—indeed stimulates—the emergence of characteristics traditionally associated with Jewish marginality that enjoy, it would appear, a much more comfortable fit than the full distribution associated with normalcy.

Jewish *galut* culture had sunk into its very pores the notion that police, violence, force, and brute power were the devices of "them" and were negatively valued. Assuming responsibility for not only exercising these sanctions but also finding it necessary to do so is or has not yet been so easily assimilated among large numbers of Israelis.

> I prefer taking [eating] shit from non-Jews. From Jews it bothers me. When Jewish kids took an eye out of a Jewish kid at our local high school—I said if it was *goyim*—I could take it. I haven't made peace with Jewish deviance— whores, thieves, murderers. If we are just people like any other—then I can live more comfortably elsewhere. Maybe there are one-half million of us [Israelis] in America because they came to the conclusion that we are just people like any other.

People like any other—but not really in the sense that for numerous Israelis the achievment of normalcy presages, legitimizes a return to the true status of the other, the stranger, the dweller on the margins or fringes. Is this indeed a picture of a people like any other or rather one of a peculiar and historically validated Jewish provenance?

Israeli sovereignty has, it can be asserted, given rise to a peculiar social pathology of overidentity that leads ironically to full unravelment of national-communal ties. "I feel that when anybody in Israel is murdered, or assaulted, or is in some way attacked—that a part of me has undergone the same treatment." The person added: "In America these things would bother me—but not personally." In Israel overidentity can and does contribute to a decision to cut oneself off from what in the long run is viewed as a heavier burden than many are willing to bear.

But how does one deal with "Jewish deviance" in the *galut*? There too history and experience if not common sense teach that Jews like other mortals are not uniformly of angelic mien and disposition. Simply, in the Diaspora almost all forms of Stygian bleakness, of social disorder can be obscured by sheer numbers and absorbed within the protective coloration of a marginal in-group existence.

> I worry for Israel! I worry because when you have upset, disorder, crime here it is twice as hard to recover as it is in the States. Because there it is big, it is established, it can absorb better—whereas Israel cannot absorb having its foundations shaken.
>
> America can afford corruption. She is big. Here we can't given our size and situation.

The "situation" is two-pronged: there we are threatened and must be strong in order to meet the threat and cannot afford a weakening of the social fabric; here we are on stage for ourselves and for others.

> I'll tell you—in 1978 I visited the FBI building in Washington and there we were told that a murder or some other crime takes place every 20 seconds in

America. It's part of their life, it's normal: 230 million people so that a million or so who deviate can be absorbed. Here it is different, much smaller; everything that happens here affects us. Here it's *us* not statistics.

In the end it comes down to this: Individual deviance in the marginal context can be attributed to sui generis factors and, more importantly, tends to have individual repercussions. Thus a Jewish thief may bring a modicum of dishonor to the word Jew but does not represent an organized mass known as Jewry when he acts. In some curious (and admittedly unjustified) sense, however, a collectivity is seen to be pilloried when such and such exists in the Jewish state. Everything tends to be done "in my name," whether it be politics, art, or crime. One can see an operative element of being hoisted on one's own pitard in the sense that a dominant Zionist point of view, a prominent element in the Israeli formal socialization process, is the notion that Israel is not only the center of the Jewish world, but represents as well the Jewish people wherever they are. This in effect was the underlying justification of the Eichmann trial and it would appear that whatever positive national aims may be associated with it, it has its decidedly counterproductive dimensions as well. It would seem that the implied burden of such a contention, is, at least for a goodly number, more than can easily be borne.

> It's hard for me to think about Arik Sharon, and Green Patrols, and Flatto-Sharon, and all the lies. It's easier for me to take on tens of millions of Americans where even if a few million are out and out fascists there are enough of the others. There is redress there and you feel it.

The speaker was associated with the radical left in Israel but even in this case a long and often moving jeremiad about the parlous state of Israel was concluded with: "Not in my name; I don't want these things in my name."

That the world is stained and blemished can be dealt with. That Israel can be so afflicted is more than many can bear.

Notes

1. Use of the term may serve an additional function that should not be lost sight of. If one says he is leaving to change his life or to improve his life the implication is of finality, permanence. One is leaving for "greener pastures," better opportunities, and so on. Use of the term *l'hitavrer*, on the other hand, suggests a therapeutic goal, which once achieved can allow for the return of the patient to his familiar surroundings reinforced, renewed, and presumably recommitted.
2. In the interview the terms *lachatz* and *metach* were used interchangeably by respondents. *Metach* is closer to tension and *lachatz* (pressure) closer to stress

in a technical sense but it was at all times clear that respondents were not distinguishing between the two. Thus, the two words will be herein used interchangeably following the usage in the interviews.

3. Two informants who had visited Egypt noted the Egyptians, who lived in a hotter climate than Israels' and who had much more to be nervous about, were on the whole kinder and more helpful to one another and to strangers than was the case in Israel.

4. As an example of how "one can't win," note the comment of a Russian *yored* who found behavior in Israel (in certain respects at least) a bit too civilized and thought correction was in order: "There is too much freedom here. You get away with murder here. If someone kills somebody you sentence him to a few years in prison and give him a color TV and then cut the sentence when it turns out that he was crazy. In that case you should kill him twice. You should kill him like a dog. In Russia there is no murder! Why? Are people better there? No—it is because they are afraid. You need some fear for the sake of order."

5. Sobel (1974: 82–84) discusses the phenomenon of short-circuiting as it relates to religious conversion.

6. I am aware of only one instance where one of the noted "deficiencies" was protested and this was an environmental issue wherein hundreds of citizens attempted to prevent the continued and progressive scarring of Mt. Carmel in order to provide gravel for the local cement factory. With this one exception (and perhaps some others of which I am unaware), Israelis show a remarkable proclivity for "making do" with whatever the political and governmental structure sets before them. Demonstrations about purely political (mostly foreign policy) or peace-related issues do take place, however, with a fair and growing degree of regularity.

7. It is not accidental or without significance that a rather well-known and oft-used action expletive used in Israel is *zbeng-gamarnu*, which freely translated means "one blow and it's all over." It suggests above all a need or tendency to take immediate action of a drastic kind in problem solving rather than lay the slow, deliberate, and systematic groundwork for achieving one's ends.

8. But even here one must enter a cautionary caveat. Differences in this respect were visible depending on whether the individual leaver was native born or an immigrant, and further whether from a Western European or American background or elsewhere. When bothered, native-born Israelis interviewed seemed to be disturbed by personalities—Begin, Peres, Rabin, etc., or by certain policies with which they disagreed. Western-born immigrants, on the other hand, seemed less concerned by personalities and were more disturbed by the aforementioned factor of unresponsiveness of the political mechanism and a feeling of nonrepresentation. In addition, they tended to be largely concerned with the possibility of bringing about change. This represents a weighting rather than an absolute cleavage so that Westerners were in many cases bothered by issues of personality and native-born Israelis by issues of unresponsiveness and the absence of the possibility of change.

9. For additional material on the factor of religion in Israeli society consult the general bibliography. Special note should be taken of Abramov (1976), Aviad (1983), Birnbaum (1970), and Liebman and Don-Yehiya (1983).

10. It would appear that the contention of so many among the observant and religiously Orthodox that they do not leave Israel, that they are not highly visible among *yordim*, is correct. Less than 10 percent of my sample were

visibly Orthodox although a considerable number claimed to be traditional in outlook and practice. It should, however, be noted that a very high proportion of those who refused to be interviewed were Orthodox. In addition, it must be emphasized that Jerusalem with its very heavy concentration of Orthodox Jews was not included in the present sample.

11. For additional material on Arabs in Israeli society consult the general bibliography. Special note should be taken of Hareven (1983), Jiryis (1974), Landau (1969), Lustick (1980), and Smoocha (1980).

12. There were three others who could point to at least one personalized (rather than personal) relationship with an Arab fellow citizen—one as a student and two in a work situation.

13. For further and systematic discussions of intracommunal tension among Jews in Israel see Ben Rafael (1982), Breznitz (1983), Deshen and Shokeid (1974), Geffner (1972), and Inbar and Adler (1977). For additional references consult the general bibliography.

14. Educated opinion suggests a much higher rate among departees than showed up in our sample. It might be that a higher proportion of young and the "illegals" is drawn from this section of the population.

15. Interestingly, the only other departees to suggest or hint that this was a key element in their decision were three additional couples who refused to be interviewed but did in the course of my attempt at convincing them make it quite plain that they were feeling a sense of second-class status. Two were of Iraqi origin and one of Moroccan origin.

16. This fell to one seat in the elections for the Eleventh Knesset in 1984, but this should not be interpreted to mean a lessening of ethnic consciousness inasmuch as other political configurations tended to take up the slack with a decidedly "ethnic" appeal. For example, a Sephardi religious party—Shas—won four seats in its first political outing in addition to the one seat retained by Tami.

17. It has been suggested that at least one reason for the seeming prominence of *edot hamizrach* among the more "hawkish" political constellations is related to the above factor.

4

America, America

*Migration on the part of an individual . . . reflects an
expectation that the individual will be better off at the
point of destination than at the point of provenance.*

—Spengler and Myers (1977:14)

The Magic Pull of America

The above quote represents an unarguable position assuming of course
that there is some understanding of what is meant when one says "better
off." But the term is sufficiently vague and no doubt intentionally subjective as to be somewhat all inclusive. Thus one can *be* better off in an
objective economic sense by earning more, having more, or being physically safer. One can *feel* better off in the sense of having a closer cultural
identity to the new society than was experienced with the old, a heightened
sense of economic security, a broader canvas for a wide range of individual
and group expression, a sense of inner peace and satisfaction, or on the
other hand a need for excitement and challenge.

The key word here is "expectation." Nobody leaves his home, his place,
his familiar surroundings—no matter how aware he may or may not be of
alternatives—unless he expects improvements in his situation.

For the tens of thousands of Israelis who have left for other countries, it is
clear that a two-fold interrelated process of push-pull is operative. On the
one hand there is far-ranging dissatisfaction on many levels with Israel and
Israeli society; on the other hand are the glittering prizes of other lands—
mostly America—beckoning with a multihued siren call of seductive
promise.

For some it is the lure of wealth and material ease. For others it is one of
expanded horizons and opportunities—artistic, cultural, educational, and
economic. Some are seeking a measure of anonymity that is felt to be
difficult to obtain in a tiny country. Others want to throw off constraints of

ethnicity, class, or even family. Some are pursuing a clouded grail wherein a true testing of one's mettle can only be undertaken on the "serious" canvas of *chutz la'aretz* rather than within the narrow, unchallenging confines of their tiny homeland. For a few it is escape—of all kinds; for others the call of adventure predominates, underscored by an overarching feeling that one owes it to oneself "to at least try."

Some leave because they never felt quite right in their skins as Israelis, and never fully identified with the national enterprise. Others leave from an *excess* of identity and a corresponding inability to deal with the blemishes of ordinary existence in the Jewish State.

Some go because in the long run Israel feels unsafe and endangered, and America promises stability and a modicum of security. For others, the lure is the relative lack of stress, the well-oiled functioning of societal mechanisms in the United States, as opposed to the constant struggle that Israel is perceived as demanding.

A few go because some significant other in their cosmos has gone before, while others because somehow or other moving to America does not really feel like emigrating at all: "What's the difference whether I live in Tel Aviv or New York? I'll always be an Israeli."

Whatever the range of "push" factors bringing one to make the decision to leave Israel, whatever the depth (or surfaceness) of dissatisfaction with life in Israel, the "pull" of America retains its historical efficacy and strength.

America might suffer riots in the streets of its cities, racial tensions,the existence of inordinate rates of crime and violence, the blight of urban areas, the decay of the countryside, ecological threats of mind-boggling proportions, high rates of unemployment—and still for the overwhelming proportion of departees it remains what it had previously been in the dreams of their parents and grandparents from Vilna to Istanbul—the Golden Land. America might be involved in war and will be perceived as a land of peace and security. There might be millions of unemployed but it is seen as the land of "endless opportunity." It might objectively demonstrate all the hallmarks of a hierarchically structured class society and will be perceived as either classless or at least endlessly fluid and open-ended. Its cities might be run by corrupt politicians and bored bureaucrats, but they are celebrated as "straight" and, above all, efficient. Large numbers among the poor and the elderly might suffer from want and deprivation ranging from food to medical care and the song of sufficiency will be heard far and wide.

As noted earlier, America must be viewed as a most successful purveyor of its own national myths. But it is clearly more than that—much more. The myth of voluptuous America is buttressed and sustained because in whatever dimension the myth might come short of "truth" it is at least in equal measure "true" and apprehendable as such by sufficient numbers to give it substance and life.

In almost all the interviews America seems to emerge as a "winner" in the sense that no matter what the topic—good or bad—the response seems to be *dayenu* (that's all right, that's good too). A perfect example was provided by a previously quoted newspaper reporter who observed that "America is still a country of fluid lines. You can rise above your class." When it was pointed out to him that many fell as well as rose, his immediate response was "that's good too." He went on to note that the positive part of the whole process was that elemental justice underlay the system as a whole: one achieves, one succeeds if one works hard; one fails in the absence of sufficient effort. On the other hand, in Israel the relationship between achievement and effort was at best clouded. America is thus seen as a corrective, a sort of social or historical gyroscope whose function or "mission" is to set the world back on course.

Curiously, and in an inordinately large proportion of interviews, Israel was seen as "class bound" and America as equalitarian. How does one explain a development of this kind in a social matrix that had achieved world attention as an exemplar of classlessness and equalitarianism? One might conclude that either it just never was the case, that radical change has ensued, or that some other process was at work. I am inclined to the latter choice, which has something to do with the assertion that Jews have traditionally made poor service employees (waiters, maids, etc.), which in turn has something to do with a historical reluctance to have one Jew set himself (or be set) above another. Hierarchy and authority seem to be constantly problematic in Israel wherein serious reservations come to the fore with respect to why "Chaim" should lord it over "Berel." Waiters would prefer to be clients, soldiers as often as not have to be enticed into acquiescence by officers, and certain types of employment actually get "shame increments" in salary.

America allows for two correctives to this situation: it is big enough and diffuse enough to "hide" the performer of socially inferior tasks, and it provides a historically familiar opportunity for a pariah structure wherein Jews tend to occupy certain more elevated struts of the socioeconomic ladder. *Goyim* are the hewers of wood and drawers of water in America!

The same "tight little ship" dimension of Israel and its obverse in the spread and anonymity of America plus the insistence on parity among Jews operates on still another level. Israel has in recent years and with particular urgency since the Six-Day War experienced an explosion of economic growth, rising standards of living, heightened expectations, and their handmaiden conspicuous consumption. With growing social and economic distinctions have come a growth in what might archaically be referred to as "jealousy." Jealousy with respect to what one's neighbor has achieved in Israel and jealousy over the apparent "ease" with which one's neighbor has succeeded in America.

> We see what others who went before us have accomplished while we here were struggling to buy an apartment.

> I don't know where the money comes from. This is a poor country full of rich people. I worked as a bookkeeper in a car agency. People would come in and slap down hundreds of thousands of shekels in cash. The country is full of thieves!

> I accept the present balance in the State as being between capitalism and socialism. What I can't stand and can't accept are all the *nouveau riche* who have been created by war and inflation.

In a society that has witnessed the growth of conspicuous consumption and the elevation of materialism to an almost ultimate value there must inevitably arise strong distinctions and those with a sense of being left behind. Visible wealth and almost vulgar consumption on the part of so many inevitably brings in its wake strong feelings of envy and a powerful desire to join the process. Israel, in this context, appears to be and *is* less promising an arena for success than is America: "Israel is small—America is big." This was repeated almost as a mantra by dozens of departees with, in the case of many, an interesting addendum that "Jews can be successful among *goyim*." The implication of course is that Jews cannot compete successfully among themselves if for no other reason than that competition presupposes losers as well as winners. As noted earlier, wealth as such did not seem so much the target of most as did a desire to either "outdo" significant others in one's firmament, to escape shame for one's inability to do so at home, or at least to achieve what was thought to be a degree of parity.

Again (and most strongly) America was viewed in terms where this kind of social pressure and even social distinctions did not apply.

> I'm impressed with America! There is equality there. The billionaire across the street buys in the same supermarket with the same dollar that I do. Here, the guy across the street from my shop—he has four shops—he doesn't buy where I buy or live where I live.

Absurd though the above might be on purely objective grounds, its subjective view of reality is what demands our attention. Israel is viewed as class bound and hierarchically structured while America is seen as a sort of equalitarian utopia. A partial answer to this dilemma might be suggested in an additional comment from the informant.

> Here, everybody has an apartment [that is, owns an apartment] but me and a few others. We're jealous and unhappy. There, most people rent apartments so I'm just like everybody else: I'm equal.

Somehow, the American system is seen as being able (or desirous) of camouflaging social distinctions wherein Israel appears bent on exaggerating them. But more importantly, I think, is the silent distinction made between competing at home and competing among the gentiles. In Israel, defeat is experienced as total and systemic; there it is episodic and correctable. In Israel, perceived failure results in shame; there the result is anxiety at worst, which as often as not serves as a goad and a stimulus to heightened effort.

While America is universally viewed as the very epitome of contemporary capitalist endeavor and laissez-faire economic organization where one might expect a fairly circumscribed role for concepts of social justice, it is social democratic and welfare-oriented Israel that is seen as rapacious, unfair, and lacking in this regard.

Kibbutzniks informed the interviewer about the shoddy competitiveness of the kibbutz and its exploitative attitudes toward hired workers. This was highlighted in the following comment, which was *not* unique:

> The kibbutz movement causes monopolies. They organize everything as a cooperative and then don't let outsiders in except as laborers, in which case they can't advance at all. People who live in surrounding areas can't rise because the kibbutz needs them as laborers—and they don't hesitate to use their considerable political influence to make sure that things stay the way they are. They become aware of nonkibbutz families only at election time when they enter the towns to try to convince the laborers to vote labor.

This exhibits dissatisfaction on the part of a person pulling up stakes without doubt—but it is a view widely shared. Departees followed observations of the above kind with thoughts about greater fairness in America or at the very least "a lack of hypocrisy about individual interests."

This theme of "national hypocrisy" and the absence of fairness was noted by a large number of interviewees. America comes through as a rough, tough potential cornucopia that rewards effort, while Israel is seen at best as a disappointment and at worst as fraudulent.

> There's a type of usurpation of the term "worker" [in Israel]. Middle class merchants consider themselves workers. This is basically a bolshevik country or as Mair Pail put it, the founding fathers really had a bolshevik mother.

Israel also does not fare well on the practical level in comparison with the United States.

> Here, people don't have anything. They work at a job without meaning, or the money they earn is not money, or conditions aren't conditions. Here, they don't pay for the work that is done. Look what happened at the Negev airfields built by the Americans. Israelis and Americans worked side by side in the same job and the Israelis got 60,000 lira a month while the Americans earned thousands of dollars. Is that fair? The Americans take care of their people.

A large number of informants expressed frustration over the felt lack of return for effort and endeavor in Israel. Israel and work in Israel just did not pay off. In a conversation with one departing couple the interviewer posited the observation that he too could earn more abroad whereupon the wife in a rather poignant fashion noted:

> You said you could earn so much more in America than you do here. But that is not the point. It could be that while that is true you still earn *enough* here while we don't and can't hope to. I am talking about a man who works twelve hours a day and works holidays, and works sabbaths and has no time to spend with his family. He works without profit! It's not the work—its the lack of return on investment.

The hope and belief in a direct, linear relationship between effort and reward in America is almost classic in its dimensions as noted and observed by dozens of departees. The American dream is alive and well—in Israel. Numerous stay-at-home Israelis have asked, "How do you explain Israelis who go to America and pump gas, wash dishes, or drive cabs while they would not consider for a moment doing the same here?" How does one explain departees who blithely noted that: "I don't expect my apartment in America to be as nice as this one. I know it will be hard. At the beginning I will go down in living standards in America"?

One can explain this only in the classic configuration of America as an open-ended cornucopia of opportunity that rewards effort. "At the beginning" implies "as a temporary measure," but surely not a permanent fixing in what is endlessly viewed as a demanding but just framework.

> We work harder and longer in the U.S. and at things we wouldn't do in Israel.

> Work here and work in America is totally different. Here you *come* to work. There you *work*.

The last quote was followed by the observation that "the difference is that all Jews think of themselves as kings. In the U.S. the shoe must fit the foot.

If you are fitted for a job you fill it. Here if the shoe doesn't fit, we stuff paper into the shoe to make it fit."

Somehow, it is thought that if one pumps gas or washes dishes in Israel, this is likely to assume permanence and will not be merely a way station on the climb upwards. This, more than any presumed reluctance of Jews to perform menial tasks "at home," serves to explain the seemingly perplexing dilemma painfully observed by many Israelis.

But America does not just "pay off": America *demands* as well. Performance is expected and the shoddy and the slipshod will not only be unrewarded but rejected as well. Critical faculties with respect to America seem to be largely suspended by emigrants who see efficiency, hard work, a fair reward structure, discipline, and numerous other virtues as being vibrant and operative. Though Americans might bewail the decline of virtues generally ascribed to the Protestant Ethic, apotheosizing in the process new standard bearers such as the Japanese and Singaporans, Israeli *yordim* see only a garden of delight. Comparisons are constantly drawn as between Israel and America in terms of work, discipline and efficiency with somewhat predictable results.

> Nobody cares! Nobody gives a damn. The workers are undisciplined. *Kviut* [tenure] is the worst enemy of the country. In the U.S. if you don't perform you are fired. Here if you don't perform they will find you an easier job where you can cause more damage.

> Why does it pay to perform well when you are rewarded for doing bad or doing nothing for that matter? Could a situation like this exist in America or any other civilized country for even one day?

A seeming contradiction appears here where on the one hand many leavers had previously excoriated an atmosphere of pressure and stress that they felt to be characteristic of life in Israel, and on the other hand bemoaned the "easygoing" nature of the enterprise that leads to sloth, inefficiency and unproductivity. "The Israeli" it is widely felt "does not earn his daily bread," and a prime cause or reason for this situation is reputed to be the aforementioned lack of "pay off" and the absence of pressure that makes one perform to a respectable norm. It is felt that "anything goes in Israel" and by contrast America is held up as a paradigm of quality and efficiency. Thus pressure—in this case pressure to perform—in America is good and positive, while pressure in Israel is not so favorably viewed. Pressure in Israel in whatever form or context is viewed as an imposition and a threat while in other places one is able to make distinctions and even see certain positive results. The same informant who condemned a certain "heaviness" in the atmosphere of Israel noted with clear approval the fact that workers in America (or at least in one factory that he visited) "have to prove themselves every day. Everyday anew. Here you don't have that. Here if you don't feel like working one day no one will fire you." The same informant—an otherwise rather thoughtful and liberal individual—observed (again with apparent approval) that in the factory he visited, "workers were afraid to lift up their heads in the presence of the boss." America is viewed as putting the fear of God into people, which results in great economic power, superb efficiency, and high quality.

Mr. H., a former American and convert to Judaism returning to the United States, put the matter thusly:

H: They work like hell in the States, because they get paid. I went to the worst factory I've ever worked in and the highest paid before I came here. They took raw hides and striped the hair off—dirty work. These guys they worked and they worked hard; they worked as many hours as they could and as long as they could and they only took their 15-minute breaks and their half-hour lunch breaks. Here they really play games, they come when they want, they leave when they want. When they come they work hard. But they don't work hard for very long, they'll take off.

I: Take off, you mean leave?

H: No, they'll stay, it's a real game how much work you can get away from. It's how much you don't have to do during a day; where I was working that's the way it was. . . . Here in the factory, it's a textile factory . . . I think that the work ethnic is bad, and I know the country can't afford it. These people need some sort of pride in what they're producing. There are so many products that I've been using, where the quality control, is terrible. Just an example—when you go and buy vanilla flavored ice cream one week, and you go to buy the same flavor the next week, it'll be cherry, or you'll have a banana flavor box with cherry on the inside; this sort of crazy thing. I guess ice cream doesn't really matter, but what matters is the export goods. It gives the country a lousy name. . . . They don't give it their all, because they're frustrated.

America represents not only "pay off," efficiency, and promise of fair return on investment but also opportunity. Opportunity in all areas—economics, social, educational, and artistic.

A fair proportion of our sample first went to America or decided to go because of various educational opportunities—either to complete graduate education or to specialize in an area not available in Israel, or to overcome the barriers of poor grades or lack of matriculation. Sophisticated and knowledgeable young Israelis are perfectly well aware that "somewhere" in that vast and forgiving land, a college, a university will be found to accept even the least promising of scholars. The American "system" is known as one where the "rigidities" of the Israeli system can be overcome. Technicians with the equivalent of two years toward an engineering degree in America cannot negotiate similar credit at Israeli institutions where they are expected to begin essentially from the beginning—if accepted at all. In Israel a technician is thought to be a technician because he did not have the talents of an accredited engineer. In the United States it tends to be viewed as an interrupted or incompleted process that can be dealt with rather than an uncorrectable act of providence. Lack of the matriculation (*bagrut*) in Israel can effectively prevent people from pursuing higher education without first undergoing a rather arduous make-up year (*mechina*) or sitting for the matriculation as an external student. In either case it is a considerably more difficult and lengthy a process than what is possible in so many places in the United States, where even those who have not completed 12 years of education can in some places and under certain circumstances be accepted at an institution of higher education. All of these possibilities, as noted above, are well understood and widely known among Israelis who see as standing between themselves and a higher degree only the price of an air ticket and a bit of initiative.

In terms of cultural opportunities here too we have commented under the "push" category in noting the difficulties innate to a small country. Clearly the opposite applies for America, which not only provides size and scope but in addition is viewed as the cultural arbiter of the Western world in numerous areas ranging from the pop to the high brow. Most informants stated their satisfaction with cultural opportunities in Israel but for about 20 percent (including *all* professionally involved in the arts) Israel was viewed as a veritable wasteland and America a Mecca. The latter group tended to excoriate Israel in terms of lack of indigenous cultural creativity and no little Philistinism.

> All cultural expression in Israel is based on war. Music, art—everything since the creation of the State is tied to war. If it is not war—it is a cheap imitation of America.

> One of the things I find very difficult in Israel is that there aren't many opportunities to play, to have a good time. There is too little high and middle culture—theater, cinema. There is very little being created and although it's improving (there are actually a couple of Israeli films now which I want to see) it's not New York, it's not San Francisco where you can just pick up a newspaper and find something you want, or that's interesting. Here, much of what is available is insulting.

Israel's leavers tend to talk and think about America in terms similar to those utilized by rural dwellers in America who are attracted by the bright lights of Broadway. Israelis, especially those with specific cultural needs or aspirations, do not so much emigrate to America as they do to New York,

Los Angeles, San Francisco, and a few other centers. In talking with them about these places as often as not an almost worshipful, even religious attitude predominates. Evidence is proffered suggesting no less familiarity with what are currently the "in" plays or most "provocative" shows in New York as in Tel Aviv. Street names and neighborhood names are "dropped" indicating intimate familiarity with "the city." "Making it" in America, or more particularly New York, is really to make it, while success in little Tel Aviv is somehow seen as marking time, as essentially preparatory. One must presume that seeing in New York a sort of cultural *Haupstadt* (capital) is not limited to Israelis. In the arts, New York is and does serve as an international magnet. My sense is that what distinguishes the Israelis from others in this regard is the tendency of Israelis to view America as not so much an "other" but as an extension of Israel. One does not so much emigrate to or leave for New York as one graduates to it.

Whatever the case might be for those emigrants with cultural needs or cultural aspirations that go beyond what is possible in a small or medium-sized country, America serves as a magnet and a goal. Most departees expressed satisfaction with Israel in this respect but for the minority who could not satisfy their needs in Israel, America was clearly the alternative of logic and choice.

While not complaining in large numbers about the absence or quality of culture as such, there is a lingering sense among many that they are "missing out on the action." "Big things" happen in New York or in America generally; little things, marginal things take place in Israel. One leaver after noting that "I don't think we are living in a cultural desert" added "but that doesn't mean that it's the end of the road, that everything is O.K." The tone of response of many *yordim* with respect to how they viewed cultural life in Israel as opposed to the United States puts one in mind of people who insist upon living in suburbs near to major urban centers even though they rarely use the facilities provided in these centers—"It's nice to know it's there and available to me if I should want it."

While comparatively few *yordim* were attracted by the existence of cultural opportunity and scope, this was not the case with respect to economic opportunity. This was viewed not in the narrower dimension of a more promising stage upon which to become wealthy (who after all does not have some fantasies along these lines) but in terms of breadth and depth, and dimensions that appear to many Israelis coming out of tiny Israel nothing short of breathtaking. Almost all interviewees in one way or another arrived at the (obvious) conclusion that "Israel is small—America is big." Two young brothers, who by their own assertion "lacked for nothing in Israel" and who in fact are leaving behind a thriving import-export firm that will be run by their father, added still another dimension to the opportunity variable. They observed that for political reasons (the Arab boycott) businessmen suffered from insurmountable restrictions in Israel that could be overcome (and then some) in the United States. America, they asserted, had unlimited horizons for energetic businessmen, whereas Israel by its very nature spelled limitation—if not by its small dimensions, then because of political, structural, or historical circumstances. These young businessmen repeated a statement heard from a fairly large proportion of departees to the effect that they were not really *yordim*. They were "creating export potential." Every interviewee who was involved or aspired to become involved in a business enterprise extolled the glories and possibilities of America. "In America," I was told over and over again, "business is not a dirty word and the government wants you to succeed." Markets are unlimited, taxes are low, financing is readily available, stability is assured, inventiveness is rewarded, and labor is disciplined. With respect to all of the above, it is felt that the obverse is true in Israel.

America is viewed as an arena for "the second chance" as no other place in the world. America is the place where three poor brothers of Moroccan origin can build an empire based on blue jeans (Jordache), a simple school teacher who could not make it at home became a multimillionaire (Riklis of Rapid American), or an immigrant from Iraq can become an arbiter of fashion (Sasson). If these heights prove too steep to assimilate, let alone fantasize about, numerous examples known to everybody can be adduced of X who could not finish the month on his salary in Israel who now owns three cars and flies "back" every summer, or Y who failed at everything but now owns a modest enterprise in Los Angeles, or W who is nearly illiterate but owns a prosperous garage in Chicago. Other examples can be found of prosperous doctors in America who worked in clinics in Israel, or holders of chairs and full professorships who failed to win tenure back home.

Almost without exception, all the interviewees were fully armed with examples similar to the above whose major thrust was that America is synonymous with possibilities. Failure, or lack of success "here" (Israel) does not define or delimit one in terms of "there" (the United States). A page can be turned, a new beginning can be undertaken in America with almost no limitations. One interviewee was a 23-year-old man who was going to join his parents, who had emigrated in order to join their eldest son who had left a decade earlier. He recounted the fact that his parents were doing well economically (they owned a grocery or as he defined it a "mini-market"), knew only Hebrew, and were in their late fifties when they decided to pick up stakes and leave for the New World. Why do two people—who own their apartment outright, own a functioning and reasonably profitable business, speak only Hebrew, have relatives in and strong ties to Israel, and are in addition approaching retirement age—decide to sell everything, pick up stakes, and go off to America to a situation where the woman works as a waitress in a cafeteria and the man (as the son tells it) "putters about" helping his elder son in his business. The answer received was, "All in all my parents are doing OK in America. They lack for nothing and they have succeeded in changing their atmosphere."

What is meant by changing one's atmosphere? Why could the change not be brought about in some less drastic context than that of emigration? One reason is that the very act of emigration is denied, especially when the move is to America, which is seen somehow as an extension of Israel—a sort of Western extremity of the Jewish State. Another reason was brought forth from the departee when he noted, "My father simply decided that he wanted a new chapter in his life." There exists no better canvas for the unfolding of new chapters in one's life—at whatever stage—than the United States. They often have no common language or familiarity with the culture, the people, or the structure—but they believe a "new chapter" or new beginning to one's life can be had there as nowhere else on the globe.[1]

Could it be that the lack of knowledge of the language and culture is viewed differently by *yordim* than by stay-at-homes? Is it possible that in fact the anonymity suggested by the above is seen as a positive value rather than a negative price to be paid by the emigrant seeking other rewards?

Anonymity—indeed a measure of isolation—promises a measure of freedom. As noted earlier, a great number of departees are in pursuit of "not caring," of not being involved, of living their own lives at their own pace. America for these seekers is a veritable paradise of not only new beginnings, but endless ones as well. "What do you think about Israelis who end up as cab drivers in America?"

> It's a pleasure to be a cab driver in America. You see ready cash and you can get to be independent fast and you can live well. Can a cab driver do that here? There is everything in America, everything. There are no limits. The United States is the embodiment of the word "country." Any Israeli who could get to America, who could overcome his fear would go in a moment.

No matter how high the praises sung of driving a cab in America, what could have been added was the implied factor of anonymity—simply the fact that one could engage in all sorts of low-status occupations without anybody knowing about it.

America is variety. There are all kinds of people from all sorts of places beginning their lives anew on a level of parity. The Israeli is not unique, not alone. The spotlight of history is removed from him. "I'll always prefer Jews to anyone else but the Americans have something deeper. They have more layers of depth which comes from their tremendous variety. Here we blend in."

"America is easier." "America is calmer." "America is cleaner." When comparisons are drawn with Israel in these respects Israel invariably emerges second best. "Not that here it is harder but that there it is easier."

> The dirt, the pushing, the shoving, the shouting—all of this is Israel and it bothers me. . . . They have it there [America], too, but there I don't feel as if I belong so it doesn't bother me.

> I don't think there is so much "push" pushing people out of Israel as there is "pull" or a magnet drawing them to the West—mostly to America. The bad things in Israel become really visible only after you have experienced something else. When I come back to Israel I see the place as really primitive.

Thus, America is seen as expansive, open, receptive, in terms of a new beginning, in terms of release from social pressure, in terms of a social mix and structure assuring parity, and in other ways as well. It is simply run better. It is the vanguard of change in all areas of endeavor. It is a place of bigness, of opulence, of safety, and of stability. "In Israel, nobody knows what tomorrow will bring. Here, people worry about what will happen in the State, and about the economic situation."

America promises as well a modicum of release from what is viewed as ceaseless struggle, a guardedness in one's behavior. It is a place that affords a sense of peace and redress, as evidenced in this interview with Mr. L.:

L: I don't think people are leaving the country to go someplace else and fight, they're leaving Israel so that they don't have to fight.

I: Why does it seem such a ready option here, and not in many other countries?

L: I don't think that it's such a ready option at all, it's very hard to leave this place. For all kinds of reasons; its very hard economically, when you start translating what you have into dollars, or sterling, or whatever you're translating into. It's not an easy thing, it's much easier to come here than leave. But I think that emotionally it's extremely hard, people see it as a weak act to leave the country, the people that I know who have left have had to gather all their resources.

I: Emotionally?

L: Emotionally. Economically, every possible way in order to get out, to make that move.

I: You're indicating or suggesting that it's almost an act of desperation?

L: Well, it's also. . . . Well, I can only talk about myself. I am going in order to, to *renew* my life which is sort of going downhill. And I suspect that that's a lot of what other people are doing, some people are obviously leaving to make a better living, economically, but I don't know about that. People who are leaving for more spiritual reasons want a larger world, one that's a bit more welcoming and they have a desire to do so, whether it's professional, political, or artistic, whatever it is. Without a sense here of opportunities, you seem to start undoing, to start fighting some of the things that are plaguing the society. It's not just organizing a neighborhood group, have a little protest and get an ordinance changed, that's not what's going on; what's required is a resocialization of major proportions! [small laugh] I don't think that people have any sense of the possibility here of this kind (at this time). They are tired!

Here one finds the life of struggle, of conflict where the challenges appear so enormous as to bring about discouragement and a desire to depart the field of battle. Every interview was replete with at least one personal tale of woe in this respect.

America is viewed as a place of freedom but not, it would appear, in the traditional sense of political and religious freedom. In this regard, Israelis do not feel particularly deprived. Freedom for the fairly high proportion of *yordim* who commented was more a function of that spirit of expansiveness, of unlimited and unbounded opportunity that is synonymous with the very idea of America. Mr. P. put it thusly:

P: Once I was in America I realized what freedom is.
I: Do you feel that America offers a higher level of freedom of speech and . . . ?
P: No, no!! If anything Israel is freer in that respect.
I: So what do you mean by freedom?
P: I can go shopping at the supermarket at 2 o'clock in the morning. I can work out at the YMCA until midnight. You can do *whatever* you want *when* you want. This country is too small for me.

Israel tends to be viewed in terms of constraint, limitation, and duty. America is seen as a sort of global candy store where everything is obtainable, no desires need be curbed—and there is no time like the present. Whatever your appetite, whenever the desire appears it can be satisfied. As a sort of counterpoint to the pioneering ethic of Israel that emphasized deprivation, simplicity, future orientation, and the group needs over individual wants, many thousands of Israelis now seek instant gratification of a personal almost idiosyncratic kind in a framework of heady hedonism. Time is being successfully turned on its head in contemporary America and among the most avid consumers of the new context is an energetic breed of ex-Israeli bent on doing to time what has historically among Jews been done to concepts of space—etherialize it out of existence and consciousness. Day is turned into night and night into day in a myriad of shopping plazas and malls where an urge to buy can be satisfied at most any hour of the day. The constraints of little Israel—where shops close at 7 P.M., and all day Saturday and half day on Fridays and Tuesdays, and all

Jewish holy days; where one cannot get a liter of milk after 8 P.M.—tend to loom large in the consciousness as freedom-denying and restrictive.

While the grandfathers of today's Israeli might have embraced time as the working context of the Jew in history, making only symbolic obeisance in the direction of space, the grandchild having rejected the bindingness of Jewish faith and thrown off the newly assumed enclosure of space is left with a passion for limitlessness that for some becomes transmogrified into being able "to work out at midnight."

The pull exercised by America to be sure encompasses many things ranging from the absurdly subjective (McDonalds hamburgers) to the more serious dimension of life opportunities, a sense of security, anonymity, privatization, and much more. For many Israelis statehood reflected the glaring needs of a particular point in historical time. But 1985 is not the same as 1948. Relativity may be an imperfectly understood dimension of philosophy and physics but its sociological import is felt on the living flesh and tends to be most clearly understood. As one thoughtful and articulate respondee phrased it:

> A man who wanders for a very long time in the desert is willing to drink water that isn't so clean and say that he is happy while someone who is sitting next to a clear spring for forty years will complain bitterly about a piece of straw falling into and dirtying his water.

The Americanization of Israeli Society

A somewhat curious but nonetheless highly significant fallout from about one-half of the interviews resulted in a denial that leaving Israel and moving to the United States was an act of emigration. Some referred to it as temporary, refusing however to put a time frame to it. Others called it a move not dissimilar to moving between Haifa and Tel Aviv. Not a few ingenuously asked what difference there was in whether one lived in New York or Tel Aviv, while still others "commuted" or planned to commute between the two countries. How in fact can one explain the development of such a phenomenon?

On a simple level one can see it as a refusal to deal with a possibly questionable act for which the individual feels personally guilty, or views as perhaps illegitimate. When all is said and done many, if not most, *yordim* do in fact experience considerable guilt and shame for having decided to break away. Even in cases where leavers somewhat aggressively state their right to live their own lives wherever they might choose to do so, one need not be the most perspicacious of observers in order to hear the strong undertones of regret and lack of complete assurance with which the position is put forth.

On another level one observes the existence of a sort of continuity with traditional Jewish praxis where being Jewish was a completely portable identity. The fact is that notwithstanding 35 years of statehood and what is perceived by both insiders and outsiders as an almost rabid level of nationalist fervor, a high degree of confusion persists with respect to whether what is being viewed is Israeli nationalism per se or Jewish ethnocentricity with a flag and an anthem. As noted earlier, there exists much confusion on this score with Israeli and Jew used interchangeably and rather promiscuously.[2] Thus, one could see in Israelis moving to America a modicum of continuity with past practice whatever the confusion it might wreak with the "national" context: Jews move; Israelis are Jews: Israelis move!

There is an additional factor in the amalgam that serves to both legitimate *yerida* and to mask it with the fictive quality of not existing at all—what might be called "the greening of Israel"[3] or a process of relentless Americanization.

Americanization is not new as an ingredient of the Israeli cultural scene nor is Israel unique among the nations of the world in falling victim to the seductiveness encompassed in the American dream. This is especially the case for nations reaching independence at this particular juncture of world history, whose communications are dominated by "the big eye" of television where the American influence is large, indeed almost inescapable. Whether or not a McLuhanesque global village constitutes the emergent pattern of the world, it is without doubt true that an aura of interchangeability has descended upon much of the earth. Things tend to look familiar whether one is sitting in São Paulo or Savannah. Green and white or blue and white highway signs dominate autostradas, autobahns, and Route 64s everywhere. Coca Cola holds sway from the People's Republic of China to Saudi Arabia and Timbuktu. Millions share sleepless nights pondering the machinations and incredible complexities of the Ewings of "Dallas"—in about as many tongues and accents as one could care to conjure. Blue jeans are the great leveller of the twentieth century, popular as much in Leningrad as in Louisville. Everyman's dream and expectations tend somehow to be spun out in Hollywood and on Madison Avenue rather than in centers closer to home, and perhaps slightly more indigenous.

Thus, there exists at least the basis for understanding when a constantly recurring notion emerges in the responses of emigrants who state, "It makes no difference where I live. I am just as much an Israeli in New York as I am in Tel Aviv." Most emigrants asserted that they foresaw no difficulties in adjusting to America, saying in fact in a number of cases that "it will be easy." For when Israelis look around their country they are able at nearly every turn and in almost every area to view a little bit of America. Israel's single television channel is almost totally dependent on imports for its entertainment shows and these tend to be predominantly American. Thus Israelis, after watching programs like "Dallas," "All in the Family," or "Starsky and Hutch," are fairly sure that America holds no shocks in store. They know where to expect violence, crime, kindness, affluence, poverty, and high and low culture. They also use television as a primer for improving their knowledge of the language spoken by a clear majority of the world's Jews—English. American television—in color—enthralls with visions of excitement, breadth, challenge, and limitless horizons. At the same time, it projects an aura of attractive mystery while dissipating fears that might be stimulated or buttressed by an excess of exotic unravelability or ignorance.

Fashion and fad seem to leap the oceans with uncanny speed so that the clothes shown on Fifth Avenue in the spring are immediately visible on Dizengoff—and perhaps more extensively distributed among wider strata of the population than in New York's own hinterland. Where once—and not so long ago—Israelis were immediately identifiable to one another and to outsiders by their unique style of dress based as it was on sandals, shorts, khaki trousers and skirts, accented by simplicity and functionality above all, they are now indistinguishable from their class and age cohorts across the seas. Imported shoes and clothes from the most advanced centers of fashion in Europe and America find a ready and enthusiastic market in Israel. Hair styles and makeup of the latest *outré* are highly visible not alone in the cities of the land but on kibbutzim as well, many of which have resident cosmeticians and visiting lectures on the subject.

The Hebrew language tends to be well sprinkled with English additions, attesting not only to the status and worldiness of the speaker but assaying as well a fact of life—the important things, the key decisions that guide and determine our lives, are made not in Hebrew but in English.[4]

Watching a society celebrate can, as Lloyd Warner and others have demonstrated, tell us much about a great deal. Where Independence Day used to be a quasi-spontaneous outburst of sheer joy and demonstrative identity with the national enterprise, it has of late increasingly approximated an American Fourth of July model of set-piece speeches and family picnics. The collective dimensions of celebration are in eclipse and the private, the individual, the idiosyncratic are on the rise. Similarly, life cycle events that only a few years ago cast a web of participation far and wide to include complete families (including the young), neighbors, friends, coworkers, etc., with all helping in the preparation of food, now tend to involve only close family members—as often as not without young people—because of the expense involved in catered affairs. The American models for marriages, bar mitzvahs, and anniversaries are fast becoming preeminent in Israel to the point where if one did not hear the language spoken at events celebrating similar occasions in New York or Tel Aviv one would be hard pressed to know in which city the celebration was occurring.

Patterns of crime and deviance, the tone of youth culture, the approach to sports, consumerism, credit buying—all have been colored by contact (both personal and via the media) with America.

"Settling accounts" in the underworld is now carried out "Chicago-style" with booby-trapped cars and bodies buried in the countryside.[5] Cries and alarms have recently been raised about teenage drinking, as statistics indicate a rise in alcoholism in the Jewish State. Consumerism—buying as much as is possible of anything and everything—has probably surpassed America given Israeli inflation and the relative "freshness" of the germ. (Rare is the Israeli who will argue over a price, be it a $50 bill for a mediocre meal in a third-rate restaurant, a dentist's fee that is based on the American schedule never mind the income level of the average Israeli, or shoddy appliances costing deluxe prices.) Sports have increasingly taken on American tones with thousands turning out to watch professional basketball where the stars (mostly American blacks, some of whom have benefitted from instant conversion to Judaism) receive NBA-type salaries.

Education over the years has moved from a European, rather elitist pattern to an American-oriented mass model. More and more Israelis are attending the university (the proportion has surpassed Great Britain) and the B.A. is becoming a *sine qua non* for middle-class credentials and less an attestation of professional competence. Part and parcel with this development one takes note of the fact that a very high proportion of Israeli university academicians did graduate and/or postgraduate work in the United States. On the lower levels enrichment and "full child development" schemes have attained a foothold where previously a no-nonsense, 3-Rs approach dominated the scene.

In leisure time pursuits, a rise can be observed in all forms of spectator sports, as well as surfing, sailing, wind-surfing, and just about anything else that has achieved popularity and acceptance on either the east or west coasts of the United States.

In marketing and merchandising the supermarket has replaced the corner grocery and the department store is inching out the specialty shop. Advertising is slick, even more sexually explicit and leering than would be permitted in the United States, and held in check only by the limitation posed by the fact that it is not permitted on television and is restricted with respect to billboards.

Plastics and the nonbiodegradable, throw-away products are sweeping the country—and littering it at the same time. The slogans "new," "improved," and "the latest" hold the same if not greater fascination for the Israeli consumer as they do for the American and are guaranteed, sure-fire marketing tools.

Magazines geared to sports, cars, sex, popular entertainment, and the "house beautiful" (to say nothing of Hebrew imitations of *Time* and *Commentary*) are making their mark.

Stereo systems and video sets sell at extraordinary prices and breakneck rates such that troubled, little Israel is reputed to have the highest proportion of videos to population in the world. One is thus able to add hundreds of American films and TV shows to the inventory already supplied by the regular television service.

Israelis who toasted *"L'chayim"* only at weddings, circumcisions, and bar mitzvahs now feel it encumbent upon themselves to keep a "decently" stocked bar and to offer guests a drink or a cocktail. (Consumption, however, still lags far behind most Western countries and the United States.)

The two-car family, though not general, is no longer the rarity it was as recently as a decade ago and the whole concept of space and distance has undergone radical change. Israelis now "commute" to jobs in the cities from suburban belts, driving for increasingly long stretches of time to arrive through smog, heat, and snarled traffic. Driving from Haifa to Tel Aviv for theater, dinner, or visiting is no longer viewed as an outrageous extravagance either in the money or time dimensions. A Sabbath dinner in the Galilee or at the seashore is not unattainable, nor is travelling up to the Golan for a day of skiing, or driving or flying to Elat for scuba diving. Mobility has become a basic need and a critical feature in the lives of tens of thousands of Israelis, although not in all respects as in America. Israelis for example are still much more tied to place, to locale than are Americans who are notorious movers, changing residences at record rates.

In concepts of space as well, prosperity and attendant Americanization have brought about change. The compact apartment with its livingroom doubling as sleeping space is out, and each succeeding year brings with it a new and expanded norm for living space. The terms "cottage," "villa," "a full *dunam* of land," "200 meters of living space," "room for expansion," "2½ bathrooms," "American kitchens," or "Live the American way" are examples of the eye-catchers used in current advertising campaigns.[6]

In almost all these phenomena we are viewing something not limited to Israel nor merely a result of deep contact with American civilization. As societies prosper, expand, and develop we tend inevitably to see corresponding changes in concepts of living space, distances, and material goods—or the good, the true, and the beautiful for that matter. Additionally, in view of the fact that America has served and seemingly continues to serve as the spearhead or vanguard of new standards for industrial and postindustrial civilization on all levels from material factors to popular culture, one should not be surprised to note its weighty influence on Israeli society as well. What other possible model could there be when all is said and done, for an emergent, noncommunist developing society, in the latter part of the twentieth century?

But differences of both kind and extent exist when comparing the relationships between Israel and America on the one hand and other countries falling into the American orbit of influence on the other.

In the previously mentioned area of language, Israel is perhaps more vulnerable to cultural upheaval being done to it than other countries. The Hebrew language is not only poor in terms of a twentieth-century, technical provenance, but poor in general given its uncanny but difficult survival as a language of ritual and scholarship alone for centuries—actually predating the expulsion of 70 A.D. When one feels the need, for example, to lustily curse one's neighbor, recourse to Arabic, Russian, Yiddish, or English is required. All terms with a contemporary technological or even mechanical nature must be invented or reinvented (or borrowed). Vulnerability to cultural—in this case linguistic—invasion under these circumstances is not only inevitable but can be catastrophic in psychosocial terms. Clearly, a culture that must submit to great ingestions of another language or languages in order to function is a culture that can only be viewed as disadvantaged if not inferior. As much justified pride as there might be over the "rebirth" of the living Hebrew language, a concommitant awareness of deep limitation and constrictiveness is also present as an unshakeable subtheme.

Israel was reborn as a state at a time where at least cultural if not political borders were crumbling. Before its institutions could sink roots or its culture achieve a degree of indigenousness, the mass communications revolution of the mid-twentieth century—television, satellite, jet travel—had opened the society to powerful and seductive influences from abroad. A law of cultural physics posits that the more powerful, more insistent, more pervasive, and more universal will supplant the weaker, more parochial culture. This is especially the case where a tremendous degree of dependence up to and including the actual physical survival of the weaker culture is clearly tied to the more powerful force.

Physical survival in the economic as well as the political sense is posited here. The Israeli economy could not sustain the country's present standard of living without massive ingestions of aid from the United States treasury and to a much lesser extent the American Jewish community. The dollar has almost replaced the shekel as the currency of the country, with many things having their value or price quoted only in dollars. The Israeli treasury is more subject to fluctuation in Congress than it is to movements in the Israeli Knesset and the Minister of Finance would probably respond sooner and with much more candor to a query from the former than from the latter. The Israeli Air Force talks in "inches" and "feet" while every other branch of the military is so tied to American supplies (notwithstanding Israel's own large defense industry) that a cutoff could effectively turn Israel back to the bow-and-arrow stage of military capability.

There are almost no Israelis who remain unaware of the extent of their dependency on the United States. Jokes might make the rounds, a certain cynicism might insinuate itself, a bit of arrogant bluster might be introduced suggesting how clever Israelis are to "get so much for so few" or how Israelis are really helping the Americans in terms of their global interests, but the end result is more hurt than joy, more doubt than assurance.

America, it might be posited, has become the alterego of Israel in political, economic, and cultural terms. America has become the mentor, the father figure looming larger than life and indeed holding the keys to life, to survival. From values to weapons the dominance of America in the lives of Israelis is perhaps without precedent given even the lack of spatial proximity and contiguity between the two countries. When not only *yordim* but many stay-at-home Israelis as well decry behavior in their society, invidiously comparing it to America, they are demonstrating the fact that they have already absorbed American standards, which are then turned in upon themselves.

The rhetoric of the political leadership of both countries suggests an intimacy and interdependency that would leave both devastated if something were to destroy or weaken the powerful preternatural bonds that tie them. In the case of Israel, the dimensions of loss are rather clear-cut, whereas in the case of America at most symbolic loss is posited. This asymmetry also tends not to be lost upon Israelis, who despite some brave efforts to the contrary, see themselves as "takers" not "givers"; they see America as mentor and Israel as ward. Thus, a deep sense of national inferiority regarding America cannot but result, and as Israelis see the influence and power of all things American on their lives and indeed their destinies, one of the questions pushing to the fore is: Why here and not there? If we dress American, dance American, fight American, and "deal" American, why not the real thing instead of the local copy? If this is "Little America," the 51st state, what difference does a short jet flight between Tel Aviv and New York really make? The difference between the two is further narrowed by a relatively small though visible group who manage to live in both places seemingly at the same time, maintaining an apartment in Jerusalem, a refurbished villa in old Jaffa, *and* a place on Riverside Drive or the east side of Manhattan.

Even for those who cannot afford this life style, the possibility of extended visits every year or so is not out of reach for a large proportion of leavers. This creates, I suspect, a feeling among many of not having left and not having arrived, of being here and there and not being able to distinguish quite where one is at any given moment.

This umbilical tie to America has, I would aver, deprived Israel as a state in terms of independence and autonomy and Israelis as human beings of a dimension of adulthood. The former is clear and needs no further explication, while the latter assertion can remain only speculative. Adulthood entails assimilating and dealing with limits with regard to aspirations and goals. One learns how to distinguish between reality and fantasy, the achievable and the unachievable, the possible and the impossible, the necessary and the borderline. But, as noted earlier in this chapter, Israelis have (at least since 1967) learned how to blur these distinctions into oblivion. Somehow the thought gained currency that little Israel—8,000 square miles, 4 million people, no natural resources to speak of—could at one and the same time build cities in the West Bank, expand industry, run a welfare economy, maintain a massive military structure, and provide a high standard of living for its people with no visible limits in sight. Israeli society has learned how to evade reality and evade paying for mistakes by its great dependence on being bailed out by aid from America. While the rest of the world has begun to think in terms of "no growth" and belt tightening and lessening of living standards, Israel has proceeded on its way with the concept of the sky's the limit. The average citizen knows that Israel is a small country with scant resources and a shaky industrial base and yet sees budget lines of millions and billions for this and that (settlements, deficits, subsidies, etc.). Thus the citizen also begins to think in these terms and shortly becomes convinced that he is not getting a fair share, or that there is so much out there in the global candy store that he, too, must reach for it.

One wonders also if the phenomenon of *shnor* (begging) has begun to show its societal effects. The country has developed a system of living on grants from outside, so why not the individual citizen? And if it is not forthcoming—an apartment, a certain sought-after job, a car, etc., then why not seek it at the same source from which the society at large draws?

Just as the society could do everything so could the individual. Do we want a trip to Europe? A safari to Kenya? A post-Christmas shopping trip to London? Why not! Videos, color television, expensive stereos, imported furniture, German beer, Dutch cheese, Parisian styles, Italian shoes? Why not! Every year a different minister of finance sings another jeremiad about imminent downfall and still the country's standard of living rises. "Wolf" has been shouted too often and not only has the wolf not appeared but the golden eggs have increased. If fairy tales are to be the measure of the citizens' lives the preferred mode is the benign to the draconic, the lulling and soft to the harsh and abrasive. Choices are not necessary, work is at best inefficacious: wishing is sufficient. And if not? Then the circle can be completed at the source—in America. Not able to apply limits to swollen and enlarged appetites for more and more, the next step up, the one additional rung of expansion sits beckoning, pulling the seeker to indulgence and hoped for satiety.

The Pull of Those Who Have Gone Before

The move to America would still prove unobtainable for many if not for the existence of still another "pull" factor—the growing Israeli community already established there. A certain critical mass has been achieved in recent years where a satisfying degree of "Israeliness"—language, foods, friendships, and family links—has become a movable and interchangeable feast sustaining those already there and beckoning others to follow. Restaurants serving felafel, houmous, tehina, and "grill" are available in the major centers of settlement. Neighborhoods where Hebrew can be heard as readily as English exist in New York and Los Angeles; local Israeli banks (L'eumi, Hapoalim, Discount, and even Mizrachi) have branches in these same centers. Hebrew newspapers from Israel are fairly accessible; Hebrew can be heard on the radio and television; Israeli "hang-outs" have been established where one can always hear a welcoming *"Nu ma nishmah?"* (So, how are you doing?). Israeli travel agents, appliance dealers, cafes, and nightclubs are, while not ubiquitous, certainly visible and satisfactorily available.

As with other immigrant groups, certain trades and occupations seem to be "taken over" by the newcomers, considerably cushioning the entry experience. Israelis seem (on the East Coast at any rate) to have cornered the market on discount appliance shops and discount sundries, while establishing a strong foothold in diamonds and jewelry, cab driving, household repair, and Hebrew school teaching.

While the above cushion is common to other groups such as Greeks and Italians, the Israelis are provided with still another corridor to American status through what might be called the "official" Israeli presence in the United States. Not an insignificant number of young Israelis ease their way into America and American life by working in one capacity or another for the Jewish and Israeli establishment. Ironic though it might be, these form a sort of hothouse for alleviating homesickness, isolation, and lack of savvy with regard to the American reality, thus easing the emigration process. One informant noted that "I would have gone crazy if I didn't get work with El Al during the first six months I was in the States." Others were less emotional but still noted the "cushioning significance" of work with the Israeli consulate, El Al, various defense and trade delegations, the U.N. staff, the UJA, Israel Bonds, the Jewish Agency, and others. Thus an additional factor pulling one to make the move is the ready availability of a supportive web of familiarity previously established by other Israelis and buttressed by the very bodies seemingly dedicated to stopping the phenomenon of emigration and in fact dedicated to the opposite—*aliyah*. No fewer than seven informants indicated that their decision to stay on in America received impetus from the existence of this network—if not an undertone of legitimacy itself, through the imposition of a quasi-official status.

> I first went to the States to be a counselor in a summer camp for two months. After the summer I had two months set aside for travelling and on the trip I met an Israeli who worked at the Israeli consultate in New York. He was a student and he asked me if I was one. I said yes (I wanted to be one) and he offered me a job in security. So I tried to get into a university and if I succeeded I would then stay to study and if I stayed it no longer mattered what kind of visa I had because with the work offered me my visa would be changed to a diplomatic one. So with a diplomatic visa I could stay on without worrying about studying *or* working.

Another type of legitimacy is conferred by the prior emigration (and success) of significant others. Senior officers in the armed service have become successful businessmen in America. Emissaries of the Jewish Agency or the Foreign Service often neglected to return home at the end of their tour abroad. Elite pilots now run ferry services out of obscure airports in Florida or Orange County. Professors decide to extend their stay in the United States "until the next sabbatical" and upon whose students the message is never lost. "My professor too is a *yored*—well let me not say *yored*; he is simply contributing from *there* instead of from *here*."

In almost every field of endeavor it is possible to point to a list of "top-notchers" who "could have made it" anyplace including Israel but chose to go to America: doctors, scientists, musicians, artists, teachers, bankers, diplomats, professors, businessmen, army officers. Even in fields where one might expect a sort of natural anchorage to the soil of the Holy Land, such as Judaica, religious functionaries, Hebrew writers and poets, journalists, jurists, one finds not a few distinguished and considerably more journeymen practitioners who have joined the move to *chutz la'aretz*. The effect of these "defections" on those remaining behind can only be surmised, but if ready familiarity with cases of these kinds is any indication then my sample would suggest that this factor acts as legitimation and an additional pull toward emigration.

Needless to add, the larger the pool of emigrants already in a given locale the stronger the pull on relatives and friends to join them. Well over one-half of the sample had close relatives already living in the United States (not including spouses bringing over their partners, which would have raised the figure considerably).

There seems to be an interesting process at work here wherein when putting aside all the objective attractions of America we find inordinate interest on the part of relatives in the United States to "bring out" their loved ones to join them. I say inordinate because after recognizing the natural desire to have parents join their children, siblings come together, or simply to rejoin families separated by distance, there still seems to be an additional dimension at work. In a number of cases the desire to have relatives join them in America seemed almost frantic as if more than mere consanguinity was being sought. Ms. B. is a good example:

I: You started to think about moving to America on your visit in 1979?

B: No, I was there in 1974 and again in 1979 and my brother tried to convince me to stay.

I: To stay?

B: To stay. America is a big and lovely country but there is nothing like Israel. But still we started to prepare the papers, without any connecting thoughts . . . really quite blindly.

Upon further questioning, Ms. B. could not quite understand her brother's near frantic desire for her to stay. He could only ask repeatedly, "What's good in Israel?" She, for her part, although going through with the move to America remained ambivalent and troubled.

B: Look, I find my America here. I don't know, maybe I want to be near my brother. I'll be close to one part of the family, but far from the others.

I: What about your parents?

B: Well, we sat and talked about it. My mother is very against going but my father is willing—but only for my sake.

The brother is trying to convince the parents to come as well and will probably succeed in reestablishing the complete Israeli based family in the United States.

In other instances I was told how pressure was brought to bear from sisters, brothers, cousins, aunts, and children to "bring the family over." One respondent put the matter in terms of a handy symbiosis:

> Well, I have three sisters in America—all married to Americans. They have been bothering me to come for years now. They tell me "we will help you." You need us for material help which we can give you and we need you because we need family. So, let's make a deal together.

Loneliness? A desire for extended family? Possibly, but one cannot avoid the suspicion that a kind of guilt is being worked through and legitimation established for the emigration. The more who come, the more who take the step—the more legitimate the individual move seems to become. A sort of cyclic device is constructed wherein Israelis already in America pressure family and friends to join them, all the while extolling in ecstatic terms the benefits to be had and then explaining their own situation in America as merely reflecting a family reality: "We are all here and nothing was left for me in Israel."

The Factor of Fad and Fashion

There would appear to exist at least two types of emigration from Israel, which could be termed "hard-core *yerida*" and "marginal *yerida*." The former comprises a range of individuals who are intent upon moving abroad for one reason or another and will not be swayed or deterred in their decision. These individuals are convinced that their place is elsewhere and Israel for them has lost the ability to command deep loyalty. Rises and drops in the popularity of *chutz la'aretz* generally or America specifically will, on the whole, not affect their decision to leave, nor will emoluments on the part of Israel draw them back once departed. Marginal emigrants are clearly inclined to make "the" move or "a" move but with this group external factors seem to play a much larger role. For this latter group factors such as economic conditions in both Israel and the receiving country are seriously weighed, as are their perceptions of "conditions" in both places with respect to a wide spectrum of factors ranging from crime to war or the threat of war.

This second group—and it is much the larger—has more of a will-o'-the-wisp character to it and is guided by, among other things, the fashionability, the "in" quality of this step. For many in this marginal group emigration is akin to something that they must get out of their systems in order to feel that they have done right by themselves. For this group phrases such as "I must give it a try," "the grass is always greener in the neighbor's yard," or even "I owe it to myself" spring readily to their lips. One receives the unmistakable impression that the people in this group tend to think of their emigration as always reversible should "the conditions be un-propitious," but there is no great tragedy if it should become permanent. It is this group that J.A. Jackson (1969:4) presumably had in mind when he observed:

> Today it is increasingly apparent that a significant number of migrants spend periods of their lives outside their country of birth, returning home and perhaps after a further period setting off again without the implications of finality usually associated with such moves.

That the move *will* in fact be final for most is clear, but just as clear is the element of ambiguity that tends to surround the move. For the marginal group to "miss out" is devastating, especially when it is all so reversible, so correctable if one desires a further change.

> I don't think we will stay in the United States but we must try. I have never been abroad and everybody else has.

> I'm satisfied with everything here—but one must try, no? A man has to try! I've never been abroad, never left the country.

The first comment is by a housewife following her husband, who made it plain in no uncertain terms that the American move was unavoidable if their marriage was to hold together.[7] The second comment was made by a body and fender mechanic going to Los Angeles to do the exact same work. The theme is "one must try," one can correct any mistakes that might be made. Sometimes the tone of response takes on a childlike, almost simplistically reverential mien as when one young man explaining the prior emigration of his parents noted:

> They had it good here economically. But they worked very hard, very hard: from morning to night. My mother said, "Let's take a vacation: we'll go to America, and see how it goes there." So they went and they stayed.

The seeming ease with which the decision to emigrate is taken is no doubt more apparent than real, but again, it does serve to highlight this "swaying in the wind—going with the drift" quality of the matter for so many. For some it has something of the Everest patina about it: "Why do I go to America? Because it is there and it is possible." Many respondents stated that Israel was "fine," "satisfying," "good," "the best"—"but we're going anyway."

For some this was merely an effort at maintaining a degree of national piety. For most who took this line, however, it did indeed reflect a strong need to make a stab for the opportunity that life and destiny had cast their way. It was sometimes stated as if it were an earned right. "After so many years here why shouldn't I try there for a few years?" What, one might well ask, does such an approach auger or suggest with respect to how one views one's life in Israel: a duty? a burden? something to be served out bearing release as an end reward?

For a considerable number the "try abroad" pattern is part of a rite of passage that has seemingly achieved a degree of sanctity in Israel. As noted earlier, finishing army service is often marked by a trip abroad, which in not a few cases results in the individual staying or having the seed of emigration firmly planted within only to bloom sometime in the future.

> Why do Jews leave Israel? Each Jew gives the next Jew the push to go. When one goes and succeeds it becomes very attractive to others . . . for example, that's what happened with me. When I was nearing the end of army service, all I would hear among the soldiers was—I'm going to Australia or I'm going to India, or America, or God knows where. Everybody was going someplace. Why? Because of the build-up of pressure and the lack of freedom we had suffered for three years. Also because many who preceded them did it, because it's popular.

Not going abroad for at least a certain period of time has begun to suggest a certain lack of vigor or ambition among the stay-at-homes. The trip abroad has become so much a part of the average Israeli's experience that a certain reverse snobism has begun to emerge among those who have *not* taken the plunge in at least visiting foreign parts. Emigrating has certainly not achieved quite this level of fashionable acceptability, but it would appear safe to assert that the former condemnation and excoriation of the phenomenon has largely disappeared. A corollary of even semi-fashionability is an inevitable smoothing of the step itself, so that much more ease is experienced by Israelis attempting to justify the step to themselves or to others. The fashionable acceptance of living abroad allows for the enhancement of privatization, of doing one's own thing: "After all, I am not doing more nor less than thousands of other Israelis when I move abroad." A statement such as the following will no longer draw extensive condemnation:

> I have come to the opinion that *I have* to be the center and not country, land or anything else. I don't feel guilty anymore! Why? I don't think it's because Israel no longer needs me; they do—but *I* have to be the center.

At the same time as it is essential to recognize an important shift in Israel with respect to how the phenomenon of *yerida* is viewed both by leavers and stayers, care must be taken not to overplay the depth of this shift. While many feel increasingly free to express sentiments such as the above, there still exists considerable ambivalence about emigration in both camps notwithstanding changes and increased fashionability. For example, the same person quoted above, an architect in his thirties, also noted not uncharacteristically:

> Everybody tried to make me feel like a traitor for leaving. But I worked on this and now I feel freed. *Yordim* should not be forced to feel bad. We should be like the Italian in this respect. When an Italian government minister

comes to New York and meets with the Italian community, he thinks of them and treats them like honored ambassadors of Italy. When our ministers come, they deal with us as deserters and worse. Don't make *yordim* feel bad about themselves. If they come back fine—if not, also fine.

Reactions to the decision to leave on the part of family, friends, and coworkers tended to fall into four areas: understanding and acceptance, opposition based on family considerations, opposition based on broader or societal considerations, and acceptance and an expressed desire to leave as well. Very few departees reported along the lines of the architect quoted above. Few were made to feel guilty over their decision, at least insofar as they were able to perceive and interpret the reactions of others. In only one case was a particularly nasty reaction recorded and that case involved young children rather than adults. "Our son was called a *boged* [traitor] at school [when he told friends about leaving] and the kids told him the plane taking him to America would crash." Most indicated that reactions were surprisingly accepting and benign (but again a degree of caution is indicated given the fact that this is being reported by the departee himself).

A lot of my friends are thinking of *yerida*. It's nothing to be ashamed of: after all, a person leads his own life.

How did people react to our leaving? With jealousy. There are many who would like to do it, but for one reason or another can't.

No one tried to talk me out of it [moving]. That's what surprised me when the whole idea took root with me about two years ago. I talked to so many people and everyone agreed with what I said. There wasn't one who said "Look— you haven't thought about 1, 2, 3, or 4." *No one* said something like that. Everyone agreed with me but said it's hard for them personally to leave and all sorts of things like that. I think that if there was something organized, some organization which could get jobs, housing and all—an awful lot of people would consider emigrating.

Has anybody expressed opposition to my decision? Yes, my mother! [laughter] But some others as well said I shouldn't go; that with my *vetek* [seniority], I have a good thing here—but a lot of these people want to go as well; at least for awhile!

Has anyone called me a traitor? No! On the contrary. You know what they told me? If you're there for a year and it's really good, do me a favor and think of me. At least five of my closest coworkers asked me to look for jobs for them.

In the absence of the rise to acceptance and near fashionability, reactions such as those recorded above would have been extremely rare. While emigration is still not considered a positive national value, it would appear that it is no longer thought of among many as quite the nefarious act as it once was. Many respondees noted the "understanding" with which their decision to emigrate was received by most, including some from within establishment centers that one might expect to be in the forefront of vociferous and condemnatory opposition—the kibbutz and the army. Of three kibbutz members interviewed all indicated acceptance and support from their kibbutzim for their decision. (Two left for personal or familial reasons and one for "artistic" opportunities.) "They (the kibbutz) accepted my decision with complete understanding, complete understanding." An army officer noted that the army accepted his decision although "they were sorry they couldn't do anything to change it" (that is, they could not provide what he needed). In the only case in the sample moving to a European country, opposition was noted not to emigration per se but because the couple was going to Germany. "Going to Germany bothered almost all our friends. If we were going somewhere else it would have been different." In some cases departees took pains to underline the factor of sympathetic understanding, saying things like "they [people] don't like the fact that we are leaving but they understand that it is the right thing for us." A variation is, "It's my life so they accept my choice."

Family rather than national or communal factors were most often cited as negative resultants of emigration. That someone would choose to leave Israel in order to go to America is, it would appear, an increasingly digestible even somewhat fashionable move in the local constellation. But that family ties would be disrupted in the process represents one of the more difficult dimensions of the act. This is especially the case with people of Middle Eastern and North African background, but for Europeans as well separation from loved ones is felt as a loss though ultimately not a barrier to *yerida*.

Clearly, the "beaten-path" effect or the fact that many significant others have preceded one has an impact on emigration to a given locality. The thought that "everybody's doing it" has an effect on all strata and all age groupings. While in many cases children were the most reluctant with respect to making the move, I was frankly surprised at the approximately 25 percent of families with children who voted their full acceptance of the move. In one case the informant noted his eldest child's reaction as being "a big experience—she wants to go very much because three or four girls in her class have already left." Others took note of the wave-like dimensions they sensed as being attached to the phenomenon: "The summer comes and everybody goes. One hears the story from the next one and wants to go." (Families with school-age children generally wait for the end of the school year before leaving.)

For some emigration has seemingly nothing to do with either Israel or America, but simply reflects a Jewish mode of existence: "The Jews love to run around: from here to there, from there to here." But for most it is a more directed phenomenon with very definite referent points in the providing and receiving country. It is not just anywhere that is desired but America specifically, which holds out not only its intrinsic attractions but glitters as well as the object of so much collective fascination. Almost everyone knows of at least one person or family who has emigrated to America. Even if it were not buttressed by any number of objective elements a situation like this would on the face of it elicit a desire for imitation on the part of many.

> It's an epidemic! I think that among us Jews it's very common to imitate one another. Everyone sees in his neighbor an equal. You were there—I want to go there too.

> This business of *yerida* has become a national sickness, a national fashion. Somehow or other people started to go and many have ended up with less than they had here—but still others follow. They send post cards with pictures of the Empire State building or the Twin Towers to their friends and never mind that they drive a taxi—but they are out there in a big world *with everybody else.*

This imitative factor, while playing a role, is not the major determinant in a decision to emigrate for most. But for a few one is shocked to learn that it is not only a factor, but indeed the *only* visible cause of emigration. In a few cases I was not able to discern any stronger motivation other than the repeated assertions of "why not?" or "we are not the only ones" or "*X* moved and look at him today." In these cases moving to America represents a slight escalation of a decision to change jobs, apartments, or locale at home. The higher the level of fashionability of the move, the wider the web of Israeli association and cohorts in the United States, the larger this group of leavers will grow. This end of the emigration spectrum involves a certain mindlessness more akin to fad than to fashion. Here people emigrate in a fit of absentmindedness rather than as a result of more reasoned or basic considerations. Here one finds individuals fearful not only of missing out, but of being left behind, of being considered in current Israeli slang *Frierim*, or soft touches. When fashion dictated travel abroad—Israelis responded unstintingly. When a latent dimension of this became distorted into emigration, a similar feeling of not allowing oneself to lag behind emerged. As one departee eloquently put it:

> After the Six-Day War a new spirit was introduced into Israel which replaced the image of the kibbutznik and the proud fighter with the lover of the foreign and the strange. Everybody started to run after the foreign and the strange. When I came to Israel in 1969 I used to have arguments with Israelis of my

age group who could not believe that any place in the world was as good as Israel. But then people began to travel, to see the big world and they realized that there *is* something out there; something beyond our little problems. And Israel lost attractiveness.

Adventure and Escape

As Israel lost attractiveness, America gained such in the eyes of many. America seemed (and seems) the perfect escape from a wide array of problems, ranging from the personal to the communal. It is gigantic in size and scope, heterogeneous in makeup, anonymous in form, and diverse in its offerings. It offers in these respects what Israel cannot. America, for many, provides at least the illusion of being "forgiving" in a way in which other nations, Israel among them, is not—so forgiving that America can even lose a war without fear that its very existence as a nation would be jeopardized. One can err in business, in job or career, in marriage, in choice of living locale and make necessary corrections when these are indicated or desired. If New York does not work out there are always 49 other states to choose from. If jeans decline in popularity, a market for mini-skirts can open up. If one's present apartment seems too small or too large, or not sufficiently posh—alternatives are readily available and relatively easy to arrange.

Israel, on the other hand, is seen as a tight little island where depredations or failures suffered in Tel Aviv are readily communicated to Haifa and Jerusalem; where failure in business in one locale can permanently impair one's ability to try again in another; where an extramarital affair in Afula might be talked about (and follow those involved) in Arad. In short, "running away" or to put it in more positive terms "beginning anew" is seen as difficult if not impossible in Israel and eminently feasible in America.

America affords one the possibility of escaping into anonymity, where Israel suggests a constant spotlight on the individual. This is especially true for all kinds of deviance (especially sexual deviance). In America two ingredients are present that remain difficult to find in Israel—acceptance and a supportive group of the like-minded. Homosexuality, while of course existent in Israel, is still largely at the closet stage (although emerging) and the kind of of supportive community of the like-inclined one can readily find in any large or medium American city is much more circumscribed in Israel.

For people who for one reason or another are not following a societally sanctioned course in their personal lives or who even might just be "off schedule," America affords escape and sanctuary. I am here referring to those respondees previously cited who noted that in order to escape family pressure (to marry, have children, buy an apartment, or follow a certain educational or career line), a move to America seemed, if not the only, then at least a desirable way of coping.

> I came back to Israel after 12 years in Italy with my parents' promise not to bother me with getting married. They broke their promise and one of the reasons I'm going to America is to get away from this pressure.

Not only is it much harder to badger one at a distance of thousands of miles, but the calculus of relationships undergoes a change revolving about the reality of separation in place of former failure to conform to parental or communal expectations. "In America," I was told by many departees, "one is free to do as one wishes without external pressures."

All respondees without exception indicated that in order to achieve desired change in their lives or life styles only departure for America would avail. Moving in Israel was seen as a palliative and essentially ineffective step. America, because of what they saw as objective reasons bound up in size and style, promised escape and salvation, while staying anyplace in Israel suggested constrictiveness and sameness.

Escape from personal problems is only one dimension of the phenomenon, however. Escape of a more existential, broader visage plays a deeper role in the decision-making process. Here again, America is seen as the mirror opposite of Israel, allowing as it does for privitization, withdrawal, and the cultivation of one's own being unencumbered by "big" ideas like redemption, national revival, Jewish fate and destiny, and other similarly weighty concepts. For thousands of Israelis there has developed a palpable tiredness with respect to "big issues" and a corresponding desire to proportion their lives more modestly in this regard than was allowable during the intense and demanding period of state-building.

> Here abroad, I am free of all obligation, all responsibility, all affiliation. I am entirely freed from the pressure-cooker within which I was raised on the kibbutz. I don't owe anything to society or to the state, or to any other framework. For me, as someone who has left the kibbutz, it is a sufficient pleasure to enjoy the world and to hang loose (*Yediot Aharonot* 1 May, 1983: 21 [Hebrew])

The young lady quoted above comes from a kibbutz that has lost forty people to emigration. They chose to leave a social framework that had earned the respect of both Israel and the world as a paradigm for social and communal concern above personal wishes and individual whim. Not only the kibbutz but all of Israel—classic symbols of the committed society of our times—have seemingly joined the rest of the Western world on the path to alienation and noncommittedness. The myths are in eclipse, the dream is tainted, and the resulting response of failure on the part of the society to elicit loyalty and identification opens the door to anomie, personalism, and defection. Where better to enjoy the new freedom than the streets of New York or the boulevards of Los Angeles? Not only do these places afford one a near perfect escape from the committedness of Israel, but because of geography if for no other reason America allows for maximum running space. "In Israel you can't escape—there is no place to run to. In America, you can always run." But again the key theme, the major element to be enjoyed and embraced in America is the freedom to throw off a burdensome sense of social and communal responsibility and to live what is viewed as the unencumbered life.

> Life here is much harder than in the States. Life there is a "bargain" and Americans don't know how to appreciate it. Americans don't know how good they have it. There problems are marginal. America has problems but you can distance yourself from the problems. You can live in a neighborhood far from crime. In America you *can get lost*. Here you can't or it is much more difficult to distance yourself from problems.

In America "you can get lost." In America you are not required to care or to be involved with the fate of the society. It is expected that you will act always in a fashion that is best for yourself. If crime exists in certain neighborhoods you can move to another, but you need not trouble yourself with inordinate pain concerning the fate or direction of society as a whole.

For some, emigration to America is seen not so much as a flight from onerous responsibility or personal difficulties as it is something of an insurance policy. This is a more literal, more basic category of escape having little to do with ego or other prosaic motivations. About 12 percent of the sample expressed interest in emigration so as to earn American citizenship, thereby being able to return to Israel armed with "papers"—a recourse should the worst happen and Israel be overcome. In this protean sense of escape we see the existence of an underlying fear among many with respect to the ultimate resolution of the Jewish-Arab conflict and other key difficulties and societal challenges.

> I might stay, but I don't feel that this country has a future. I worry not for myself, but for my children. There just doesn't seem to be a solution.
>
> The country is about to go bankrupt and I don't want to be here when the thing explodes.
>
> Two of our children have American passports and two don't. I want to be in America long enough to get passports for these two—just in case.

The irony of this point of view cannot be lost on either Israelis or Jews in the Diaspora who apparently view each other's domiciles as possible places of refuge should "the worst happen." Israelis so often can be heard scornfully explaining Diaspora fund raising for Israel as an "insurance policy," a place to run to should the anti-Semites begin to rampage. Clearly, however, this represents a two-way street with at least a proportion (no doubt well exceeding the small proportion in the present sample) seeing in America a safe harbor in the storm yet to come.

Escape, sanctuary, refuge—all are key elements pulling, inviting one to try one's luck in what I have called the "great candy-counter of America." But the pull, the attraction would remain a dormant fantasy, an idle spinning of wheels were it not for the existence of a responsive behavioral framework within which these idylls can be acted out. One finds this in the oft-referred to penchant of Israelis to travel as far and as often as possible, and in the spirit of adventure whose roots and origins one can only guess about.

Clearly, travel is at least as much a form of escape as it is a desire to see the other side of the mountain. Where in certain societies and perhaps in other times, a natural first response to trouble in one's environment is to seek cause and attempt to confront the situation *in situ*, that is not necessarily the Israeli response. Perhaps because of historical factors that remain deeply rooted in the Jewish psyche, for Jews the ever beckoning response to difficulty is flight, or its very opposite—denial. Jews have been notorious for being among the last to discern an irremediable change in their fortunes in certain contexts and acting accordingly. Obversely, however, Jews have also been notorious for the portability of their lives—being able to live a nomad-like existence when circumstances so dictated, spreading out to the four corners of the globe. Given a natural tendency to make virtue of necessity, Jews have grown somewhat fond of mobility, portability, of a certain anchorlessness in their lives. Thus whatever else the idea of travel might suggest it also reflects a type of response to trouble of all kinds and degree.

One respondee innocently records the response of his kibbutz-member mother to the Likud electoral victory saying:

> Mother, of course, would prefer that I should be with her, but after the elections she said, "Well, now you lift your legs and travel, resting wherever you will. It's bad enough that we can't do it—at least you should enjoy yourself."

To enjoy oneself means "moving," being "mobile," even to an apparently sedentary mom who probably really does want her son to remain near. The response to a problem seemingly as abstract as an unfavorable electoral result is an unmistakable and totally uncamouflaged message to flee. To be free, to be safe, one must be consummately mobile above all.

For some departees the aspect of escape is buried in a miasma of justifications bound up with a sort of self-delusion about the entire step (emigration) as ultimately benefiting Israel in one way or another. Two brothers in the import-export business previously cited insisted that they were not emigrants really. One said: "I am not a *yored*. I'm going for business and that's good for Israel. I am creating export potential." Another felt that every Israeli should be sent abroad for a period of time "to learn" so as to improve the quality of life and expand horizons.

> I think it [America] is a school for life. I think that National Insurance [Bituach L'eumi] should create a program which would send everyone abroad—at least once in a lifetime. It will prove the best of schools.

To some extent travel is viewed as a device by which a perceived sense of parochialism and isolation can be overcome. Various departees explained how their leaving was not so much an escape as an experience that could smooth the rough edges left by life in Israel. A few suggested that they learned how to drive properly only after a stint in America. Some claimed a commitment to civil discourse and behavior came about only as a result of experiencing the American crucible. Similar claims were made for work habits, tolerance for differing points of view—even an appreciation for Judaism. In the final analysis, it is clear that travel represents an attempt to abandon a specific path in order to embrace another. In asserting the preferability of life styles in *chutz la'aretz*, and more specifically in America, a rejection of the Israeli pattern is implied, though this rejection is consciously refuted and denied by most. This rejection tends to be obscured by various devices, the most prominent of which is an emphasis on the positive—the affording of the possibility to learn, to expand one's horizons through "adventure" (which is another word for travel).

> If only I could afford it I would move to a different country every couple years. If there were no problems with language and kids I would really like to do it.
>
> In Israel everything is ordinary—I've been there. But America was a chance to widen my horizons, to have more opportunity. Also, I love adventure.
>
> I've lived here 40 years and I don't see any reason not to go out and see something different. Call it adventure—I'm not opposed to the word.

Almost all interviewees denied that their leaving meant a cessation of contributing to the development of Israel. Almost all saw their departure as an adventurous step in personal terms that ultimately would redound to Israel's good. Almost none saw themselves as rejective of Israeli values or society, although highly and vociferously critical of them and seduced by America and American values. Somehow American values became in their minds the true Israel, which was being temporarily obscured but with proper nurturance could again spring forth. Some actually viewed themselves as potential vessels for the better transmission of these "true values" back to Israel—following, of course, a stint abroad and a taste of life's great adventure.

Notes

1. This example was not an isolated one. Others in this category included a retired policeman in his late fifties, and a few widows and widowers, most with at least one child living in America, who saw America as opening up horizons that could not even be thought about in Israel, let alone approached.
2. This results, among other things, in no little mischief being done to the concept "Israeli Arab." For both Arabs and Jews the phrase rings hollow and does anything but roll off the tongue with ease.
3. "Greening" in this case refers both to the widespread presence of green cards, as immigrant work visas are known, and the "dollarization" of the Israeli economy. Recently, a minister of finance was finally forced to resign for positing a formal agenda along these lines.
4. Thus Israelis who have "backing" seek "action" on the basis of "ideologia" without however being "fanati"; they are trying always to be "liberali" and "fair." The way to be "OK" is to be willing to go "fifty-fifty," thereby avoiding "conflict" and possibly helping to bring about "reforma." A walk down an Israeli main street might be similarly rewarding with signs flashing the availability of "American ice cream," "milk shakes," "hamburgers" to be had at the "New York delicatessen," or the "Broadway" or the "California milk bar." An Israeli youngster can be overheard ordering his friend to "hands-up," while his older brother will be playing "basketball" down the block, where he will be engaging in such exotic moves as the "fast-break," "jump-shot," and "hook-shot." The parents of both will be contemplating how to spend the "weekend." The parents of our youngsters might write a "check" (though they have an "overdraft") for the purchase of a "sweatshirt" and "training suit" for the children, and another to cover the cost of repairs to the "clutch" and "brakesim" of the family car. One could go on and on but the point has now doubtlessly been made.
5. Breaking and entry crime has surpassed European rates and is approximating the American level, although violent crime is still well below American rates.
6. One of the main attractions for the nonideologically committed for buying property on the West Bank is the possibility of more space, more rooms, more land for less—much less—than can be arranged for on the other side of the green line. A veritable orgy of competition has emerged over how grotesquely large a house one can build there for relatively little money. The winning entry thus far (known to the author) is a 19-room villa in one of the Samaria settlements. An additional grotesquerie is to be seen in the sales pitch for Nofim, another Samarian town where each house will be supplied with a personal computer for

"doing the shopping." The surrounding area seems closer in its form and con-
ditons to the sixteenth century than to the twentieth.
7. Very often the wife goes reluctantly in order to save the marriage. The husband
seems in almost all cases to be the main pusher of emigration.

5

The Diminished Dream

The desire for travel and adventure can presage many elements, as noted in the previous chapter, among which is a wish to escape a situation viewed as negative. Indeed, a simple explanation of why people migrate, as S. Eisenstadt has observed, must take cognizance of this most basic and elemental factor.[1] Note has been taken throughout the present work of a decline of binding myths and of a heightened sense of dissatisfaction with the national enterprise. These factors must be seen as occupying a central place in the motivational structure underlying emigration from Israel.

Stated very plainly the sustaining image or dream of what the Jewish State was to be (in its myriad and diverse understandings) has been weakened and dimmed with (and by) the passage of time. Thus Israel, for many departees, is viewed as a "failed," "inefficient," or at best "underpowered" America. This, in turn, leads to some of the befuddlements noted at the end of the preceeding chapter and results in confusion as to where basic values or ideals of Israeli society can best be realized. Additionally, for some leavers a sense of having been personally hurt or badly dealt with by Israeli "society" and its various organs results in feelings of "they didn't do right by me," which further unravels ties to the national undertaking.

Thus both factors—a sense of personal victimization at the hands of society *and* a growing dissapointment with the direction of change being undergone in the country—must be seen as important elements in both the motivational and the legitimation matrixes underlining the emigration phenomenon.

How It Used to Be: Israel as It Is and as It Was

Emigrants are not the only category of humankind who suffer the effects of a nostalgic reordering of the past wherein among other things the present never quite stacks up to what has gone before. Somehow watermelon was sweeter, movies were better, cars were handsomer, life was less complicated in by-gone times—usually when we were younger. Similarly, we tend to apothesize our environment, our society, in much the same way and for much the same reason. Leaders always seem more imposing and achievements grander in the past than they do in the present.

In listening to the comments of leavers about the Israel they are leaving and the Israel which, as it were, left them, one is met with a sense of déjà vu. A very high proportion of departees observed that the country had turned if not sour, then at least something very different from the elevated paragon remembered from their youth.

Almost all interviewees noted, for example, the change in their personal observance of Independence Day as symbolic of a change in the quality of the collective undertaking. This can be seen in the following interview with a husband (H) and wife (W) about to emigrate:

I: How did you spend last Independence Day? What did you do, do you remember?

H: Yes, I remember. [He asks his wife] Do you remember?

W: We went to a party . . .

H: Yes, we went to a party, with the kids. [She's still trying to talk but he overrides her.] If you want to know what the difference is between the parties we once had, and the ones today, well, it's a huge difference. A huge difference. Night and day, night and day. Maybe it's nostalgia, but Independence Day, as children, I remember, there was such happiness, you felt it, there wasn't a house in Hadar without a flag. There wasn't a house. And there wasn't any need for public service notices, it was spontaneous. At 7:00 there was a siren in the Memorial Garden, and at 7:05 you would feel the change from Memorial Day to the Independence celebrations. It's true that it made a lot of people feel bad, especially parents who lost a child. How can you turn a switch from sad to happy? But most of the people weren't in mourning, most of the kids weren't mourners, and you could see the spontaneity in their expressions of joy. Also Memorial Day, when there was the siren, you wouldn't see a car on the road, not one car moving would you see, even the Arabs, they would stand too. This time I left the house just before the siren and it caught me just going, so I got out of the car, of course, but cars went by. Maybe it's a generalization, but at least two, three cars went by. I don't know, maybe they didn't hear it, in the middle of Hadar. . . .

I: So you don't feel the same happiness, in the public, and within yourself?

H: One brings the other. You get a lot from the environment that you live in, from society. I remember that such a happiness would burst out on Hertzl Street. They would dance until two, three at night, but dancing [excited]. With all their heart. When there was a parade on Independence Day, I remember my father had tears when we saw the soldiers go by. He was in the Hagana, he fought; you see, then it was something else, maybe we've gotten used to the idea that we're an independent State, or that people don't care, or that the pressures of life push it aside. Look today, they dance and are happy, but it's not what it once was.

A perceptible change has occurred in the way the national day is observed and this is clearly not without meaning and impact. The interviewee quoted above who spoke of the difficult but understandable tie-in between Memorial Day and Independence Day commenting on his sense of changes in public behavior was touching upon a most important and complex point of national cathartic ritual. The pattern has not changed but the degree of public participation and no doubt involvement has. For any outsider who witnessed this curious juxtaposition of mourning and joy during the earlier years of statehood (and even today) the impression tends to be considerable.

The Memorial Day for the nation's fallen begins 24 hours prior to Independence Day and is launched with a blast of the air raid sirens covering every corner of the country. All places of public entertainment—theaters, cinemas, concert halls, cafes—close down, while programming on television is exclusively dedicated to the cultivation and elucidation of the price in human terms paid for independence. The streets of town and village fall quiet and an air of communal reflection covers the land, which is again jolted on the morrow when at mid-morning the sirens again wail bringing everything to a standstill. Cars and trucks stop in their tracks; workers lay down tools in the factories; farmers leave the plow; pupils close their books; housewives cease their labors while the entire nation stands at attention against the eerie wail of the sirens. Ordinary affairs are then resumed until night when in most of the cities and towns of Israel the period of mourning and remembering is brought to a close with elaborate displays of fireworks, by programs in the parks and streets, speeches, bonfires, parties, and dancing through the night. Independence Day itself was in the past celebrated by military parades and air force flyovers, but in recent years these have given way to more pacific delights such as folk dancing, pageants, communal picnics, public exhibitions, and so on.

Nothing in the outward organization of these linked national events has changed but changes have occurred in the way they are related to. The private family picnic or a few families getting together are more and more in vogue. The collective functions are less popular, with the significance of the change not being lost on many of the participants. It reflects a lessening of collective enthusiasm and passion and a growing dimension of privatization. Almost none of the interviewees celebrated the event as they had in the earlier days of statehood, and almost all saw in this not only a symbol of decline in collective involvement but a sense of personal loss as well. Most people had to think for a few moments in order to recall what they had done or how they had celebrated the past Independence Day. Many rather sheepishly—almost ashamedly—told about the family picnic, which was as often as not commented upon (voluntarily and without probing) as a "dull and unworthy" affair. Almost all (as in the lengthy quote above) compared the last observance very negatively with the remembered ones of the past where something above and beyond the narrow concerns of family or the individual was central.

Something clearly has been sensed to have been lost from the halcyon days of early independence, and the celebratory pattern is most reflective of this sense of loss. In place of the elevated dream of Zionism realized, one finds a growing weariness expressed in the lessening ability or desire to come together for purposes of collective enhancement. Increasingly, and somehow reflective of this change, there has been a growing demand to separate the twinned occasions of Memorial Day and Independence Day. This stems, I feel, from a lessening ability to empathize with the gaiety and gift of independence while retaining an all too palpable ability to feel and conceptualize what is viewed perhaps as an increasingly expensive arrangement.

While Independence Day affords us what might be called a macro-conception of the diminishing dream, departees take note of details ranging from an increasingly jaundiced view of "today's youth" to matters such as Zionism, work, collective responsibility, and even a departed sense of *joie de vivre*.

In place of past consensus and willingness to sacrifice most respondents were able—indeed eager—to note a massive decline. One observed that in place of group-orientation Israel has elevated "a personal survivalism in the really worst sense of the word." Others took note of money replacing serious values and almost everyone had something to say about a growing atmosphere of difficulty. "There are disturbances in daily life all along the way. Wherever you go and whatever you do—there are disturbances. Strikes, bad labor relations, wild prices. . . ." A number of interviewees commented about low labor morale and low productivity, while still others took note of what they thought of as the insidious results of cheap Arab labor replacing Jewish labor. One respondent claimed to be leaving the country as a result of being squeezed out of the building trades by the ready availability of Arab replacements.

Extensive comment was made about the past involvement of youth in the various pioneering movements as opposed to today, where the discoteque is an increasingly dominant theme. The decline of simplicity in everyday life was bewailed and the development of conspicuous consumption condemned in elders as well as among the youth.

Most bemoaned was what they considered to be the decline of Zionism. Some thought it had been fulfilled, thus becoming irrelevant. Others thought it had run out of "ideological fuel," while in one case the respondent felt it had become "gutless" and effete. For most, a general theme of diminishment was expressed in a growing "greyness" associated with the enterprise:

> When my parents came they were Zionists but they aren't anymore. They came with certain ideals—they were after all coming to the Land of Israel, the Holy Land. Today, it is not like that: they just live here. They live the daily life of the country, the greyness of it, the goodness of it, and everything in between. Once they were involved with everything which went on—they were part of all sorts of organizations whereas today they just live ordinary lives. They were involved with the community, with the society, but now they are more private, more involved with what's closer to them—their family.

This, in effect, was another way of describing a loss of collective purpose or direction. A number of respondents, indeed a majority, indicated (though phrasing the matter differently) that "everything is going downhill." Some saw this being expressed in growing taxation with lessened benefits to the citizen. Others saw it in the Americanization process:

> We have surpassed the original America itself . . . the thing is we don't know limits, we lose proportion. This country used to be wonderful but we lost our purpose. If you don't have a purpose, life isn't worth living. Look at Ben Gurion. Not that I agreed with everything he did—far from it. But he had a purpose, a vision which the nation could follow—to build a state. When we fulfilled that purpose, that goal, we didn't have another as a nation, a group. We have lost our *direction*, so people go off in many different *directions*.

The above informant observed that *yerida* is a direct fallout of purposelessness and the fact that the vision is in eclipse. Sameness has afflicted what was viewed by so many as unique. National tasks have been replaced by personal ambition, and even obscured and stymied by personal quirks.

> In the past journalists didn't write the muck they write today. At the creation of the State there was a feeling of a great undertaking and the positive was emphasized. I read those papers when I was young and they informed at the same time as they strengthened us. But in this as in other things, matters are getting worse and worse and I have no idea how to change things.

Zionism itself has become a quasi-pejorative term. Zionism has come to be identified with preachiness, high-blown thoughts, foolish selflessness, and misplaced ideological zeal. Increasingly, it is difficult to define a Zionist, but relatively simple to define a non-Zionist. The latter is a realist, a survivor, a striver, a no-nonsense, down-to-earth proficient grappler with the verities of his time and place.

Perhaps the central facet of diminishment with respect to Israel as a vision was the illusiveness of a deep-down good feeling one should have about living in the first Jewish commonwealth in 2,000 years. For most respondents the fact that being an Israeli did not totally transform consciousness was interpreted as a sign of conclusive failure. Where was the warm feeling of oneness knitting together all the diverse strands of the House of Israel? Indeed, in place of a feeling of unity one was witness to acts—reputed or actual—of discrimination, prejudice, even hatred and violence between Jew and Jew. Instead of feelings of instant kinship and closeness one felt suspicion and otherness within the Jewish fold and not just along ethnic lines. Class and hierarchy in a society in flux, in formation, can be and often are problematic phenomena. This is particularly true within the sociohistorical context of the Jewish reality. "Who made thee a Prince and a judge over us?" (Exodus 2:14) represents something more telling than a biblical throw-away line.

Where in fact was the safety to be enjoyed from a sovereign existence when in fact living in Israel and being an Israeli in the middle and latter part of the twentieth century constituted perhaps the most dangerous domicile for Jews? Where was the sought for homogeneous Jewish society when in fact Israelis were living as a majority in only the most tenuous sense of the term? Israelis found themselves part of what would appear to be a centrifugal force moving toward a Diaspora framework of "living with the gentiles," summed up in what on the surface appears to be a thrust toward sovereignty and dominance. I here refer to the paradoxical policy of the most nationalist sectors of the population that blithely insisted on the introduction of an additional one million Arabs through annexation of the West Bank, positing that adding one million non-Jews to an already shaky demographic structure would not "constitute a problem." And while this program is advanced by nationalist activists, it appears to be widely accepted or at the very least elicits widespread indifference among large numbers of the population.

Where is the enthusiasm one expected to find at every turn with the occupation of State Building? How explain to oneself the existence—indeed the predominance—of the commonplace and the routine with little to enthrall and carry one away on the soaring wings of a great adventure? How does one make one's peace with the many stains and blemishes marking what should have been (had the script been followed) pure and blameless: crime and deviance in the Jewish state; conflict between religious and secular Jews; great and yawning gaps between rich and poor; constant and repeated wars? Are we not in a tailspin moving us inexorably away from the pristine vision toward an abyss of folly and smashed dreams?

Among the great majority of those interviewed, the sense of a lost age of innocence was returned to again and again in diverse fashion:

> I don't know how to explain it—but once things were different here. Young people were all in youth movements . . . they behaved differently, they thought differently. Everything is worse today than it was in the worst time of *tzena* [austerity].

> People, certain people put up barriers to separate us. It is in their interest to do so. This was not the dream of the founders, of men like Ben Gurion and Sharett.

> Once we [Jews] worked—now we work the *boursa* [stock exchange]. Once we took pride in our achievements for the nation; now we boast about how much "I" got. Once we looked always to the future and today we speak after only 35 years of the good old days.

For many departees life in Israel has assumed the dimensions of an interregnum, a formless void wherein the old values, the old verities have been supplanted by new ones that as yet either lack definition or look suspiciously like what is available in the *galut*—and better there.

They Did Not Do Right by Me

It would be perverse and incorrect to assume that the vast majority of *yordim* leave either as a result of disillusionment or of a smashed collective vision of Elysium. For many leavers the disappointment is of a subjective nature having little or nothing to do with the decline of myths or the tarnishing of dreams. For these individuals it is simply a matter of Israel not "giving" them enough, or believing that they have not been dealt with fairly by the society. Some see it in terms of ethnic disabilities wherein their Eastern origins have been held against them. As noted earlier, relatively few departees were willing to attribute their decision to leave to ethnic discrimination but I have no doubt that this does not truly reflect actual feelings, and that in fact the ethnic factor does play a role of some importance in some departees' decision to move.[2]

A sense that the "country has screwed me," while not exclusively limited to emigrants of Eastern background, tended to be highly concentrated in this group. Among many departees from these sectors of the population one was privy to an underlying whine to the effect that not so much has life been unkind to them as has the State of Israel. Here, personal hurt, failure, or frustration was invariably placed against the backdrop of societal constrictiveness or malignancy.

Though largely denying that the ethnic factor played a role in the decision to leave, it cannot be without significance that virtually all inter-

viewees who expressed a deep sense of bitterness about the country
stemmed from these groupings. Mr. A., the owner of a small rather marginal business, expressed many of the sentiments heard from others in a
rather pithy, often crude and somewhat simple manner. I will try to re-
produce segments of the interview with a minimum of editing in an effort
to preserve tone and emphasis.

A: Why did I decide to leave? Well, my father isn't a millionaire and
      when I got out of the army—after three years—I didn't have anything
      to eat on the outside. But I started this store and it was hard, very
      hard. I borrowed a bit, I scrounged a bit and I got to be more set up
      than most guys who leave the army. After three years in the army *no
      one* in the government helped, nothing, not a thing, zero: not with an
      apartment, not with a loan to live on like they give new immigrants—
      we didn't get those conditions. This hurts me and it hurts a lot of
      other young people that we can't get anything from them. I'm a young
      man; I'm looking for something out of life. I don't want to say that
      I'm not a Zionist or that I don't love the State—God forbid; I do, I
      love the State but I also love having some money and maybe to be
      truthful, a little more.
I: Very clear!
A: Yes, very clear and I know that here I won't reach that. I have many
      friends who went to America and today they are very big, very big—
      you can't talk to them about less than a half million dollars.
I: How did they earn so much in just a few years? [He does not answer
      directly.]
A: Look, you know Jordache? If they had stayed in Israel they would
      have been nothing. They wouldn't have made it.
I: But how many success stories are there like that?
A: Mister, maybe there aren't too many like that but it's an example that
      shows Israelis and at the same time gives you a pain in the heart.
      These guys were completely poor here; they were nothings in Israel;
      they didn't have food to eat, and that's the way they would have
      stayed. But he went to America and made it big and *now* he is big in
      Israel too. That's the way for people like us to get big here—do it first
      in America. Well, if it was good enough for them, it's good enough for
      me. It's possible that I'll come back to live here in another 20 or 30
      years, but first I have to make it.

      Look Mister, I don't want to lie to you and say I love the State and I'm
      a Zionist and they can take three years from my life, and every year a
      month or two of reserve duty and because this is my country I'm
      willing to "eat hay" for it—no, I don't say that, I'm honest. I'm
      looking for something more, I like to live, my wife wants all sorts of
      things that I can't give her here. About half a year ago we went to buy
      a refrigerator. Tens of thousands of lira, and tens of thousands for
      other appliances, which we could put together in America with a

month's work. Here, God, I don't know how many months I have to work for it.

If the State would help us, if the State would only help us it could be that I would change my mind about going even now.

Believe me—I don't like New York: I like my own country even though the people living in it aren't so ay-yay-yay and I wouldn't leave it if I knew that I could get to what it takes to survive here. But I feel that it's not good for me here, and it won't be. I'm in the business three years already and I haven't gotten ahead.

I: What about noneconomic things that you mention like reserve duty and army? Do these influence your decision making?

A: Naturally, naturally! It's also what made my brother-in-law leave—in his case it's the *only* reason for his leaving. At the time of the Yom Kippur war he had just gotten married. Well, there's nothing to be done about that—a war broke out. They took him to the army for eight months, exactly eight months—no more, no less. They originally took him for two months and just kept adding on to it, and adding on to it. At work, at his job he was pretty well placed, pretty high up before this happened, and after four years on the job they fired him. Very simply fired him. And he was attached to his work; he couldn't leave it; he loved it. He worked with guys who he grew up with, who were friends from childhood.

I: Why was he fired?

A: Why? Well, for eight months he didn't come to work.

I: But under the circumstances that's against the law.

A: Mister, don't be naive! Look, in eight months they had to have a substitute for him, yes? So maybe they liked the substitute better and believe me there are ways to arrange a thing like that. So now he is out of the army and out of work and he wasn't about to work at some menial job like cleaning or something. He needed a real job, so mother helped him to emigrate to America.

I: And now?

A: Now they are doing fine. They have a house—well, they don't own it, but they have a house, a car, and a kitchen with all the appliances, all brand new. They live well.

I: Are there other reasons, like the threat of war?

A: Yes, I'll tell you, it's a question that I didn't think you'd ask. It's hard for me to say yes, because it's not nice. But I'll tell you, "yes" and I'll tell you why. I'm scared that one day my children will die for this State. I really didn't think you would ask this question, but since you've already asked it, I'll tell you the truth. I know someone who lost two children on the same day: on the same day he lost two people. Believe me, in my heart this hurt me. I don't want to feel that one day this State—mind you I'm willing to give the State a lot—that this State will take my children. I'm not willing to give part of my soul and

I now think if there is a war and even if I tell him [my son] not to go he'll have the "blood" [guts] to go, and of that I'm scared. I won't make children for the government here!

Any day a war can start here and if not a war, terrorism. I would be scared to go out today if I lived in Nahariya or Qiryat Shemona.

I: But earlier you spoke of the dangers involved in living in New York.

A: But Mister, one thing hurts me and that is that it happens in *my* country. There, it's not my country, but I must live in my own country in fear? Fear that I can be walking in the street and a bomb will go off, or a whole car will "go up." A couple of times recently they even closed the sea to protect us from terrorists.

But I could accept this if the State would today give me—not me alone but all of those getting out of the army—something to get us started in life. If instead of the few hundred lira a month they paid during service or the miserable 20,000 lira demobilization "gift," they would give us an apartment—give *not* loan—and give a loan of about a million to start a little business, then I wouldn't leave.

I: Do you think that other countries give . . . .

A: [interrupts]But there is no other State which steals years out of your life!

The major thrust of this respondent's complaint is that the State not only did not give him enough but took too much. The State takes the best years of one's life for army and reserve service and then (in the reference to his brother-in-law) does not even protect one's livelihood. The State does nothing to supply adequate housing or give servicemen a proper start in business. The State does not assure price stability or a rational economic framework that would give people the opportunity to purchase goods at the rate one could in a "good" country like America. The State does not even properly protect the people from the rampages of terrorists and the threat and reality of war.

How much of this represents a causative chain reaction and how much a legitimating framework for a decision already taken? The two, I would aver, are inextricably mixed and the emigrant extensively quoted above fits solidly into a matrix suggested by N.H. Frijda (1961:85) wherein emigration comes about through:

1. Dissatisfaction, usually of an economic nature with the migrant's native land.
2. A special stimulus to leave either through the *pull* of ties with emigrants or the *push* arising from an orientation which differs from that of the community and of a lesser degree of adhesion to that community and the people who comprise it.
3. A more specific motive . . . in the shape of longings which already contain the germ of "somewhere else."

For many of those leaving stemming from an Eastern community, "somewhere else" represented, I am convinced, an effort to set matters right in ethnic terms. The economic framework represents the stated or manifest goal, but cries to the effect that the State "did not do right by me," that justice is unobtainable in Israel, or that recompense for suffering is unavailable represents in many cases a telegraphic affirmation of the latent element of a sense of deep-seated insult and hurt.

This is not to suggest that only departees of Eastern origin feel or express this kind of reaction, or that the departure of Easterners is to be explained in a unidimensional framework of a sense of ethnic discrimination. Easterners and Westerners tend to leave as a result of the same constellation of factors, albeit with shifting emphasis and underpinnings that must be highlighted and explicated. Practically all leavers expressed disappointment with the state of the national enterprise, but subtle and not-so-subtle differences emerged among the differing groups with the Westerners expressing more dispassionate disappointment and the Easterners more personal hurt. Westerners tended to feel that objective circumstances prevented them from "making it" in Israel, while Easterners tended more to feelings of diabolism, unseen plots, and absent justice.

> When a judge tells me that "your truth was not as convincing as his lies," I know that something is rotten. Here the Jews eat each other up alive. There is no justice. . . . Here it is who you are and who you know.

The above respondent, a small businessman of Iraqi origin, was referring to a lost court case involving him and an Ashkenazi political figure. For him personal disappointment was expressed in global terms.

Others took note of societal injustice so pervasive, so deep as to require especially cosmic correction:

> Nobody thinks of the little man here. Oh, I don't mean big things . . . I mean the little things like helping him to solve his problems, like helping him to get through the bureaucracy. But for this I think you'll have to tear down the State and start all over again.

The above respondent, a secretary of Turkish background, felt helpless against the forces of the State that she saw as unhelpful at best and malicious at worst. The State was viewed as an instrument of cold indifference in the hands of forces not controllable or amenable to intervention on the part of simple citizens such as herself. The State is viewed as responsible for providing basic needs of the citizenry—among these apartments—and its failure to do so represents a failure of much broader and deeper dimensions.

> Another reason (after slave wages) for people leaving the country is housing. In other places in the world there exists housing for young couples for which you can pay in subsidized low rent. Here, it doesn't exist. If a young married couple doesn't have an apartment they have to live with parents, and if parents can't help them, they are really in trouble. I work like an ass (forgive the expression) all my life and what do I have, what can I get? Nothing!

It is the State—the society—that has failed to establish a proper ratio between expenditure of effort and visible benefit. The State has not set up a fair system for the provision of shelter, for the collection of taxes, for the distribution of rewards and duties, or for the dissemination of justice. Even in an area of presumed state sensitivity—defense—one sees evidence of mistreatment.

> Two of my brother's children were hurt by *katyushas*. What did the State do for those families, or those apartments which were damaged? In my opinion she didn't pay the full price to those people. My sister suffered a loss—her apartment was damaged—and the curtains that she bought for 100,000 pounds were destroyed, were ripped. What did they tell her? Sew it up with a needle and thread.
>
> For other things she did get paid, but again not for the full value. I know that in the last instance of shelling, a house on Eilat street was hit, and a woman's fridge was burnt out because of the resulting electrical short-out. But because the *katyushas* didn't directly hit her house, they told her, "Lady, the damage isn't from the *katyushas*." And that is what makes people bitter, and ask themselves: "What is this place giving me?" There are a lot of unemployed, there isn't much work for the people. We pay the same taxes, like those paid outside (we do have a 7 percent reduction, but that's not at all meaningful). I'm not saying it can all be expressed in money, there's nothing in life that can be described in terms of money, but . . . there is no motivation, except for Zionism, to keep people in this area.

Money is not so much the issue here as is a sense that nobody cares, that there are no defending powers between the distant, unapproachable State apparatus and the needs and desires of the powerless.

As noted earlier, this attitude while most persuasively expressed among Eastern leavers is not exclusively so. People of European origin as well expressed feelings of subjective deprivation as an outgrowth of the structure of Israeli society, but their expression of this assumed less of a minority group pique and more of a broader societal critique. Rather than tales of how government deprived them or their friends or family members, one tended to hear more structural criticism that resulted in personal deprivation (for example, criticism of government land policy that made it impossible for "people like me to build a private home," horror tales of bureaucracy that "stymied natural business or creative talents," "unfair distribution of reserve duty," or vendettas on the part of the income tax authorities).

Whether of Eastern origin or not, the bottom line was simply that Israel in one way or another, for one reason or another, just did not provide enough of what was required and as such did not or could not elicit unbending fealty.

Migration and *Yerida*

So what can be said about the departure of tens of thousands of Israelis abroad to seek their destinies on foreign shores in foreign climes? Can the departure from Israel be "explained" in the same fashion as, say, that from Italy or Greece? Is it different and if so how? If it is different, are there historical and structural factors stamping this particular migratory movement with the mark of the *sui generis* not relevant or applicable in other cases? In short, are we dealing here with a case study in international migration or a phenomenon known as *yerida,* or "going down"—as in declining, fading, or failing?

As with so many questions dealt with in the present work, complete clarity to say nothing of simple answers, are not readily at hand. To the best of my knowledge emigrants from other lands are not labelled in quite so judgmental, so ontological a fashion either by those left behind at the country of origin or by the emigrants themselves. Thus, from the starting point of our analysis—defining and labeling the act or process as well as the actors—we are confronted by a rather singular situation with little parallel material to provide guidance.

I do not suggest that migration has ever been viewed in neutral tones in all places. In given historical circumstances, a reaction similar to the feeling of many Israelis that emigration represents desertion has been visible. Kingsley Davis (1977) suggests that there exists a deeply ingrained fear of depopulation that is understandable in universal terms and thus is applicable to the Israeli scene.[3] Among the reasons he adduces is the assumption that if conditions are good in any given place people will not leave. But if people leave, then conditions must be bad or threatening to become so, thus easily engendering growth of concern about the wisdom of remaining *in situ* or raising questions about the vigor and survivor instincts of those not taking the necessary steps to protect their own interests. This should especially be the case among populations lacking a long tradition of sedentary life and a high degree of rootedness. In speaking about rooted and unrooted men, Robert Lane (1962: 303) comments with regard to what motivates the former to want to stay put and the latter to move:

> The conflicting motives in these two kinds of cases are different. For the rooted, they center about a fear of strangeness, loneliness, and the unfamiliar; for some of the unrooted, they embrace in part a desire to run away from trouble, to chuck it all, *to be someone else and act like someone else in a setting that would support this different self-image.* (emphasis added)

To be someone else, to act like someone else—can this not be said to constitute the essence of the bifurcated man, the rootless wanderer, the stranger? Are these not conditions known if not wholeheartedly embraced in Jewish praxis?

I would assert that the reaction to departure from Israel on the part of both stayers and leavers represents a partial recognition of the continuity involved in this praxis and the inability (in the short term at least) to shake off its implications for reconstituting a national land-rooted existence. In this sense if in no other, *yerida* is not merely a case study in contemporary migration, but rather a phenomenon with substantial valence and heavy implications not only for the Zionist enterprise in Israel but for the Jewish people as well.

For peoples or individuals leaving behind deep-seated ties to place, clime, language, myth, and imagery, the wrenching experience of seeking "somewhere else" extracts a significant psychosocial toll. Thus Morrison and Wheeler (1978:75-84) were no doubt correct in noting that "the image of elsewhere"—the propensity to move on—was (and is) most significant in the unfolding of the American dream where the centrality of the "new" achieved an uncanny prominence. They were wrong, however, in asserting the "Americanism" of the phenomenon. It is clearly more related to objective, time-gauged elements of a particular people's or group's history and is thus just as much "Jewish" as it is "American." Simply stated, for those who lack deep physical roots in place (though roots are not limited to this dimension), the image of elsewhere, the possibility, indeed the attraction, of moving on demands a lessened price. Edward Shils (1978:418) in an insightful essay on migration observed that "it must be accepted that immigration results in some loss of what is objectively valuable to the immigrants and their descendants. They lose their language and a sense of historical continuity with their ancestors and their ancestral place . . . they lose their imagery and their consoling proverbs and adages."

But what if one has little to lose in the first place? Or if one's cultural baggage is so eminently adaptable or portable so as almost not to experience the loss?

For Israelis, going to America carries with it a sense of almost complete familiarity, of moving from one known cultural context to another. It is not viewed as terribly different or strange. Thus the entire act of removal, of immigration, tends to take on (partially) a dimension of nonseriousness—

almost as if what was occurring was a nonevent. For many the act is more comparable to a rural-urban or intercity move rather than one involving the crossing of cultural, political, or linguistic borders.

In this sense if in no other, Israeli society in evincing concern—even a kind of panic—at the perceived growth in *yerida* is reacting realistically to a threat that could prove utterly pernicious. Fear of depopulation is not only a fear that things are better "over there" but reflects a deep concern for the continued existence of the fragile national enterprise. Put differently, Greece might have to worry about the depopulation of the Peloponnesus and the overcrowding of Athens but need not overly concern itself with the survival of Greece as a nation-state. The same may be said for every other country experiencing a high degree of out-migration, but one would hesitate to assert the same with respect to Israel. And this is either known or sensed by those who stay as well as those who leave.

The portability of Jewish identity has been collapsed for many into an Israeli identity and this has and will continue to play havoc with any and all attempts to formulate a vision of national rootedness. The Israeli finds it relatively easy to slip off to America not only because of prior Amer-ricanization of his surroundings, but because he is prepared to see his Israeliness as a slightly expanded, slightly modified expression of his Jew-ishness—and Jewishness can be as American as apple pie.[4]

In most migratory situations the act of leaving one society and moving to another enjoys a certain sociological discreteness. In the case of *yerida* a certain dialectic has emerged that requires that it be interpreted not discretely—but rather as resulting from a failure of *aliyah*. As long as it can be demonstrated that one can have a strong Jewish identify and satisfy the various demands (lighter or heavier as one chooses) of Jewish faith in the Diaspora and in addition enjoy the fruits of the wide world rather than the parochial narrowness of Israel, then *why not?*[5]

Thus emigration from Israel must in fact be seen as somewhat different in many dimensions from general emigration. In some ways it should be viewed as a prime example of what Petersen (1970: 53) has called a con-servative migration wherein "people move geographically in order to re-main where they are in all other respects." Here I mean, of course, in order to retain an earlier conception of Jewish mobile polity and sociology al-though to be sure there exists also the dimensions of new horizons and new challenges. But the major thrust is in a return to the age-old conception of *Eretz Yisrael* as a metaphor rather than a city on a hill. Petersen suggests that people move either to innovate or conserve. I am suggesting that while both factors play a role in the *yerida* phenomenon, the accent must be placed on the latter rather than the former—and not alone in the pre-viously discussed framework of a return to marginality and the status of the stranger. A conservative ethos is being expressed when two different respondents made serious (and honest) arguments to the effect that *chalutziut* (pioneering) at this juncture might be best addressed in the *galut* rather than Israel, which has "made it" and entered upon a stage of routinization. Both emphasized the decline of challenge with the realized state but also saw in the phenomenon of emigration a sign of the "maturing" of Zionism: choice could now be added to and temper necessity. In combating the routinization of life and the closure of the ordinary, emigrants are reaching out to recapture what has been lost to them and to reassume center stage.[6] Tradition and culture do not die easily nor are they transformed with ease. Petersen (1970:52) is right when he observes that social groups tend to remain as they were (mobile or stable) "unless impelled to change, for with any viable pattern of life a value system is developed to support that pattern." The historically sanctioned pattern of the Jews was one of mobility rather than stability, and while one must agree with Petersen that one cannot explain modern immigration surges on the basis of a kind of restlessness inherited from ancestor nomads, an element of continuity with ancient cultural patterns is both understandable and reasonable.

But can one reasonably attempt to analyze (and thus explain and understand) *yerida* from contemporary Israel only on the basis of a powerful historical model of continuity with the dominant cultural patterns of the past? Trying to understand why people leave Israel is part of the general problem of trying to understand why people migrate at any time and from any place. I would agree with Guillet and Uzzell (1976:11) when they state:

> At first glance, it might appear that if we could only compile a list of all the "true" reasons or all the right population characteristics, we would know why people move, if not how they decide to move. The same forces that impel social scientists towards such a compilation also invite us to create systems of referential semantics, and the same fallacy would foredoom such efforts to failure. Just as no list of kinship terms can explain the meaning to me of this aunt, in this situation, on this day, so no list of reasons for moving can explain the meaning of this particular decision to move. Meaning grows out of, and remains situated in context.

Clearly emigration from Israel and to the United States cannot be fully understood only by reference to the embracing of marginality or a fear and rejection of at least the implications of sovereignty. "Migration," as Taylor (1969:101) observed, "does not take place *in vacuo*." It involves origins and destinations—which is another way of saying pushes and pulls. These factors exist and inform the phenomenon of *yerida* no less than they do other migratory movements of our times and indeed of all times. People leave

Israel and go elsewhere because of a number of dissatisfactions and expected improvements involving origin and destination. Israelis who go to America do so expecting "things" to be better there than they are in Israel. They do so not because Israel is impossible but because the prospect of America is so much more promising.

Bogue's (1977:178) suggestion that migrants decide to move for reasons other than "desperation or dire necessity" holds for Israeli emigrants as it does for so many others in the contemporary context. The overwhelming majority of those interviewed for the present study were interested in improving their lot by emigrating rather than expressing anything even remotely akin to motives based on "dire necessity." Costs and benefits of staying or leaving were reviewed and weighed by most departees, and while the process could not be described as an exercise in pure rationality, it certainly, in most cases, reflected the fruits of thought and essentially serious concerns. As G. Beijer (1969) found in studying patterns of international migration, the factors of ambition, hope, zest for adventure, desire for new beginnings, and not least economic opportunities all play a role in the motivational package. These factors are no less operative among *yordim*! In today's world where degrees of permanence and finality are less and less attributable to behaviors and acts ranging from marriage to migration, one sees that "today's man differs from yesterday's in that his propensity to move, temporarily or 'for keeps' appears to be greater and obstacles in the way of his movement fewer" (Spengler and Myers 1977:13). Richmond (1969:280) has attempted to argue the proposition that migration is becoming or has become something of a norm in the contemporary context:

> Migration becomes a norm of behaviour at least for selected age and occupational groups, and is two-way or, more exactly, multi-directional. Individual migrants in post-industrial societies are of the "transilient" type who do not necessarily settle permanently in any one locality and yet are not "rootless," or alienated or marginal men in the sense in which these terms were understood.

Richmond contends that "contemporary migrants are frequently 'men of two worlds' able to move easily from one to the other" and that in fact "classical studies of immigration have tended to exaggerate the problem of 'marginal man torn between the irreconcilable demands of different cultures" (266). Following a similar line of development Shils (1978:424) makes the point that the spread of science and what might be called universal or world culture has made immigration easier with the possibility of participation serving as a stimulus to migration. And when the contributing and receiving societies are perceived as being so close in outlook, values, and behavior—as in the case of the United States and Israel—then the process might almost seem inevitable given the existence of open gates at both ends of the spectrum.

> The greater the similarity between the culture and the way of life of the former place of residence and the new one the less likely a migrant will experience cognitive dissonance or role strain. Similarly, when the ethnic sub-system and the wider society reinforce each other in emphasizing certain goals and values there is a greater probability of geographical movement and social mobility between them (Richmond 1969:266).

Richmond (1969:264-65) argues to the effect that migration might be looked at in terms of life choices rather than as a closed circle of push-pull forces, a sort of a social causality network of ineluctable stimuli and reactions. He attempts to counter Eisenstadt's claim that every immigration movement is motivated by the migrant's feeling of some kind of insecurity and inadequacy in the original social setting, asserting that "migration may be an end in itself, satisfying a desire for new experience, adventure, or fulfilling cosmopolitan or international values. . . . In contemporary industrial and post-industrial societies, migration is also closely related to the occupational career cycle and may be regarded as a normal means to the end of occupational advancement."[7]

So taken have recent theorists been with the presumed "normalcy" of migration that the question of optimality has been raised with, among others, the economist Joseph Berliner asking how much movement is consistent with social benefits and health, only to be answered in most contemporary fashion by Neuberger (1977:474) who asserts that "from the point of view of individual utility maximization any migration that provided gains to the individual migrants would constitute a movement toward an optimum even if both regions were to lose thereby."

Thus, if rural out-migration ruined the countryside and created slums in the urban receiving areas, it would be optimum (positive?) if the individuals involved preferred it. There is a growing school that views migration in what Berliner (1977) refers to as "bullish" terms, or as a globally positive act. An extreme in this direction was voiced by M.R. Reul (1971:6) who suggests that professions such as social work must learn to "deal with migration as a normal stage in the life cycle of man much like birth and death, health and illness." A growingly perceptible movement seems to be afoot moving us away from the stability model to one of mobility, from communal orientation to an almost Rabelaisian individualism: Migrate— it might be good for you!!

But perhaps not. Again Berliner in a most humane and perceptive fashion has taken note of the possible affects on society as emigration grows. His comments fit well with the proposition of Kai Erikson discussed earlier wherein he observed that a "crime wave" need not be a statistical phenomenon but rather a definitional one and thus one having potential psychological and social impact. In talking about the milieu of emigration Berliner (1977:459) states:

> From week to week one's neighbors change. No one needs to tolerate an imposition upon him by another, or to work out accommodation with a testy neighbor. One simply splits and sets up a pad elsewhere. People flee that which makes them uncomfortable, and thereby flee that which makes them human.

We flee what makes us uncomfortable, that which makes us feel unsafe or threatened, that which fails to satisfy individual or culturally determined needs. In this sense *yerida* is of course no different than any other presumed migratory causal chain except that *yerida* reflects a higher degree of cultural continuity than would be, let us say, the case of the migration of Turks or Norweigians. However "normal" an artifact of contemporary life some theorists might posit migration has become, it still, I would argue, represents a deviant rather than a normative act in the history of most societies. This is not the case with the Jews and the impact of this truth must be absorbed.

Most theorists and researchers of the migration phenomenon have observed that a major factor underlying migration is prior migration. Berliner (1977:459) has mused that "migrating is like sinning; after you have done it once, it is easier to do it again." Researchers have agreed that a previous record assures further trips to the fount more than anything else. Lee (1969:296), for example, noted:

> Also operating to increase migration is migration itself. A person who has once migrated and who has once broken the bonds which tie him to the place in which he has spent his childhood is more likely to migrate again than is the person who has never previously migrated.

Petersen (1970:63), in support of this proposition, states the matter in even stronger terms: "Once it is well begun, the growth of such a [migration] movement is semi-automatic: so long as there are people to emigrate, the principal cause of emigration is prior emigration." Petersen adds that "other circumstances operate as deterrents or incentives but within this kind of attitudinal framework."

Countering this notion in the specific case of *yerida* one must take note of the fact that a high and growing proportion of leavers are Israeli-born and have in fact not previously migrated. Here too, however, Berliner (1977: 459) observes that the children of migrants are more likely to be migrants themselves because "intelligence and education are related to mobility and because the inertia threshold is likely to be lower."

Thus an argument is made to the effect that migration is at the very least positively correlated with a generational (or historical) predisposition, and if this be the case, the matter of *yerida* is rightly seen as terribly threatening and indeed an actual danger to the continuance of Israeli society. *Yerida* is indeed a form of and related to other phenomena of migration but largely epiphenomenal rather than resultant, in A.H. Hobb's terms. It is caused and sustained by other than specific socioeconomic conditions and its causes must be sought largely in the deep folds of Jewish history and culture rather than the everyday specifics of the Israeli milieu. These provide the context, the format, and the stated or manifest etiology—but the fault lies elsewhere.

Notes

1. Eisenstadt (1954:3) makes the following interesting observations with respect to immigrants' motives for moving:
   1. He may feel that the original society does not give him enough to maintain physical existence, or to ensure his or his family's survival within it.
   2. His emigration might be stimulated by the feeling that certain instrumental goals (economic and other satisfaction) can not be satisfied at home.
   3. He may feel that he cannot fully identify (feel solidarity) with people and society.
   4. He may feel that his society does not afford him the chance of attaining a worthwhile pattern of life. (paraphrased)

   He adds that "the stability of any society depends on an optimum number of its members finding satisfaction and gratification in all four of these spheres in accordance with society's institutional arrangements. Lack of gratification in any of them necessarily upsets social stability, and gives rise to various processes of social change."

2. My sense is that if one could split Jews of Eastern origin into three major camps—(1) Iraqi and Syrian, (2) Moroccan and North African, and (3) Yemenite—the scale of bitterness willingly expressed over the ethnic issue would follow the above order of placement. Iraqi informants tended to be most out-spoken over this factor, though their overall objective socioeconomic positioning is more promising than either of the other two broad groupings. This, of course, is not surprising and most adequately explained both theoretically and prac-tically. People of Moroccan origin or background tended to occupy a middle rung, while Yemenites claimed to feel no particular discrimination and ex-pressed little or no bitterness over their positioning in Israeli society.

3. Davis (1977: 161-62) avers that throughout history population grew in good times and declined in bad. People naturally came to equate population growth with normality and population decline with catastrophe.

4. Approximately two-thirds of the respondents fit this category of people who have collapsed or made no distinction between a national identity as Israelis and a religioethnic identity as Jews. The remaining one-third, however, was either

unconcerned by the Jewish dimension of their identity or even consciously rejective of it admitting that if they were to affiliate as Jews in America it would be only to preserve links with Israel. For this strong minority among informants an Israeli national identity more akin to a "normal" conceptualization was either in process or had taken root.

5. A fair number of respondents suggested that being Jewish was easier in the Diaspora than in Israel because in the Diaspora one had to work at it or consciously choose to affiliate rather than have it decided by circumstances. It was felt that individual choice and the effort involved in personally choosing represented a more genuine "fit" with the Jewish experience than a form of state religion as existent in Israel.

6. Kai Erikson (1966: 112-13) talks of the malaise setting into Puritan New England following upon the excitement stage and quotes a beautiful passage from Perry Miller (*Errand in the Wilderness*): "If an actor playing the leading role in the greatest dramatic spectacle of the century were to attire himself and put on his make-up, rehearse his lines, take a deep breath and stride onto the stage, only to find the theatre dark and empty, no spotlight working, and himself entirely alone, he would feel as did New England around 1650 or 1660. For in the 1640s during the Civil War (in England) the Colonies so to speak, lost their audience."

7. Another way of putting the matter is in the view expressed by Lee (1969: 296) that "the characteristics of migrants tend to be the intermediate between the characteristics of the population at origin and the population at destination."

Bibliography

Books

Abramov, Zalman S. *Perpetual Dilemma: Jewish Religion in the Jewish State.* Jerusalem: World Union for Progressive Judaism, 1976.

Antonovsky, Aaron, and Arian, Alan. *Hopes and Fears of Israelis: Consensus in a New Society.* Jerusalem: Academic Press, 1972.

Antonovsky, Aaron, and Katz, Abraham David. *From the Golden to the Promised Land.* Jerusalem: Academic Press, 1979.

Aviad, Janet. *Return to Judaism: Religious Renewal in Israel.* Chicago: University of Chicago Press, 1983.

Avi-Jonah, M. *The Jews of Palestine: A Political History from the Bar Kochba War to the Arab Conquest.* Bristol: Western Printing Services, 1976.

Avineri, Shlomo. *The Making of Modern Zionism: The Intellectual Origins of the Jewish State.* London: Weidenfeld and Nicolson, 1981.

Beijer, G. "Modern Patterns of International Migratory Movements." In *Migration*, ed. J.A. Jackson. Cambridge: Cambridge University Press, 1969.

Ben Rafael, Eliezer. *The Emergence of Ethnicity: Cultural Groups and Social Conflict in Israel.* Westport, Conn.: Greenwood Press, 1982.

Berger, L., ed. *Immigration and Israel's Survival.* Jerusalem: Office for Economic and Social Research, The Jewish Agency, 1975.

Berliner, Joseph S. "Internal Migration: A Comparative Disciplinary View." In *Internal Migration: A Comparative Perspective*, ed. Alan A. Brown and Egon Neuberger, New York: Academic Press, 1977.

Birnbaum, Ervin. *The Politics of Compromise: State and Religion in Israel.* Rutherford, N.J.: Fairleigh Dickinson University Press, 1970.

Bogue, Donald J. "A Migrant's Eye-View of the Costs and Benefits of Migration to a Metropolis." In *Internal Migration: A Comparative Perspective*, ed. Alan A. Brown and Egon Neuberger. New York: Academic Press, 1977.

Breznitz, Shlomo, ed. *Stress in Israel.* New York: Van Nostrand Reinhold, 1983.

Curtis, Michael, and Chertoff, M. *Israel: Social Change and Structure.* New Brunswick, N.J.: Transaction Books, 1973.

Davis, Kingsley. "The Effects of Outmigration on Regions of Origin." In *Internal Migration: A Comparative Perspective*, ed. Alan A. Brown and Egon Neuberger. New York: Academic Press, 1977.

Davis, Uri. *Israel: Utopia Incorporated, A Study of Class and Corporate Control.* London: Zed Press, 1977.

233

Deshen, Shlomo A., and Shokeid, Moshe. *The Predicament of Homecoming: Cultural and Social Life of North African Immigrants in Israel.* Ithaca, N.Y.: Cornell University Press, 1974.

Eisenstadt, S.N. *The Absorption of Immigrants.* London: Routledge and Kegan Paul, 1954.

———. *Israeli Society.* London: Weidenfeld and Nicolson, 1967.

Eisenstadt, S.N., and Bar Yoseph, Rivkah, eds. *Integration and Development in Israel.* Jerusalem: Israel University Press, 1970.

Elizur, D., and Elizur, M. *The Long Way Back: Attitudes of Israelis Residing in the United States and in France Towards Returning to Israel.* Jerusalem: The Institute of Applied Social Research, 1974.

Elon, Amos. *The Israelis: Founders and Sons.* New York: Rinehart and Winston, 1971.

Erikson, Eric. *Dimensions of a New Identity.* New York: Norton, 1974.

Erikson, Kai T. *Wayward Puritans: A Study in the Sociology of Deviance.* New York: John Wiley and Sons, 1966.

Etzioni-Halevy, Eva. *Political Culture in Israel: Cleavage and Integration Among Israeli Jews.* New York: Praeger, 1977.

Fein, Leonard J. *Israel: Politics and People.* Boston: Little, Brown, 1967.

Foerster, Robert F. *The Italian Emigration of Our Times.* New York: Arno Press Reprint [1919], 1969.

Frankel, William. *Israel Observed: An Anatomy of the State.* London: Thames and Hudson, 1980.

Friedlander, Dov, and Goldscheider, Calvin. *The Population of Israel.* New York: Columbia University Press, 1979.

Frijda, N.H. "Emigrants—Non-Emigrants." In *Characteristics of Overseas Migrants*, ed. G. Beijer. The Hague: Government Printing Office, 1961.

Gainoor, Itzhak. *Steering the Polity: Communication and Politics in Israel.* Beverly Hills: Sage Publications, 1982.

Geffner, Edward. *Sephardi Problems in Israel.* Jerusalem: World Sephardi Federation, 1972.

Ginor, Fanny. *Socio-economic Disparities in Israel.* Tel Aviv: Tel Aviv University, 1979.

Greenberg, Harold I. *Israel Social Problems.* Tel Aviv: Dekel Academic Press, 1979.

Greenwood, Davydd. *Unrewarding Wealth: The Commercialization and Collapse of Agriculture in a Basque Town.* New York: Cambridge University Press, 1976.

Gruber, Ruth. *Israel on the 7th Day.* New York: Hill and Wang, 1968.

Guttman, Emanuel. "Religion in Israeli Politics." In *Man, State and Society in the Contemporary Middle East*, ed. Jacob M. Landau. New York: Praeger, 1971.

Hareven, Alouph, ed. *Every Sixth Israeli: Relations Between the Jewish Majority and the Arab Minority in Israel.* Jerusalem: Van Leer Jerusalem Foundation, 1983.

Hasdai, Yaacov. *Truth in the Shadow of War*, trans. Moshe Kohn. Tel Aviv: Zmora, Bitan, Modan, 1979.

Hazelton, Lesley. *Israeli Women: The Reality Behind the Myth.* New York: Simon and Schuster, 1977.

Herman, Simon. *Israelis and Jews: The Continuity of an Identity.* New York: Random House, 1970.

Inbar, Michael, and Adler, Chaim. *Ethnic Integration in Israel.* New Brunswick, N.J.: Transaction Books, 1977.

Isaac, Rael Jean. *Israel Divided: Ideological Politics in the Jewish State.* Baltimore: John Hopkins University Press, 1976.

_____. *Party and Politics in Israel: Three Visions of a Jewish State.* New York: Longmans, 1981.

Jackson, J.A., ed. *Migration.* Cambridge: Cambridge University Press, 1969.

Jacobson, Dan. *The Beginners.* New York: Macmillan, 1966.

Jaffe, Eliezer D. *Pleaders and Protesters: The Future of Citizen's Organizations in Israel.* New York: American Jewish Committee, Institute of Human Relations, 1980.

Jansen, C. "Some Sociological Aspects of Migration." In *Migration*, ed. J.A. Jackson. Cambridge: Cambridge University Press, 1969.

Jiryis, Sabri. *The Arabs in Israel*, trans. Inea Bushnaq. New York: Monthly Review Press, 1976.

Kanaana, Sharif. *Socio-Cultural and Psychological Adjustment of the Arab Minority in Israel.* San Francisco: R. and E. Research Associates, 1976.

Keniston, Kenneth. *The Uncommitted: Alienated Youth in American Society.* New York: Harcourt Brace, 1965.

Kimche, Jon. *Can Israel Contain the Palestine Revolution?* London: Institute for the Study of Conflict, 1971.

Kraines, Oscar. *The Impossible Dilemma: Who Is a Jew in the State of Israel?* New York: Bloch, 1976.

Krausz, Ernest, ed. *Studies of Israeli Society.* New Brunswick, N.J.: Transaction Books, 1980–1983.

Lamdany, Ruben. *Emigration from Israel.* Jerusalem: Falk Institute, 1982.

Landau, Jacob M. *The Arabs in Israel: A Political Study.* London: Oxford University Press, 1969.

Lane, Robert E. *Political Ideology.* New York: Free Press, 1962.

Lee, Everett. "A Theory of Migration." In *Migration*, ed. J.A. Jackson. Cambridge University Press, 1969.

Leslie, Clement S. *The Rift in Israel: Religious Authority and Secular Democracy.* London: Routledge and Kegan Paul, 1971.

Liebman, Charles S., and Don-Yehiya, Eliezer. *Civil Religion in Israel: Traditional Judaism and Political Culture in the Jewish State.* Berkeley: University of California Press, 1983.

Lind, J. *The Trip to Jerusalem.* London: Jonathan Cape, 1974.

Lissak, Moshe, and Gutmann, Emanuel, eds. *Political Institutions and Processes in Israel.* New Brunswick, N.J.: Transaction Books, 1974.

Lustick, Ian Steven. *Arabs in the Jewish State: Israel's Control of a National Minority.* Austin: University of Texas Press, 1980.

Luttwak, Edward, and Horowitz, Don. *The Israeli Army*. London: Allen Lane, 1974.

Marmorstein, Emile. *Heaven at Bay: The Jewish Kulturkampf in the Holy Land*. Oxford: Oxford University Press, 1969.

Matras, Judah. *Social Change in Israel*. Chicago: Aldine, 1965.

Meyer, Lawrence. *Israel Now: Portrait of a Troubled Land*. New York: Delacourt Press, 1982.

Morrison, Peter A., and Wheeler, Judith P. "The Image of 'Elsewhere' in the American Tradition of Migration." In *Human Migration: Patterns and Policies*, ed. William H. McNeill and Ruth S. Adams. Bloomington: Indiana University Press, 1978.

Naipaul, V.S. *India: A Wounded Civilization*. New York: Knopf, 1977.

_____. *Among the Believers—An Islamic Journey*. New York: Knopf, 1981.

Neuberger, Egon. "Internal Migration: A Comparative Systematic View." In *Internal Migration: A Comparative Perspective*, ed. Alan A. Brown and Egon Neuberger. New York: Academic Press, 1977.

Orr, Akiva. *The Un-Jewish State: The Politics of Jewish Identity in Israel*. Ithaca: Ithaca Press, 1983.

Patai, Raphael. *Cultures in Conflict*. New York: Herzl Press, 1961.

_____. *Israel Between East and West: A Study in Human Relations*. Westport, Conn.: Greenwood Press, 1970.

Petersen, W. "A General Typology of Migration." In *Readings in the Sociology of Migration*, ed. Clifford Jansen. Oxford: Pergamon Press, 1970.

Poll, Solomon, and Krausz, Ernest, eds. *On Ethnic and Religious Diversity in Israel*. Ramat Gan: Institute for the Study of Ethnic and Religious Groups, 1975.

Pourcher, G. "The Growing Population of Paris." In *Readings in the Sociology of Migration*, ed. Clifford J. Jansen. Oxford: Pergamon Press, 1970.

Reul, Myrtle R. "Migration: The Confrontation of Opportunity and Trauma." In *Migration and Social Welfare*, ed. Joseph W. Eaton. New York: National Association of Social Workers, 1971.

Richmond, A.H. "Sociology of Migration in Industrial and Post-Industrial Societies." In *Migration*, ed. J.A. Jackson. Cambridge: Cambridge University Press, 1969.

Ritterband, Paul. *Education, Employment and Migration: Israel in Comparative Perspective*. Cambridge: Cambridge University Press, 1978.

Rolbant, Samuel. *The Israel Soldier: Profile of an Army*. South Brunswick, N.J.: T. Yoseloff, 1970.

Rosen, Harry M. *The Arabs and the Jews in Israel: The Reality, The Dilemma, The Promise*. New York: The American Jewish Committee, 1970.

Rossi, Peter H. *Why Families Move: A Study in the Social Psychology of Urban Residential Mobility*. Glencoe, Ill.: The Free Press, 1955.

Roumani, Maurice M. *From Immigrant to Citizen: The Contribution of the Army to National Integration in Israel—The Case of the Oriental Jews*. The Hague: Foundation for the Study of Plural Societies, 1979.

Samuel, Edwin. *The Structure of Society in Israel.* New York: Random House, 1969.

Schiff, Gary S. *Tradition and Politics: The Religious Parties of Israel.* Detroit: Wayne State University Press, 1977.

Schnall, David J. *Radical Dissent in Contemporary Israeli Politics.* New York: Praeger, 1979.

Schweid, Eliezer. *Israel at the Crossroads,* trans. Alton Meyer Winters. Philadelphia: The Jewish Publication Society of America, 1973.

Selzer, Michael. *The Aryanization of the Jewish State.* New York: Black Star Publishing, 1967.

Segre, V.D. *Israel: A Society in Transition.* London: Oxford University Press, 1971.

_____. *A Crisis of Identity: Israel and Zionism.* Oxford: Oxford University Press, 1980.

Shama, Avraham, and Iris, Mark. *Immigration Without Integration: Third World Jews in Israel.* Cambridge, Mass.: Schenkman, 1977.

Shils, Edward. "Roots—The Sense of Place and Past: The Cultural Gains and Losses of Migration." In *Human Migration: Patterns and Policies,* ed. William H. McNeill and Ruth S. Adams. Bloomington: Indiana University Press, 1978.

Shimshoni, Daniel. *Israeli Democracy: The Middle of the Journey.* New York: Free Press, 1982.

Shokeid, Moshe, and Deshen, Shlomo. *Distant Relations: Ethnicity and Politics Among Arabs and North African Jews in Israel.* New York: Praeger, 1982.

Shumsky, Abraham. *The Clash of Cultures in Israel.* New York: Columbia University Press, 1955.

Simmel, Georg. "The Stranger." In *The Sociology of Georg Simmel,* ed. Kurt H. Wolff. New York: Free Press, 1950.

Smoocha, Sammy. *Israel: Pluralism and Conflict.* Berkeley: University of California Press, 1978.

_____. *The Orientation and Politization of the Arab Minority in Israel.* Haifa: Institute of Middle East Studies, 1980.

Sobel, B.Z. *Hebrew Christianity: The Thirteenth Tribe.* New York: John Wiley and Sons, 1974.

_____. "Unease in Zion: The New Israeli Exile." In *Diaspora, Exile and the Jewish Condition,* ed. Etan Levine. New York: Jason Aronson, 1983.

Spengler, Joseph J., and Myers, George C. "Migration and Socioeconomic Development: Today and Yesterday." In *Internal Migration: A Comparative Perspective,* ed. Alan A. Brown and Egon Neuberger. New York: Academic Press, 1977.

Stendel, Ori. *The Minorities in Israel.* Jerusalem: The Israeli Economist, 1973.

Stock, Ernest. *From Conflict to Understanding: Relations Between Jews and Arabs in Israel since 1948.* New York: Institute of Human Relations Press, 1968.

Stone, Russell A. *Social Change in Israel, 1967–1979: Attitudes and Events.* New York: Praeger, 1982.

Stonequist, Everett V. *The Marginal Man.* New York: Russell and Russell, [1937] 1961.

Tabori, Paul. *The Anatomy of Exile.* London: Harap, 1972.

Talmon, J.L. *Israel Among the Nations: Reflections on the Jewish Statehood.* New York: The City College, 1968.

Tamarin, Georges R. *Forms and Foundations of Israeli Theocracy.* Tel Aviv: Shikpul Press, 1968.

Taylor, R.C. "Migration and Motivation: A Study of Determinants and Types." In *Migration,* ed. J.A. Jackson. Cambridge University Press, 1969.

Thompson, William I. *Evil and World Order.* New York: Harper and Row, 1976.

Tuan, Yi-Fu. *Topophalia.* Englewood Cliffs, N.J.: Prentice-Hall, 1974.

———. "Space, Time, Force: A Humanistic Frame." In *Timing Space and Spacing Time,* Vol. I, *Making Sense of Time,* eds. T. Calstein, Dan Parkes, and Nigel Thrift. London: Edward Arnold, 1978.

Weingrod, Alex. *Israel: Group Relations in a New Society.* New York: Praeger, 1965.

———. *Reluctant Pioneers.* Ithaca, N.Y.: Cornell University Press, 1966.

Weller, Leonard. *Sociology in Israel.* Westport, Conn.: Greenwood Press, 1974.

Winthrop, Robert C., ed. *The Life and Letters of John Winthrop.* New York: Dacapo Press, 1971.

Yehoshua, A.B. "The Golah: The Neurotic Solution." In *Between Right and Right,* trans. Arnold Schwartz. New York: Doubleday, 1981.

Zucker, N.L. *The Coming Crisis in Israel: Private Faith and Public Policy.* Cambridge, Mass.: M.I.T. Press, 1973.

Zureik, Elia T. *The Palestinians in Israel: A Study in Intercolonialism.* London: Routledge and Kegan Paul, 1979.

Zweig, Ferdynand. *Israel: The Sword and the Harp—Controversial Themes in Israeli Society.* London: Heinman, 1969.

Articles

Adler, Israel, and Hodge, Robert W. "Ethnicity and the Process of Status Attainment in Israel." *Israel Social Science Research* 1 (1983): 5–23.

Al-Qazzaz, Ayad. "Army and Society in Israel." *Pacific Sociological Review* 16 (1973): 143–65.

Alport, E.A. "The Integration of Oriental Jews into Israel." *The World Today* 23 (1967): 153–59.

Antonovsky, Aaron. "Toward a Refinement of the 'Marginal Man' Concept." *Social Forces* 35 (1956): 57–62.

Arian, Asher. "Elections 1981: Competitiveness and Polarization." *Jerusalem Quarterly* 21 (1981): 3–27.

Avineri, Shlomo. "Letter from Israel: Political Trends under the Begin Government." *Dissent* 27 (1980): 27–35.

Avruch, K.A. "Gush Emunim: Religion and Ideology in Israel." *Middle East Review* 11 (1978–79): 26–31.

Ben-Ezer, Ehud. "War and Seige in Israeli Literature after 1967." *Jerusalem Quarterly* 6 (1978): 80–93.

Benismon-Donath, Doris. "Social Integration of North African Jews in Israel." *Dispersion and Unity* 12 (1971): 68–100.

Bernstein, J. and Antonovsky, A. "The Integration of Ethnic Groups in Israel." *Jewish Journal of Sociology* 23 (1981): 5–23.

Bizman, Aharon, and Yehuda, Amir. "Mutual Perceptions of Arabs and Jews in Israel." *Journal of Cross-Cultural Psychology* 13 (1982): 461–69.

Cohen, Erik. "The Black Panthers and Israeli Society." *Jewish Journal of Sociology* 14 (1972): 93–109.

––––––. "Ethnicity and Legitimation in Contemporary Israel." *Jerusalem Quarterly* 28 (1983): 5–23.

Cohen, Percy S. "Ethnic Hostility in Israel." *New Society* 22 (1963): 14–16.

––––––. "Ethnic Group Differences in Israel." *Race* 9 (1968): 303–10.

Coser, Lewis. "Afterthoughts on the Israeli Elections." *Dissent* 28 (1981): 411–13.

Deshen, Shlomo. "Of Signs and Symbols: The Transformation of Designations in Israeli Electioneering." *Political Anthropology* 1 (1976): 83–100.

Ettinger, Shmuel. "Zionism and Its Significance Today." *Forum on the Jewish People, Zionism and Israel* 28/29 (1980): 9–20.

Garcia, Sandra Anderson, "Israeli Arabs: Partners in Pluralism or Ticking Time Bomb?" *Ethnicity* 7 (1980): 15–26.

Goldberg, Harvey. "Introduction: Culture and Ethnicity in the Study of Israeli Society." *Ethnic Groups* 1 (1977): 163–86.

Goldberg, Milton M. "A Qualification of the Marginal Man Theory." *American Sociological Review* 61 (1941): 52–58.

Golovensky, David I. "The Marginal Man Concept." *Social Forces* 30 (1952): 333–39.

Gonen, Jay Y. "The Israeli Illusion of Omnipotence Following the Six Day War." *The Journal of Psychohistory* 6 (1978): 9–20.

Gordon, Leonard. "Reflections on Inter- and Intra-Group Relations in Israeli Society." *Jewish Social Studies* 36 (1974): 262–70.

Green, Arnold. "A Re-Examination of the Marginal Man Concept." *Social Forces* 26 (1947): 167–71.

Guillet, David and Uzzell, Douglas. "Introduction." *New Approaches to the Study of Migration* 62 (1976): 1–11.

Hofman, John E. "Social Identity and Readiness for Social Relations Between Jews and Arabs in Israel." *Human Relations* 35 (1982): 727–41.

Jiryis, Sabari. "The Arabs in Israel, 1973–79." *Journal of Palestine Studies* 8 (1979): 31–56.

Kass, Dora, and Lipset, Seymor Martin. "Israelis in Exile." *Commentary* 68 (1979): 68–72.

Kats, Rachel. "Concerns of Israelis: Change and Stability from 1962 to 1975." *Human Relations* 32 (1982): 83–100.

Lazar, David. Israel's Political Structure and Social Issues." *Jewish Journal of Sociology* 15 (1973): 23–43.

Lehman-Wilzig, Sam. "Public Protest Against Central and Local Government in Israel." *Jewish Journal of Sociology* 24 (1982): 99–115.

Leibman, Charles S. "Religion and Political Integration in Israel." *Jewish Journal of Sociology* 17 (1975): 17–27.

_____. "Extremism as a Religious Norm." *Journal for the Scientific Study of Religion* 22 (1983): 75–83.

Leibman, Charles S., and Don-Yehiya, C. "Israel's Civil Religion." *The Jerusalem Quarterly* 23 (1982): 57–69.

O-Dea, Janet. "Gush Emunim: Roots and Ambiguities." *Forum on the Jewish People, Zionism and Israel* 25 (1976): 39–50.

_____. "The Religious Aspect." *Forum on the Jewish People, Zionism and Israel* 26 (1977): 39–41.

Peres, Yochanan. "Ethnic Relations in Israel." *American Journal of Sociology* 76 (1971): 1021–47.

Rofe, Yacov, and Weller, Leonard. "Ethnic Group Prejudice and Class in Israel." *The Jewish Journal of Sociology* 23 (1981): 101–11.

Rosen, Sherry. "Intermarriage and the 'Blending of Exiles' in Israel." *Research in Race and Ethnic Relations* 3 (1982): 79–102.

Rosenberg, Bernard. "The Arabs of Israel." *Dissent* 27 (1980): 161–70.

Rosenfeld, Henry. "The Class Situation of the Arab National Minority in Israel." *Comparative Studies in Society and History* 20 (1978): 374–407.

Rosenstein, Carolyn. "The Liability of Ethnicity in Israel." *Social Forces* 59 (1981): 677–83.

Roshwald, Mordechai. "Theocracy in Israel in Antiquity and Today." *Jewish Journal of Sociology* 14 (1972): 5–42.

Rotenstreich, Nathan. "The Israeli Society and Its Values." *Forum on the Jewish People, Zionism and Israel* 1 (1976): 5–14.

Schweid, Eliezer. "New Ideological Directions After the Six Day War." *Dispersion and Unity* 19 (1970): 40–53.

Selikar, Ofira. "Ethnic Stratification and Foreign Policy: The Attitudes of Oriental Jews Towards the Arabs and the Arab-Israeli Conflict." *The Middle East Journal* 38 (1984): 43–50.

Sharkansky, Ira. "How to Cope with the Bureaucracy." *Jerusalem Quarterly* 6 (1978): 80–93.

Shoufani, Elias. "Israeli Reactions to the War." *Journal of Palestine Studies* 3 (1974): 46–64.

Shuval, Judith T. "Emerging Patterns of Ethnic Strain in Israel." *Social Forces* 40 (1962): 323–33.

Sigal, Clancy. "Israeli Youth: Peace in Their Time?" *New Society* 44 (1978): 479–81.

Smoocha, Sammy. "Black Panthers—The Ethnic Dilemma." *Society* 9 (1972): 31–36.

Smoocha, Sammy, and Peres, Yochanan. "The Dynamics of Ethnic Inequalities: The Case of Israel." *Social Dynamics* 1 (1975): 63–79.

Sobel, B.Z. "To the Four Corners." *Moment* 8 (1983): 18–21.

Sprinzak, Ehud. "Gush Emunim: The Tip of the Iceberg." *Jerusalem Quarterly* 21 (1981): 3–27.

Stock, Ernest. "An End to Ideology? Israel at the Polls." *Forum on the Jewish People, Zionism and Israel* 1 (1977a): 5–21.

_____. "Jewish State and Arab Citizens." *Forum on the Jewish People, Zionism and Israel* 1 (1977b): 42–51.

Toren, N. "Return to Zion: Characteristics and Motivations of Returning Emigrants." *Social Forces* 54 (1976): 546–58.

Weingrod, Alex. "Recent Trends in Israeli Ethnicity." *Ethnic and Racial Studies* 2 (1979): 55–65.

Weissbrod, Lilly. "Religion as National Identity in a Secular State." *Review of Religious Research* 24 (1983): 188–205.

Yishai, Yael. "Interest Groups in Israel." *Jerusalem Quarterly* 11 (1979): 128–44.

_____. "Israel's Right-Wing Jewish Proletariat." *The Jewish Journal of Sociology* 24 (1982): 87–98.

Yuval-Davis, Nira. "The Bearers of the Collective: Women and Religious Legislation in Israel." *Feminist Review* 11 (1980): 15–27.

Unpublished Materials

Lahis, Schmuel. "Israelis in America." Report submitted to the Jewish Agency, Jerusalem, February 4, 1981, mimeographed.

Pini, Herman, and LaFontaine, David. "Israeli Immigration to the United States and Los Angeles." M.A. thesis, Hebrew Union College, Los Angeles, 1983.

Ritterband, Paul. "Out of Zion: the Non-Returning Israeli Student." Ph.D. dissertation, Columbia University, 1969.

Books, Monographs, and Reports in Hebrew (Titles Translated)

Altshuler, Mordechai. "Immigration and Dropping-Out Among Jews from the Soviet Union." Jerusalem: Sifriat Shazar, The Institute of Contemporary Jewish Studies, 1977.

Blecher, Mario, and Goldberg, Yitzhak. "Returning Migrants—Expectations as Opposed to Reality: Immigrants from Western Lands." Jerusalem: The Falk Institute, 1978.

Elizur, Dov, and Elizur, Miki. "Israelis Living in the United States and Their Readiness to Return to Israel." Jerusalem: The Institute of Applied Social Research, 1973.

_____. "To Stay or to Emigrate." Jerusalem: The Institute of Applied Social Science, 1975.

Israel, Central Bureau of Statistics. *Statistical Abstract of Israel.* Jerusalem: Hamakor Press, nos. 31, 32, 33 (1981, 1982, 1983), Hebrew and English.

Levy, Shlomit. "The Desire to Remain in Israel." Jerusalem: The Institute of Applied Social Research, 1975.

Peres, Yochanan. *Ethnic Relations in Israel.* Tel Aviv: Sifriat Poalim and Tel Aviv University, 1976.

Articles in Hebrew (Titles Translated)

Aciezra, Avraham, and Zarhi, Shaul. "Emigration from Israel—Its Dimensions and Causes." *B'shaar* 22, no. 145 (May–June 1979): 206–13.

Ben-Kochav, Ezra. "On Emigration," *Maase Choshave* 8 no. 2 (April 1981): 4.

Chakak, Herzl-Balfour. "Emigrants from Zionism—An Interim Report on the Public Controversy Concerning Emigration." *Kivunim* 13 (November 1981): 177–81.

Della Pergola, Sergio. "Quantative Aspects of Emigration from Israel." *P'tachim* 3–4, no. 51–52 (September 1980): 35–42.

Elizur, Dov, and Shye, Samuel. "The Tendency to Re-Migrate of Israelis Living in the United States and France." *Megamot* 21, no. 3 (May 1975): 324–33.

(No author), "Emigration from Israel." *P'tachim* 3–4 no. 51–52 (September 1980): 7–34.

Galezer, Eliahu. "The Curse of Emigration." *Ha'uma* 19, no. 63 (May 1981): 13–19.

Gaon, Yoram. "With Good Will, with a Loving Outlook, with Grace and Mercy." *B'maracha* 21 no. 250 (September 1981): 12–13.

Harel, Yecheskel. "Zionist Policy and Emigration from Israel." *P'tachim* 3–4, no. 51–52 (September 1980): 42–48.

Kenan, Amos. "Letter to an Emigrant." *P'tachim* 3–4, no. 51–52 (September 1980): 48–50.

Lahis, Shmuel. "Israelis in America." *P'tachim* 5–6, no. 53–54 (March 1981): 76–77.

Lamdany, Reuven. "The Emigration from Israel." *Rivon L'Qualkala* 116 (1983): 462–78.

Leket, Yehiel. "The Emigrants." *Migvan* (March 1981): 11–13.

Peli, Pinchas. "The Problem of Emigration in Ideological and Historical Perspective." *P'tachim* 3–4 (51–52) (September 1980): 52–55.

Paz, Eli. "The Emigrants." *Migvan* 50–51 (August–September 1980): 27–29.

Rabi, Zion. "Emigration from Israel, 1948–77. *Rivon L'qualkala* 25, no. 99 (December 1978): 348–58.

Rak, Shalom. "How to Make Peace with the Idea of Emigration." *B'Eretz Yisrael* 116 (June 1981): 21.

Sabatello, Eitan. "The Emigration from Israel and Its Characteristics." *Bitfutzot Hagola* 19 no. 85–86 (Summer 1978): 63–76.

Shapira, Rina, and Ben Yizhak, Shula. "Emigration from Israel—Inferior Material or a Lack of Spirit?" *Iyunim B'chinuch* 36 (February 1983): 5–24.

Shilansky, Dov. "A Negative Phenomenon from the Moral and Economic Viewpoint." *B'Eretz Yisrael* 112–13 (February–March 1981): 9.

Steiner, Moshe. "A Basic Approach to the Problem of Emigration—What Is It?" *B'Eretz Yisrael* 111 (January 1981): 6–7.

Tadmor, Yeshayahu. "The Great Danger in the Phenomenon of Emigration—Its Normativeness." *Skira Chodsheet* 27, no. 10 (December 1980): 13–16.

Wilner, Meir. "Drop-Outs, Emigration and Zionism. *Arachim* 6, no. 56 (December 1979): 4–7.

Index

DATE DUE

DEMCO 38-297